PECULIAR LANGUAGE

DEREK ATTRIDGE

PECULIAR LANGUAGE

CORNELL UNIVERSITY PRESS

LITERATURE AS DIFFERENCE

FROM THE RENAISSANCE

TO JAMES JOYCE

ITHACA, NEW YORK

First published 1988 by Cornell University Press.

Library of Congress Cataloging-in-Publication Data

Attridge, Derek.
Peculiar language.

Bibliography: p.
Includes index.
1. Joyce, James, 1882–1941—Language.   2. Style,
Literary.   3. Criticism.   I. Title.
PR6019.09Z52564   1988   823'.912   87-19060
ISBN 0-8014-2057-1 (alk. paper)
ISBN 0-8014-9407-9 (pbk.) (alk. paper)

Printed in the United States of America

FOR MY MOTHER
MARJORIE JULIA ODELL

CONTENTS

ACKNOWLEDGMENTS

O NE of the pleasures of completing this book has been to look back over the years of its growth and to appreciate for the first time just how many generous individuals its pages bear witness to, albeit imperfectly and for the most part silently. I can mention only a few here by name, but my thanks go to all who assisted, knowingly or unknowingly. Suzanne Hall's participation in every aspect of the project from start to finish has been immeasurably important. Robert Young and Maud Ellmann challenged me into rethinking old positions, and generously shared their expertise. Helpful comments on draft material came from Margaret Ferguson, Morris Halle, Daniel Javitch, William Keach, Sandra Kemp, Bella Millett, Mary Nyquist, Julian Patrick, David Quint, Frank Stack, Edward Tayler, and Penelope Wilson. Others who encouraged, advised, and helped in various ways were Bernard Benstock, Jacques Berthoud, Jonathan Culler, Jacques Derrida, Daniel Ferrer, John Hollander, Peter Keating, Colin MacCabe, Jean-Michel Rabaté, Richard Rand, Arden Reed, Christine Roulston, Fritz Senn, and Samuel Weber. Students and colleagues in the English Departments of Southampton and Rutgers Universities and the English Studies Department of Strathclyde University made numerous valuable contributions along the way. I am glad to acknowledge financial assistance from the British Academy, the Carnegie Trust for the Universities of Scotland, and the Fulbright-Hays Program. My thanks go also to the many individuals and institutions whose invitations to lecture provided the occasions for the papers that

Acknowledgments

lie behind most of these chapters and to the audiences whose questions and comments stimulated further work on them.

Earlier versions of some parts of this book have appeared as follows: chapter 2 in *Literary Theory/Renaissance Texts,* ed. David Quint and Patricia Parker (Baltimore: Johns Hopkins University Press, 1986): chapter 4 in *Post-structuralism and the Question of History,* ed. Derek Attridge, Geoff Bennington, and Robert Young (Cambridge: Cambridge University Press, 1987); chapter 5 in *MLN* 99 (1984): 1116–40; part of chapter 6 in *James Joyce: The Centennial Symposium,* ed. Morris Beja et al. (Urbana: University of Illinois Press, 1986); and chapter 8 in *Genre* 17 (1984): 375–400. I am grateful to the editors and publishers of these journals and collections for permission to reprint.

Although they are linked by their concern with a common and recurring set of problems and follow a historical trajectory, chapters 2 to 8 address particular issues through discussions of specific texts, and there should be no difficulty in reading them independently of one another or out of sequence.

DEREK ATTRIDGE

New Brunswick, New Jersey

REFERENCES

FULL references are given in the list of works cited at the end of the book; citations in the text are usually by author and short title. Exceptions are as follows: in chapter 2 otherwise unidentified page references are to George Puttenham's *Arte of English Poesie,* edited by Gladys Doidge Willcock and Alice Walker. In chapter 3 all page references for the Preface to *Lyrical Ballads* are to *The Prose Works of William Wordsworth* vol. 1 (elsewhere cited as *Prose*), and Coleridge's *Biographia Literaria* is referred to as *BL*. In chapter 4 all page references to Saussure's *Cours de linguistique générale* are to both the standard French edition and the English translation by Wade Baskin. In the last four chapters references to *Ulysses* and *Finnegans Wake* take the conventional numerical form (see chapter 5, note 16, and chapter 7, note 10). *A Shorter Finnegans Wake* is referred to as *SFW*. Line references to Joyce's writing give the first line of the quotation only. In quotations, otherwise unacknowledged translations are my own; I have modernized Renaissance printing conventions and changed "then" to "than" where appropriate.

PECULIAR LANGUAGE

Chapter 1

Introduction: The Peculiar
Language of Literature

How can the language of the poet, asks Wordsworth in the Preface to *Lyrical Ballads,* "differ in any material degree from that of
all other men who feel vividly and see clearly?" If it were possible—
which he doubts—the poet might "be allowed to use a peculiar language when expressing his feelings for his own gratification, or that
of men like himself. But Poets do not write for Poets alone, but for
men" (*Prose* 1:142-43). Wordsworth's challenge is a powerful and lasting one: if literature is a distinctive use of language with its own very
special and unusual codes and practices, it is accessible only to the few
who are in a position to acquire familiarity with those codes and
practices. It is at best elitist and at worst solipsistic. But writers have
traditionally, and understandably, made a different claim for their
work: that it speaks beyond the small circle of those with a professional commitment to literature, that it can engage with the language
and the thoughts of everyone who speaks the same tongue, and that it
attains thereby the power to intervene in the ethical and political life
of a community or a nation. To push this claim too far, however, is to
endanger the existence of literature itself as a distinct entity, for if
literature does *not* employ a special language, from what does it derive
its appeal and its strength? There is nothing in its armory but language, and if all its linguistic weapons are borrowed, they are likely to
be more forceful on their own terrain.

The desire to make one's text different, which drives every writer

1

other than the scribe (and not even the scribe is always exempt from it), is radically qualified by the desire to make it effective—to please, to move, to teach, to change. But the desire to produce effects has to operate within an already existing and highly complex cultural formation, with its own deep-rooted notions of art and aesthetic value premised upon a potent and persisting conception of literature as difference. In attacking the belief in some "peculiar language" that belongs only to literature, Wordsworth is posing the question of difference with particular force; but his very challenge to the concept is evidence that literary language is "peculiar" in the other sense, a very odd language that is and is not the same language we use to think, to prove, to govern, to mourn, to dream.

This, at least, seems to be the only conclusion to be drawn from the discussion of the question by literary practitioners and commentators throughout the Western cultural tradition. Aristotle remarks on the appropriate style for poetry that

> a really distinguished style varies ordinary diction through the employment of unusual words. By unusual I mean strange words and metaphor and lengthened words and everything that goes beyond ordinary diction. But if someone should write exclusively in such forms the result would either be a riddle or a barbarism. A riddle will result if someone writes exclusively in metaphor; and a barbarism will result if there is an exclusive use of strange words. . . . It is therefore necessary to use a combination of all these forms. The employment of strange words and metaphor and ornamental words and the other forms of speech that have been mentioned will prevent the diction from being ordinary and mean; and the use of normal speech will keep the diction clear. (*Poetics* 1458a)

As one of many possible examples from the other end of the tradition we may turn to a highly successful general book on the language of literature which uses the methods of modern linguistics, Geoffrey Leech's *Linguistic Guide to English Poetry*. In the introduction the author raises briefly the question of the relationship between poetic language and "ordinary" language—the latter adjective, significantly, between quotation marks. He lists three complicating factors in discussing this relationship, the first and third of which are:

> (1) Poetic language may violate or deviate from the generally observed rules of the language in many different ways, some obvious, some subtle.

Both the means of and motives for deviation are worth careful study. . . .
(3) Most of what is considered characteristic of literary language (for
example, the use of tropes like irony and metaphor) nevertheless has its
roots in everyday uses of language, and can best be studied with some
reference to these uses. (5-6)

Both Aristotle and Leech perform a double and contradictory gesture that has been made again and again in the history of Western
discourses on the language of literature, from classical accounts of
poetic diction to the repeated attempts within modern literary theories—Russian Formalism, Prague and Parisian structuralisms, American stylistics, British discourse analysis, and many others—to find a
way of defining literary language against a norm from which that
language is at the same time derived. The conception of the special
language of literature which we inherit from the Western aesthetic
tradition seems to be based on two mutually inconsistent demands—
that the language of literature be recognizably different from the
language we encounter in other contexts, and that it be recognizably
the same. As O. B. Hardison, commenting on the passage from Aristotle quoted above, observes, "we now face a paradox. Poetic diction
should be clear and should therefore use standard words. At the same
time, it should be distinguished and should therefore use unusual
language. Clarity and distinction are in some sense antithetical" (256).
Hardison's use of the term "paradox" signals the unamenability of
this problem to solution by means of the normal procedures of reason. In the late sixteenth century George Puttenham also emphasizes
the paradoxical nature of the demands made upon the literary writer;
he introduces his discussion of "ornament poeticall," the major section of his *Arte of English Poesie*, by remarking that requisite to the
perfection of poetry is a "maner of exornation, which resteth in the
fashioning of our makers language and stile, to such purpose as it
may delight and allure as well the mynde as the eare of the hearers
with a certaine noveltie and strange maner of conveyance, disguising
it no litle from the ordinary and accustomed: neverthelesse making it
nothing the more unseemely or misbecomming, but rather decenter
and more agreable to any civill eare and understanding" (137). The
artistic transformation that renders language strange and novel
seems, at the same time, somehow to make it more decent and agreea-
ble; and the word "nevertheless" hints at the double bind involved.

3

Introduction

This contradictory demand has continually exercised writers, critics, and theorists, and shows no signs of disappearing; any magazine with reviews of current writing is likely to contain praise for the achievement of both linguistic authenticity (the accurate evocation of the tones and rhythms of speech, for instance, or the capturing of a particular regional or social dialect) and linguistic distinctiveness (the original "voice" or verbal texture that makes a particular poet or poem worth noting among the mass of examples). In periods of literary revisionism or revolution the issue is always taken up as a matter of practice, whether manifested as a drive to emphasize or as an attempt to expunge the distinctiveness of literary language; and it is also a recurrent feature in theoretical discussions, which have tried repeatedly to fix and specify for all time the difference between literary and nonliterary uses of language. Often this question of difference is treated as a question of *deviation,* on the assumption that there exists a given and stable norm in terms of which literary language, as a subsidiary practice, has to be understood. This approach to the issue is, in effect, an attempt to eliminate the instability and uncontrollability of sheer *difference,* a relationship in which both terms—neither of which is given or stable—exist only in relation one to the other.

In the chapters that follow I examine some nodal points in this history, specific instances of theoretical and literary texts that deal with or exemplify this recurrently troubling (but, in terms of literature and literary theory, highly productive) issue. I do so in order to explore contrasts and similarities, to investigate the abiding fascination of the question and the apparent impermanence of all the answers. It is not my purpose to search for a solution to the dilemma—I do not, for instance, believe with Aristotle that the answer is to look for a point along a scale at which both these demands are met—because our notions of the "literary," and the functions of literature within our culture, depend on just this oscillating and unstable relationship. It cannot simply be a matter of "getting the balance right," for the two properties both lie at the heart of literariness. The difference of literary language from ordinary language is its defining feature, that which *makes* it literary; yet at the same time literary language is continually judged in terms of its closeness or faithfulness to ordinary language. There is also a long tradition of thought which regards the original and in some sense essential state of language as poetic, thus defining "ordinary" language against the norm of literary language; this apparent reversibility of the terms is further evidence of the impossibility of quantifying and fixing the relationship.

Although the notion of deviation has been frequently used, in some form or other, to fix the potential uncontrollability of literary difference, there has always been an understandable reluctance to propose fully explicit rules for the production or determination of literary language in relation to the norm. Literature must not, in the final analysis, be a matter of mechanical procedures; the whole cultural institution of art rests on the assumption that aesthetic practices are teachable *only up to a point*—beyond which some unprogrammable and ultimately ineffable principle has to be invoked. This conception of literary language brings further dangers in its train, however; having invoked the notion of deviation to escape the vagaries of difference, we seem to find ourselves with an equally unpredictable and uncontrollable principle, one that is, moreover, central to the distinction between "true" art and that which merely conforms to the external properties of the genre in question. This principle goes by different names at different times—"decorum," "taste," "judgment," "genius," and "imagination" among them—but whatever the changes in the context in which the names function, and hence in their exact meaning, the principle always serves the crucial purpose of putting the final determination of art beyond the reach of rules or statable, quantifiable generalizations. It is no exaggeration to say that every corner of the literary domain—creation, reading, teaching, criticism (academic and popular)—makes use of some such principle, undefinable by definition but indispensable. At the same time the operation of the principle must be disguised or denied, because a categorization (of good art and bad, of literature and nonliterature) that admitted to being entirely beyond the realm of objective demonstration would carry little weight.

There have been two major assaults on this problematic issue in recent times, carried out in the names of structuralism and sociology. Structuralism is premised on the convertibility of any cultural judgment into explicit rules; just as every detail of the linguistic practice of speakers and hearers can—in theory—be formally specified, so every detail of literary practice should be similarly specifiable, given the appropriate formal machinery. Without entering the arena of literary judgment, structuralism attempts to make explicit the principles upon which all judgments depend. Deviation is therefore a favorite device of structuralism, and the demystification of terms such as taste and imagination an obvious goal. This ambitious program has, however, not been realized. No doubt one reason is the practical difficulty of analyzing such a large and complex field of human behavior (if the rules of the English language remain, after prodigious efforts, a matter of dispute, how much less likely we are to agree on the rules of literary interpretation); but the theoretical foundations of the project are themselves open to question, for they assume a model of transcendent objectivity which has long been discredited in the physical sciences from which structuralism originally, by way of Saussurean linguistics, acquired it. The claim to stand completely outside the field of study, and to make assertions about it that have no effect upon it, is one that must be dubious in any discipline but especially in the study of cultural phenomena. Structuralism on principle leaves out of account those properties of literature, literary criticism, and literary theory which most obviously set them apart from the objects of the physical world: their existence within and determination by a shifting web of socially produced relations, judgments, and distinctions, and their consequent openness to change and cultural variation.

The other project, therefore, is to examine the social and institutional structures within which literature is constituted and controlled, the forces that determine, in any time and place, what counts as "literary." This sociological project entails a careful and systematic consideration of the question of taste and its determination by a particular social group—what Pierre Bourdieu has called, in the most detailed study to have been made of this issue, "the self-legitimating imagination of the 'happy few'" (*Distinction*, 31). However, the history of literature and of attempts to define the "literary" demonstrates that the relation of literature to its sociocultural matrix is not simply a matter of an inert substance subjected to mechanical shaping; literature has the power to raise questions about the very processes that define and perpetuate it, and one of the achievements of literary theory in recent years has been to elicit and channel that power in the service of a skeptical engagement with disciplines that depend upon a notion of absolute knowledge and fully grounded truth (whether in the name of empiricism, idealism, metaphysics, materialism, rationalism, or religion—to give a few labels that misleadingly imply the possibility of easy categorization).[1] The sociological approach to the

---

[1] That literary theory with this object or with this effect has met with resistance, or has been accommodated to more familiar paradigms and thus deprived of its power, is understandable, because recent theory questions some of the most ingrained of our

question of literariness does not escape this critique. For all its value in exposing the social and political dimension of literary judgments, it operates in terms of the same model of transcendent objectivity as structuralism.

The debate about literary language and its distinctiveness has had, within modern European cultural history, three obvious turning points: the movements we label Renaissance, Romanticism, and Modernism. The three chapters that follow examine one representative theoretical text on language from each of these movements. Although the selection has an unavoidable element of the arbitrary about it, one aim of the discussion in each case is to show the centrality of the particular text to the aesthetic arguments and the literary practice of the period in question. I could have devoted the entire book to any one of these turning points, moving from the chosen text to others of its time, but my hope is that the close discussion of one text will be sufficient to indicate how other related texts could be read to extend and refine the argument for that particular period. What is gained by this series of close-ups is both a sharper sense of the distinctiveness of the intellectual (and linguistic) texture of each period's encounter with the question and a demonstration of the persistence and intractability of the problem, which will open the way to a different perspective on the whole issue. At the same time I hope through my own interpretative encounters with these texts to exemplify some of the complexities of the activity of reading, of "making sense" of a verbal construct that has survived translation across time and space. It is these complexities that make reading an unending and unendable endeavor. In my view, nearly all literary theory and criticism (notably that which has been informed by the methods of linguistics) founders on the narrowness of its own assumptions about the processes of reading, and it is a highly questionable a priori judgment that renders the reading of literature—or of any written text—as a single, homogeneous activity capable of being explained in terms of definitions, taxonomies, and rules.[2]

---

habits of thought. Paul de Man's suggestive discussion of this issue, "The Resistance to Theory," adumbrates many of the points I attempt to illustrate and develop in this book. See also Robert Young's valuable account of de Man's criticism and its reception in *Political Literary Theories*.

[2]As with reading, so with writing—no particular practice is neutral or ahistorical. My own engagements with specific texts owe more, I believe, to the example of Jacques Derrida than to any other writer, or reader, I have read. One does not, of course,

Introduction

The text I have chosen as an example of the way in which the problem presents itself to the Renaissance is Puttenham's *Arte of English Poesie,* a book whose suitability to my purposes stems not only from its direct handling of the issue of the linguistic distinctiveness of poetry in terms highly characteristic of its period but also from its relatively low rank in the accepted ordering of Renaissance critical texts. Puttenham works with a certain doggedness and lack of sophistication through the problems that present themselves and in so doing throws into sharp relief the tensions and contradictions of his enterprise—which is, generally speaking, the same enterprise on which his more illustrious compeers are engaged. The choice of a Romantic text in English on the question of poetic language almost makes itself; but again, there is a particular value in Wordsworth's Preface to *Lyrical Ballads* other than its centrality and its influence. The Preface, too, is the work of someone who cannot be called a master of theoretical prose, and in the sometimes wooden, sometimes convoluted turns of its argument we find footholds for a reading that exposes the underlying difficulties of the project which a more polished writer of discursive texts might have smoothed away. In both these texts the question of literary as distinct from nonliterary language is often posed in the terms of a wider distinction, that between art and nature, which provides the poles between which the entire discussion moves. We shall find that although the terms themselves are not as common in later periods, the polarity they represent remains a fundamental one.

Choosing a theoretical text to represent Modernism's revaluation of language is a less easy matter, and in this case I have used rather different criteria (and strayed beyond the English tradition and beyond writing that directly addresses questions of literature). I have done so partly because an example of Modernist literary practice—and its theoretical repercussions—is the main focus of the remainder of the book. The discussion of literary language which has formed part of the "theory explosion" of the last thirty years, and which can be seen in large measure as an inheritance of Modernism, has probably been influenced more by one text on language than any other: Saussure's *Course in General Linguistics,* published posthumously in 1916. This text both marks and participates in the shift from the

---

simply *choose* the way one writes or reads, so this statement is in part the record of a historical and geographical situation, as well as the grateful acknowledgment of an experienced indebtedness.

8

historically based philological studies of the nineteenth century to the linguistic theory of the twentieth, and in so doing it liberates language from a certain myth of transparency and dependence upon the real. The linguistic experiments of Joyce, Pound, Eliot, Woolf, Faulkner, Stein, and so many others, although they may have proceeded in ignorance of the *Course in General Linguistics,* certainly grew out of the new possibilities introduced by this shift. To examine Saussure's text, therefore, is to engage with a set of arguments of crucial importance to the new directions taken by European and American literature in the opening decades of this century. At the same time it is to intervene in the current debates about the importance of the Saussurean revolution to our conceptions of literature and its place in society and history.

In each of these three case studies I have no option but to focus on a few features of the text in question. By taking specimens from my specimen, I am able to give particular attention to aspects of the argument which seem to me especially interesting and especially representative of the larger cultural problems at issue. Thus in Puttenham's case I look closely at the operation of the idea of "decorum" in literary creation and judgment; in Wordsworth's I concentrate on the attempt to ground poetic language in "the real language of men"; and in Saussure's I examine the opposition of synchrony and diachrony, with particular reference to its function in the discussion of etymology. A further point I would like to make at the outset is that all three texts are examined as texts, not arguments conducted at some prelinguistic conceptual level and then translated into words. I take patterns of repetition and opposition, the sequential ordering of material, the use of figures, all the features that come under the heading "rhetoric," as relevant to an analysis of the text's attempt to stabilize a sliding set of terms and ideas. There is no assumption on my part that a text on the topic of literary language could ever function as pure, monodirectional argument or simple conceptual algebra; hence I am in no way trying to find fault with a text in showing that it moves in more than one direction at once, that it is at odds with itself, that it conceals yet bears traces of the effort entailed in such concealment. These features are characteristic of language whenever it is used to prove or persuade, endemic to the operation of all philosophical writing, and necessarily present in any argument that sets out to fix the nature of literary language. That Puttenham, Wordsworth, and Saussure provide a fertile terrain for a reading alert to such features is testimony not to their lack of success (success is not to be measured in terms taken from mathematics or physics) but to their comprehensive and vigorous engagement with the issues. Though I am disabled from seeing them, I am well aware that my own text contains similar tensions and fractures, and my hope is that these will be regarded in the same positive light.

The second part of the book, moving further into the twentieth century, turns from "theoretical" texts to more strictly "literary" texts, to measure modern accounts of the distinctiveness of literary language against the actual practice of Modernist writing. One writer in particular has come to stand for experimentation with literary language as defined in relation to nonliterary language. When Leech, in his *Linguistic Guide* (24), is discussing the "creative" use of language, the example he gives of "poetic" creativity is not poetry at all as commonly understood, but this:

Eins within a space and a wearywide space it wast ere wohned a Mookse.

That is, of course, a sentence (or at least a linguistic sequence) from Joyce's *Finnegans Wake,* a text that not surprisingly comes to hand when the theorist is looking for an indisputably deviant specimen of literary language. *Finnegans Wake,* although usually banished to the very edges of the literary canon as an unassimilable freak, can also, it appears, function as the canonical instance of the "literary" itself. The charge usually brought against Joyce's last work is, of course, that is has "lost touch" with ordinary language—that it has, in effect, answered to one of the contradictory demands contained in the definition of literary language at the expense of the other. Ironically, Joyce's immense difficulties in securing publication for his early collection, *Dubliners,* stemmed from precisely the opposite problem: his refusal to exercise artistic censorship upon the linguistic material he drew from Dublin talk and Dublin topography. *Ulysses* occupies a curious middle position: impropriety has been detected both in its extravagant departures from ordinary usage and in its refusal to depart from ordinary usage—in, for instance, incorporating taboo words, clichés, lengthy unstructured lists, and stretches of prose in the style of nonliterary documents. It is one of those works (other examples might be *Gargantua and Pantagruel* and *Tristram Shandy*) which seem to satisfy neither of the contradictory demands made by the literary tradition—or, to put it more positively, that build the contradiction into their fabric and derive from it some of the enjoyment they transmit to the reader.

It seems appropriate, then, to utilize Joyce's two later books as quarries, not in order to offer any kind of general comment on their methods and contents but to provide material on which to base an inquiry, from a postmodern perspective, into some of the frequently adduced characteristics of literary language. Joyce not only took to new extremes some of the time-honored licenses of literature—the exploitation of multiple meaning, the deformation of syntax and lexis, and the loosening of discursive structures, for example—but used them in such a way as to provide a commentary on their function and constitution. "Commentary" is perhaps not the right term, because it suggests a privileged metatext that is able to observe an innocent text; Joyce's insights are presented in the form of intratextual and intertextual practice, and it takes a particular kind of reading to construe them as commentary. Such a reading is what I attempt, while at the same time I hope to share some of the pleasure to be found in Joyce's experiments—a word that might be taken quite literally, for the textual phenomena in question can be understood as tests of linguistic properties designed to show that the operations of language and the processes of reading are more varied, more complex, more entertainingly uncertain than most of our metatextual theories will allow. Joyce, perhaps more than any other writer, exploits the uncertain play between the two contradictory guises in which language presents itself to its readers: as a system of forms, in completely arbitrary relation to the meanings that those forms carry, and as impulses of imitation and motivation, constantly moving toward (though never reaching) a solidification of the connections between the sounds or shapes of language and their significances. (The first pulls literature toward the pole of "art," the second toward the pole of "nature.") The two linguistic theorists who play major roles in this book, Saussure and Jakobson, although largely in agreement on their general view of language, come down on opposite sides of this fence; for Saussure, apparent instances of motivation such as onomatopoeia are marginal phenomena, but for Jakobson they represent, in his phrase, "the essence of language." Joyce's texts contradict neither. It is the principle of arbitrariness, allowing infinite combinatory possibilities of form and content, which provides Joyce with his material and scope, while it is the principle of motivation, the never-fading desire on the part of the language-user to find or to make a system of signs in which form

11

and content indissolubly cohere, which produces the energy and pleasure by which Joyce's texts, and their readings, are propelled.

In tracing some of these issues through examples of Joyce's writing,
I pay particular attention to two other features of his work which are
of crucial importance in any discussion of literature as difference but
which are strongly resistant to objective analysis or description (that
resistance being part of their importance as aspects of the literary).
One is the relation between language and the erotic, or language and
the body; the other is the relation between language and the comic, or
language and laughter. (These relations are, of course, themselves
closely related.) I do not attempt to overcome that resistance to analysis and offer no descriptive framework or explanatory theory; but my
hope is that in keeping these questions alive while discussing Joyce's
language I reinforce the continuity between the domains of the literary, the erotic (in its widest sense), and the comic, all of which, I would
argue, derive their power from their evasion of taxonomic and analyt-
ical procedures. They are all fields, that is, in which prediction—the
central plank in scientific method—is impossible, because to predict
accurately is at once, and in the same gesture, to falsify the very
prediction one is making. That Joyce's achievement involved a challenge to literary conventions and to sexual taboos and was above all a
comic achievement are not fortuitously conjoined aspects of his work,
and if I have not attempted to present any argued thesis about their
relationship, I hope at least to have remained alert to what Wordsworth at one of his most remarkable moments calls "the grand elementary principle of pleasure," a principle always central to the experience of literary texts and yet so often omitted when literature is
discussed analytically, politically, or theoretically.

One feature of literary language which has frequently been singled
out as a distinguishing mark is the mimetic use of its physical existence as a sequence of sounds (and occasionally shapes). Joyce, while
revealing that his skill in this domain is as great as any writer's, also
shows that our explanations of this phenomenon consistently fall
short of its multiple and shifting modes of operation. The "Sirens"
episode of *Ulysses* is in part an exploration of this issue, and chapter 5
of this book follows through some of Joyce's mimetic maneuvers in
this episode, examining their significance to propose a new way of
conceiving the long-admired operations of onomatopoeia while at the
same time recognizing both the importance of what they represent in
literary discourse and their resistance to exhaustive analysis. The fol-

lowing chapter takes up the issue of linguistic deviation, looking particularly at Joyce's manipulation of expected language formations at the levels above the word: the syntactic rules that govern the sentence (concentrating on the "Sirens" episode) and the looser norms that operate at higher levels than the sentence (with special reference to "Eumaeus"). In doing so, it considers the relation between language and ideology as manifested in the verbal representation of the body and its desires, and it exemplifies a reading of Joyce's text which exposes some of the operations of that ideology.

The last two chapters take up *Finnegans Wake* as the ultimate test case for positivist or structuralist accounts of literary language. They argue for the critical and theoretical usefulness of regarding this text not as a marginal and easily dismissible member of the literary tradition but as the most complete manifestation of the distinctive qualities of that tradition. The claim implied in such an argument is that the radical force of Joyce's writing has not been fully registered in the literary studies (and practice) of the anglophone world, and that if it were registered in a thoroughgoing way, it would necessitate a revaluation of all our practices of writing, reading, and criticism. Whether such a revaluation is in fact desirable and/or possible is less a theoretical question than a pragmatic question concerning the society and the institutions within which those practices occur. To begin to spell out the justifications for and the consequences of a shift of this kind is perhaps to enhance the possibility of its occurring but is not to endorse it for any particular place and time. Every literary practice is caught up in a wider set of cultural practices, themselves part of a political fabric in which they serve a variety of ends; to argue the desirability of a change in literary activity or understanding for a particular moment, therefore, is to engage, knowingly or unknowingly, in a much wider discussion. Ultimately, all literary questions have to be posed—and indeed are posed—in this context, and one of the main aims of this book is to give historical and theoretical force to this point. It would require a much longer analysis of contemporary cultural and political experience than can be contained in a single volume, however, to argue a position with regard to future practices in writing and reading in the literary domain (and across whatever boundaries have been culturally established as constituting that domain). So my brief discussions of Joyce's limit text can only begin to clear the space that has to be open before such an analysis can be attempted. A subsidiary aim is to encourage hitherto reluctant readers to pick up the *Wake*, not as a Herculean labor to be undertaken or a foreign territory to be visited with guidebook in hand but as a storehouse to be explored for the same literary pleasures they enjoy finding, perhaps in less abundance, elsewhere.

Chapter 7 locates the strongest reason for the status of *Finnegans Wake* as a literary pariah in its lexical distortions, involving a careful examination of the difference between two apparently similar literary devices, the pun and the portmanteau. Although the latter would seem to take the deviance of literary language to an extreme, reminding us of Aristotle's warning against riddles and barbarisms, it affords a glimpse of language's modes of operation which even the pun conceals. The following chapter considers the distinction drawn in many critical and theoretical works between what is central to a literary text and what is digressive, and it shows by means of the apparently extraordinary case of *Finnegans Wake* that this is not a stable or a self-evident distinction. In so doing, it illustrates once more that insofar as literary language can be thought of as distinctive, such distinctiveness constitutes a challenge to all accounts of—and attempts to control—the operations of language (including the drawing of firm distinctions between literary and nonliterary) while at the same time manifesting with particular salience the ways in which all forms of language are constituted within political, social, and historical contexts.

The emphasis on this last point may seem out of place in a work primarily concerned with the close examination of examples of literary and theoretical writing, but it will be found that the discussions point consistently and ineluctably beyond the covers of the books that contain the examples. All the texts discussed, from the *Arte of English Poesie* to *Finnegans Wake*, raise the question of literature's place in the society that produces and situates it. In pursuing the question "What constitutes—or has been taken to constitute—the literary use of language?" the answers that offer themselves most immediately are, it is true, formal ones, and there is much to be learned by following them through. Such answers, however, always lead from the properties of the text to the activity of the reader in interpreting the text, in choosing this feature rather than that feature to take cognizance of, in responding to the cultural positioning of the text as reflected in its mode of presentation. And to understand the reader's activity (and to de-idealize this hypostatization so that the object of our interest becomes instead "readers' activities") we have to move to wider cultural and social questions.[3] Even here, I would argue, the problems remain unsolved: Why does the culture privilege certain kinds of language and certain modes of reading? Such a question can receive an answer only when we reach the realm of political and economic relations, the structures of power, dominance, and resistance which determine the patterns and privileges of cultural formations. Or, more accurately, all our questions change radically when we reach this point, and we see that the answers we were hoping to find do not exist. The answers to the new questions—questions about the formation of "taste" as an aspect of class relations, about the power structures and political alignments of educational institutions, about the ownership and operation of the publishing industry and the communications media (all questions to be asked afresh for every historical period and cultural formation)—have to be sought by means of a very different kind of study. Even then we would not reach "objective" answers, standing safely distant at last from the unreliable and unpredictable texts, for the texts themselves would pose questions—including political questions—that would reverberate strongly in the wider sphere.[4] Moreover, such a study would necessarily be part of the struggle of interpretations which is itself part of the wider political struggle, with its

[3]Mary Louise Pratt has written valuably on the danger of generalizing from arguments constructed on the basis of idealized linguistic situations; see "The Ideology of Speech-Act Theory" and "Linguistic Utopias."

[4]De Man argues that attention to "literariness," as the category of which literary theory treats (and which it perhaps constitutes), can free discourse from naive assumptions about the relation between linguistic and natural reality, which have a strong ideological hold. "It follows," he continues, "that, more than any other mode of inquiry, including economics, the linguistics of literariness is a powerful and indispensable tool in the unmasking of ideological aberrations, as well as a determining factor in accounting for their occurrence. Those who reproach literary theory for being oblivious to social and historical (that is to say ideological) reality are merely stating their fear at having their own ideological mystifications exposed by the tool they are trying to discredit. They are, in short, very poor readers of Marx's *German Ideology*" ("The Resistance to Theory," 11). Bourdieu's *Distinction*, highly impressive both in its detailed empirical investigation and in its theoretical sophistication, is finally limited by its refusal to allow any force to the questions raised about its methodology and assumptions by what de Man calls "literariness." That the process whereby social judgments are formed and propagated, however complete its determination by socioeconomic factors, will always include, de jure, the potential to exceed and outstrip all possible objective accounts of it, is something that the sociologist, working within the scientific tradition, cannot accept. Saussure's work on language is caught within a similar problematic, as will be seen in chapter 4.

own conscious or unconscious goals and rules, and one would never stop (one could never stop) offering readings of texts to be worked over, modified, or rejected, in many places and at many times.

This book, though it makes no attempt at the sociopolitical study I have outlined, aims to show why the domain of literature and of literary theory cannot provide its own self-sufficient and lasting answers to the question of the distinctiveness of literary language, however revealing the answers it proposes may be about the characteristics of literature and the operations of interpretation and evaluation in our culture. If art, as manifested in concrete examples as they are responded to in specific situations, always exceeds the rules and codes adduced as its determinants—and one of my objects is to show that this is necessarily the case—then the judgments that control its status and function as art must be related to the wider context in which they are formed, sustained, and modified. At the same time, however, these case studies aim to indicate some of the reasons why textual interpretation, in both the narrower and the wider domains, will always remain more a matter of power and persuasion, legitimacy and authority, rhetoric and poetry, than of demonstration, definitiveness, and truth.

Chapter 2

Nature, Art, and the Supplement
in Renaissance Literary Theory:
Puttenham's Poetics of Decorum

Nature and Art

A NY attempt to examine the ways in which the question of literary language was conceived of and discussed in a period as historically and culturally distant from our own as the English Renaissance involves difficulties that cannot finally be overcome. We cannot step outside the structures of thought and habits of mind with which we perceive the past, nor can we make ourselves fully conscious of the motivations and assumptions that propel our investigation and determine what we see and what we give weight to. However, as long as we recognize that our findings can never be verified, and that many "historical" readings have come to look, with the further passage of history, like little more than the enlisting of past texts in current theoretical and ideological battles, we ought to be able to muster sufficient skepticism and scrupulousness to perform a useful task of recovery and revaluation.[1] Certainly, the attempt to read texts of the

---

[1]Among those who have acknowledged the difficulty of the project, and who have offered advice on carrying it out, are Michel Foucault in *The Archaeology of Knowledge* and Frank Lentricchia in *After the New Criticism.* Two essays that deal with the problem in relation to the Renaissance are Thomas M. Greene, "Anti-hermeneutics" (see especially 143-46) and Michael McCanles, "The Authentic Discourse of the Renaissance." Sometimes the advice amounts to little more than "try as hard as you can," although Foucault and McCanles give a clear indication of the necessary intractability of the problem.

past in the light of their own determination by different discursive (and sociopolitical) systems can be a valuable means of gaining some purchase on the preconceptions and habits that both constrain and facilitate our own thinking, even if the contrary perspective that we might establish will itself necessarily be subject—in ways we cannot know—to prevailing modes of thought.

But there are dangers of closeness as well as of distance. Current discussions of literary and linguistic theory in the European languages are in a direct line of descent from those discussions I am proposing to reexamine; differences in fundamental assumptions will be much easier to see than the continuities that run between then and now (and begin, of course, further back in history). It is necessary, therefore, to direct attention also to similarities between the discursive systems of the past and those of the present and to attempt a defamiliarization that will make possible an analysis of both. One way of doing so is to ask how the features of discourse being examined relate to the systems of cultural and political dominance and subservience, inclusion and exclusion, in which they occur and to consider the possibility of historical continuities at this level as well. I shall touch on only a very few aspects of this question; the role played by gender in the determination of the literary, for instance, is an important issue that deserves full-length study but can be only raised here in the hope that it will be pursued elsewhere.

The text I use to exemplify the Renaissance's posing of the question of literary difference is George Puttenham's *Arte of English Poesie*, first published in 1589.[2] This treatise, often regarded as a charming but unsophisticated and inconsistent potpourri of Renaissance commonplaces,[3] may be read as a quite strenuous attempt to articulate

[2]I use the edition by Gladys Doidge Willcock and Alice Walker (which includes a long introduction on such problematic matters as authorship and dating—matters that have no direct bearing on my argument here). Page references are given in the text.

[3]The first published reference to it, by Sir John Harington in "A Brief Apology for Poetry" (1591), was derogatory; Harington remarks that "the poore gentleman laboreth greatly to prove, or rather to make Poetrie an art" and compares him pointedly with "M. *Sidney* and all the learneder sort that have written of it" (G. Gregory Smith, *Elizabethan Critical Essays*, 2:196-97). The note of condescension (as well as the unfavorable comparison with Sidney) has been echoed by many later commentators. Smith in his introduction to *Elizabethan Critical Essays*, after praising Sidney and Daniel, includes Puttenham's work among "essays of less sustained power" (lxx). Baxter Hathaway opens his introduction to a modern facsimile of Arber's 1906 reprint with a warning that "one must shut one's eyes to the book's many shortcomings" and later

crucial problems having to do with the status of poetic language within a specific linguistic and cultural framework. Not only does it show clearly the parameters of Renaissance discourse in regard to this issue, but it also offers a clearer view than a more recent text might do of the tacit boundaries to our own confrontations with related questions. In particular, to the degree that it appears fissured or self-contradictory it may reveal conceptual inconsistencies or blind spots over which the passage of later intellectual history has laid down a veneer, but which are still present in our own thinking. Puttenham's treatise is especially useful in this respect because it does not exercise to the full the rhetorical and persuasive powers that are, in part, its subject—unlike, for instance, Sidney's roughly contemporary *Apologie for Poetrie*, where tensions and contradictions tend to disappear under the immaculate surface of courtly *sprezzatura*.[4]

Although we no longer automatically divide the world around us, or the actions of men and women, into the broad and exclusive categories of Nature and Art, the traces of this mental habit are everywhere to be found, from theories of poetic language to the theological debate over contraception. The distinction between nature and art (I shall dispense with the honorific capitals, except in quotations) was, of course, a classical and medieval commonplace as well as a Renaissance and post-Renaissance one. Its history, its ubiquity, and its importance in sixteenth- and seventeenth-century English literature have been ably surveyed by Edward William Tayler in *Nature and Art in Renaissance Literature*, and it is with some of Tayler's formulations of the relationship between the two terms that I begin. Tayler finds that although the pairing of nature and art is to be met with at every turn in Renaissance writing, the relationship between them is presented in remarkably varying terms: "Nature and art were combined, accord-

---

complains about the work's "flippancy, its popularization and watering-down of theory for court consumption," applauding it rather faintly as a "more than adequate summation of a traditional approach to poetics" and a "synthesis of commonplaces" (v, xxiii–xxiv). W. K. Wimsatt and Cleanth Brooks refer to Puttenham's "uneven collection of jokes and conceits and the theoretical hints which he musters to introduce them" (*Literary Criticism*, 234). The "accuracy" of such assessments is not the issue; more important is what kind of reading such attitudes produce and are produced by.

[4]Two readings of the *Apologie* which highlight some of these contradictory processes are those by Margaret W. Ferguson in *Trials of Desire*, chap. 4, and Ronald Levao in *Renaissance Minds and Their Fictions*, chap. 5. On Sidney's *sprezzatura*, see also Daniel Javitch, "The Impure Motives of Elizabethan Poetry."

ing to a writer's temperament, training, and purposes, in innumerable and sometimes contradictory ways" (27). The contrast between the two most characteristic views of the dichotomy could hardly be more extreme: "When Art is viewed eulogistically—as the product of man's 'erected wit', of a faculty not entirely impaired by the Fall, of a faculty capable of rational creativity—then Nature usually signifies the unformed, the inchoate, the imperfect, or even the corrupt. . . . When, on the other hand, Art is viewed pejoratively—as mere imitation, falsification, reprehensible counterfeit, or even perversion—then Nature signifies the original, the unspoiled, the transcendent, or even the perfect" (36). Yet in spite of the contradictory uses to which the pairing was put, there appears to have been widespread agreement on its validity as a means of dividing the entirety of human experience. Tayler calls the pairing "indispensable to the thinkers of the Renaissance" and adds that "the use of one term seems automatically to suggest the other, as if the absence of one of the words must betray the fact that the subject has been examined incompletely" (21).

Universal assent as to the dichotomous character of experience, the appropriateness of these terms to label the divisions, and their absolute mutual dependence—and widespread disagreement as to the significance of the division and the meaning of the terms themselves: this curious phenomenon is made even more curious by the fact that contradictory positions are often to be found within a single author. "On one occasion," writes Tayler, "a writer may maintain that Art perfects Nature, on another that Art perverts Nature" (30), and among the writers who betray inconsistencies in their various accounts of the distinction Tayler includes not only Renaissance poets and theorists but Plato, Aristotle, Seneca, and Cicero. Arthur O. Lovejoy and George Boas, in *Primitivism and Related Ideas in Antiquity*, also stress the ambiguities in the way Plato and Aristotle handle the terms: the latter, for instance, puts forward an equivocal notion of art, which, "in so far as it consists in the transformation of a thing by an external agency, rather than by the spontaneous self-realization of the essence," is "antithetic to 'nature'" but, in the guise of education, instruction, and rigorous discipline, is "necessary to supplement" nature (189). (We might note the verb Lovejoy and Boas choose to convey the relation of art to nature in Aristotle's writing; they use it again in summarizing Cicero's view that the arts are "a necessary supplement to nature" [247].) Several writers have discussed the complexity of the term "nature" (and its equivalents, "physis," "natura," and "kind") in the history of Western thought and discursive practice. Lovejoy and Boas concentrate on the term's varied use as an ethical norm (chap. 3 and an appendix that lists sixty-six meanings). Elsewhere Lovejoy enumerates the functions of "nature" in eighteenth-century aesthetic discourse, emphasizing both the centrality and the instability of the concept: "'Nature' has, of course, been the chief and most pregnant word in the terminology of all the normative provinces of thought in the West; and the multiplicity of its meanings has made it easy, and common, to slip more or less insensibly from one connotation to another, and thus in the end to pass from one ethical or aesthetic standard to its very antithesis, while nominally professing the same principles" (*Essays in the History of Ideas*, 69). Raymond Williams's assessment of the term's importance is similar to Lovejoy's: "*Nature* is perhaps the most complex word in the language. . . . *Nature* is a word which carries, over a very long period, many of the major variations of human thought" (*Keywords*, 184, 189). Williams says of this complexity: "What can be seen as an uncertainty was also a tension: nature was at once innocent, unprovided, sure, unsure, fruitful, destructive, a pure force and tainted and cursed" (187). Other accounts that stress the term's polysemy are C. S. Lewis's fifty-page discussion in *Studies in Words* and A. E. Pilkington's essay "'Nature' as Ethical Norm in the Enlightenment."

Nature, then, appears in Renaissance writing and in the classical texts upon which that writing drew as both the principle of perfection and the principle of imperfection—and so does art, in a contrary or complementary relationship. How are we to characterize such an unstable and apparently self-contradictory distinction? Is it sufficient to refer to the changeableness and variety of opinion and to attempt to extract some compromise "balance" between nature and art as representing the best possible Renaissance position on the matter? Or is radical instability in some way intrinsic to the distinction and to its function within the discourse of the period?[5]

[5]Tayler's emphasis is not so much on the contradictoriness as on a reading that will minimize it. Thus he writes of the classical authors mentioned: "There are passages open to primitivistic or 'naturalistic' interpretation, but the balance in all of these minds falls finally against Nature in the sense of the spontaneous and unreflective" (51). J. W. H. Atkins, in *English Literary Criticism: The Renascence*, comes to a different conclusion about the same texts, finding that nature (or reason) is the final court of appeal. Thus he quotes from a passage by Quintilian (*Institutionis Oratoriae* 9.4.120) in which the writer is advised in matters of rhythm to take nature for a guide (166)—but he omits

Nature, Art, and the Supplement in the Renaissance

The Supplement and the Pharmakon

The opposition of nature and art is, of course, related to several other divisions typical of Western thought, among them the literal versus the figurative, wisdom versus eloquence, dialectic (or logic) versus rhetoric, object versus sign (or representation), speech versus writing, and nature itself versus nurture, or convention, or culture. Jacques Derrida, in discussing several of these dualisms as they occur in a variety of texts, literary and philosophical, from Plato to Ponge, has sought to show that they do not and cannot function as stable, given, mutually exclusive oppositions of which one member is primary and self-sufficient and the other secondary, exterior, and dependent. His deconstructive readings do not by any means invalidate the distinctions in question or find fault with the texts that rely on them; on the contrary, they enhance the significance of the texts as cultural indexes by tracing within them much more than the writer's conscious intentions. As Derrida puts it in *Of Grammatology*, "The writer writes *in* a language and *in* a logic whose proper system, laws, and life his discourse by definition cannot dominate absolutely. He uses them only by letting himself, after a fashion and up to a point, be governed by the system. And the reading must always aim at a certain relationship, unperceived by the writer, between what he commands and what he does not command of the patterns of the language that he uses" (158).

As tools for the task at hand, I take two of Derrida's best-known strategic terms, or *brisures*. These are not critical or philosophical *concepts* (the concept of the "concept" is one of the questions at issue) but words taken from texts under discussion which offer, in their own peculiar double allegiances, levers to shift some of the Western mind's most fixed assumptions. (Derrida, we must remember, is using a rhet-

---

the last part of Quintilian's sentence, which reads "none the less there will always be some principle of art underlying the promptings of nature" (Loeb ed.). Madeleine Doran is another who seeks a principle of "balance" to reconcile contradictions, in her discussion of "Art *vs.* Nature" in Renaissance writing (*Endeavors of Art*, 54-70), while Edwin M. Duval, discussing a similar inconsistency in Montaigne's "Des Cannibales," explains it as a deliberate demonstration of the mutability of human judgment ("Lessons of the New World"). It is perhaps Longinus who achieves the most skillful accommodation between the two terms: after giving several reasons why effects of the sublime in literature require art as well as nature, he comments, "Most important of all, the very fact that some things in literature depend on nature alone can itself be learned only from art" (*On Sublimity*, 463).

orical and not a logical or dialectical method: we are not being shown a previously veiled "truth" but by a certain kind of persuasive language are being freed from the narrow paths we have hitherto traveled. But the distinction between "rhetorical" and "logical" which I have just made is itself subject to deconstruction; Derrida's practice is not absolutely different from the way philosophy has always functioned.) One of these hinge-words Derrida finds at crucial junctures in Rousseau's writing: *supplément* (together with its related forms), a word that can mean both that which *supplements* something already complete in itself and that which *supplies* what is missing from something incomplete in an important respect—"two significations," writes Derrida, "whose cohabitation is as strange as it is necessary" (*Grammatology*, 144). (The English word *supplement* is not quite as self-divided but serves as the most convenient translation: think of the two ways of perceiving the *OED Supplement*, as a later and subsidiary addition to a work that has long stood as complete and exhaustive and as that which makes the *OED* complete and exhaustive.) These two meanings are, of course, quite contradictory according to normal logic, and one would assume that, for any given occurrence of the word, only one meaning is possible. But Derrida demonstrates that certain central dichotomies in Rousseau's writing are related in a way that renders both meanings appropriate at the same time: what is offered as mere addition, in other words, also makes up for an important lack—and is seen as threatening because of its tendency to usurp that to which it should be only peripheral (see *Grammatology*, 144-64). Education, for example, which is for Rousseau inherently secondary in that it adds to the perfect, innocent development of nature, is called upon to perform a crucial function in making up for weaknesses in the "natural" constitution of every child. (In trying to think about this elusive knot of relations, it is important to hold on to the fact that *reason* can never grasp the structure of supplementarity because reason is constituted by the *rejection* of supplementarity, the rejection of any possibility that an entity can be both itself and not itself—a rejection that goes back to the beginning of the Western philosophical tradition.) In "Plato's Pharmacy" (*Dissemination*, 61-171), Derrida offers a reading of the *Phaedrus* in which the word *pharmakon* is seen to operate in a similarly double way: as that which is added to the natural organism, it can mean both poison *and* beneficial medicament, and, rejected as the former, it inevitably returns as the latter, restoring perfection to the naturally flawed body. Something of its self-contradictoriness exists in the connotations of the word *drug,* an artificial addition to the body's natural intake which can be either a vicious or a remedial supplement. As we shall see, neither these terms themselves nor the unstable relations that they represent are remote from sixteenth-century discourse.

The Decorous Art of English Poetry

The stability and mutual exclusiveness of the opposition between nature and art seems to be a necessary foundation for Puttenham's enterprise, which is the composition of a manual setting out in detail what can be said about English poetry as an art of language. At first sight the distinction, as it operated for an Elizabethan, seems solid enough: "nature" refers to that which occurs *naturally,* or by *kind,* by virtue of what a thing is in all its fullness and self-sufficiency, "art" to that which is contrived by an *artificer* working upon the given materials of nature. Every object or specimen of behavior which is not natural is artificial (or "artful"), and vice versa. Human beings behave naturally by following *instinct* and artificially by learning and following the *rules* of the art in question. The connection between art and rules is always very close. Puttenham gives as the accepted definition of art "a certaine order of rules prescribed by reason and gathered by experience," and he states that poetry was not an art "until by studious persons fashioned and reduced into a method of rules and precepts" (5).[6] (Although this notion may seem completely foreign to later conceptions of art which regard artifice and rules with hostility, I shall argue in the following chapter that the difference is not as great as first appears.) An art is therefore by definition *teachable,* and an "Art" of English poetry is designed to teach (and to further) that art by setting out its rules and precepts. The first of the three books of Puttenham's *Arte,* entitled "Of Poets and Poesie," is not strictly speaking of this kind; it is partly a defense, partly a description and a

---

[6]On the importance of rules in Elizabethan conceptions of art, see my *Well-weighed Syllables* (138-43 and passim). Puttenham's association of rules with *reason* marks another dimension of the question which it is not possible to broach here (though it is implicated, as I suggested earlier, in the very procedures we are using). I simply note that reason can appear on the side of either nature or art, depending on whether the latter is seen as perverter or perfecter of the former (see Tayler, 27-30 and passim, and Duval, 103).

24

history of poetry. But Book Two, "Of Proportion," and Book Three, "Of Ornament," which together account for more than three-quarters of the work, set out without stinting on detail the two methods by which natural language is altered by the art, or artifice, of the poet— by being organized into lines of regular verse and stanzas, and by being enriched with rhetorical figures. (Puttenham's definition of poetry is a strictly formal one, unlike, say, Sidney's, whose treatise is primarily an apology for *fiction*, whether in verse or in prose.)

Again and again Puttenham stresses the artificiality of art and its distance from nature. Book Two deals with intricate rhyme-schemes, complex stanza-forms, highly intellectualized visual devices, and the adoption of the elaborate forms of classical versification into English. It uses a metaphoric language that is not at all that of the natural world but that of other craftsmen, the skillful musician dealing in harmony and cadence, for instance, or the fine jeweler (Puttenham is full of admiration for the Oriental verse that he has had described to him as "engraven in gold, silver or ivorie, and sometimes with letters of ametist, rubie, emerald or topas curiousely cemented and peeced together" [92]). Book Three begins with an image designed to fix firmly the distinction on which the entire discussion depends: just as "great Madames of honour . . . thinke themselves more amiable in every mans eye, when they be in their richest attire, suppose of silkes or tyssewes and costly embroideries, than when they go in cloth or in any other plaine and simple apparell. Even so cannot our vulgar Poesie shew it selfe either gallant or gorgious, if any lymme be left naked and bare" (137). The costly embroideries of poetry are, of course, "figures and figurative speaches, which be the flowers as it were and coulours that a Poet setteth upon his language by arte" (138).[7] Nature is to art as the naked is to the clothed, the literal to the figurative, the prosaic and everyday to the poetic. This third book is largely taken up with Puttenham's engaging catalog of the figures of rhetoric according to his own scheme of classification: the "auricular," which delight the ear alone, the "sensable," which inveigle the mind, and the "sententious," which bring pleasure to both. Puttenham's

[7]The use of "flowers" as a frequent metaphor for rhetorical devices is an interesting one. Although so habitual in this context that it could clearly be used (as here) without any connotations of the natural, it becomes elsewhere a hinge between the natural and the artificial. One of the places where this happens, of course, is where the art of the gardener (in some respects the paradigmatic art-form) is in question; we shall encounter an example later in this chapter.

25

poetics seem to represent a view of art as something defined *against* nature, which would tend to be associated with the instinctive, the savage, the uncivil, the ignorant—a view for which there is a great deal of evidence in his time and which retained at least a degree of force until the later eighteenth century, when art begins to claim for itself those "natural" qualities, renaming them "spontaneity," "sincerity," "innocence," and so forth. But to read Puttenham only as a representative of this Renaissance commonplace is to ignore much that is present in his text, and it is worth pausing on a few of the places at which something more complex— and much less easy to describe— is happening.

In the title to the second chapter of Book One Puttenham announces in general terms the position that the entire work is going to defend and elaborate: "That There May Be an Art of Our English Poesie, Aswell as There is of the Latine and Greeke" (5). In substantiating this claim, Puttenham is faced with the same problem that faced all defenders of vernacular poetry in the Renaissance: the prosody of the modern-language verse traditions, as far as it was understood, seemed to lack the intense degree of organization of Latin and Greek verse, by which every syllable was weighed and measured and given an appropriate place in the line. One response, repeated all over Europe throughout the sixteenth century, was to attempt to create similar metrical forms in the vernacular. The other was to look for organizing principles of equivalent intricacy and reliability in the vernacular tradition itself. It is typical of Puttenham's open enacting of the contradictions within the intellectual fabric of his age that he attempts both, scarcely making an effort to reconcile the two radically different solutions and unintentionally providing evidence both for the impossibility of a quantitative system of meter in English and for the prevailing lack of insight into the structures of English verse.[8]

But the problem goes deeper, for it is one aspect of a more generalized dilemma that lies at the heart of the humanist program of *imitation*. The only goal vernacular verse can set itself, given the controlling assumptions of humanism, is to match its model, classical verse; yet because that model is taken to be the absolute standard, the

[8]See Attridge, *Well-weighed Syllables*, 217-19. The disparity between the two arguments is usually taken as an indication that they were written at different times (see Willcock and Walker's Introduction to Puttenham's *Arte*, xliv–liii). If this view is accepted, we still have to account for the fact that Puttenham did not correct the earlier argument but merely added the latter one—as a supplement.

perfect exemplar, vernacular verse is necessarily condemned always to fall short.[9] This is our first example—one we need not dwell on—of the problematic of the supplement: vernacular verse necessarily is only an addition to the already complete and fully realized body of classical verse, and if it appears to be making claims to be an improvement on, or a substitute for, classical verse, which it must do to escape perpetual secondariness, it constitutes a threat to the latter's exemplary status and therefore to its own raison d'être. Any assertion of the merits of modern as compared with classical verse, therefore, must somehow involve at the same time a counterassertion, or the humanist program will disintegrate.

In his attempt to deal with this issue early in Book One, Puttenham calls on the opposition between nature and art to argue that English versification is quite different from, and as good as (but, significantly, not better than), that of Latin and Greek. The argument is that the English rhyming type of verse, to judge from historical evidence and reports of travelers, is "the first and most ancient Poesie, and the most universall, which two points do otherwise give to all humane inventions and affaires no small credit." So, Puttenham can boast, "our maner of vulgar Poesie is more ancient than the artificiall of the Greeks and Latines, ours comming by instinct of nature, which was before Art or observation" (10). At the very beginning of his art of English poetry, Puttenham seems to be privileging nature over art, instinct over rules. Not surprisingly, he quickly adds a qualification, that such priority is only priority in *time*, like the priority of the naked over the clothed or the ignorant over the learned. This addition seems to go to the opposite extreme, demolishing the case for the vernacular by associating it with the naked and the ignorant, but Puttenham is reluctant to let the earlier argument go and attempts a highly unstable compromise: "The naturall Poesie therefore being aided and amended by Art, and not utterly altered or obscured, but some signe left of it, (as the Greekes and Latines have left none) is no lesse to be allowed and commended than theirs" (10). Naturalness manages to be both an inherent advantage and, in a metaphor at least as old as Aristotle, a weakness in need of the aid and amendment of art. (Not until Daniel's *Defence of Ryme* [1603] is the argument for the

[9]The tensions within the Renaissance program of imitation have been ably brought out by several scholars, notably Thomas M. Greene, *The Light in Troy;* Terence Cave, *The Cornucopian Text*, especially chap. 2; Margaret Ferguson, *Trials of Desire*, especially chap. 2; and David Quint, *Origin and Originality in Renaissance Literature.*

natural superiority of vernacular versification carried through without flinching—and that entails the abandonment of a large part of the humanist program.)[10]

In a later chapter of Book One, Puttenham firmly reasserts the slightly shaken superiority of the artificial over the natural, sharpening the criticism of his own appeal to nature and its twin associates, universality and antiquity. Poetry is praiseworthy not only "because I said it was a metricall speach used by the first men, but because it is a metricall speach corrected and reformed by discreet judgements, and with no lesse cunning and curiositie than the Greeke and Latine Poesie, and by Art bewtified and adorned, and brought far from the primitive rudenesse of the first inventors, otherwise it might be sayd to me that *Adam* and *Eves* apernes were the gayest garmentes, because they were the first, and the shepheardes tente or pavillion, the best housing, because it was the most auncient and most universall" (23). But now the whole argument in favor of English versification is threatened, and nature has to be reintroduced in another attempt to reconcile the irreconcileable: "It is not my meaning but that Art and cunning concurring with nature, antiquitie and universalitie, in things indifferent, and not evill, doe make them more laudable" (23). Art, it seems, must in some way agree with nature even though it is defined against nature. And lest this requirement should seem to throw the ball entirely back into nature's court, there is the important qualification "in things indifferent, and not evill." The role of the artist is to identify what is evil in nature and therefore not to be followed. In this way nature is "corrected and reformed by discreet judgements." Poetry is modeled on nature yet somehow perfects nature (in the same way that, in the example of supplementarity noted earlier, modern poetry is both modeled on and yet perfects classical poetry). The concept of nature is self-divided (and is therefore not strictly a concept): it stands both for that which is itself, in total self-sufficiency, and that which is necessarily incomplete and in need of repair.

But there is a further difficulty. Insofar as art departs from nature itself (and not just flawed nature) and is constituted as art by that departure, it is in some sense essentially *un*natural. The figures of rhetoric have always been defined as transgressions of the norms of what Puttenham, like many of his successors through to the present day, calls "ordinary" language. In his chapter "Of Figures and Figur-

---

[10]See my discussion of Daniel's *Defence of Ryme* in *Well-weighed Syllables*, 232-34.

ative Speaches," Puttenham is perfectly explicit about this: "As figures be the instruments of ornament in every language, so be they also in a sorte abuses or rather trespasses in speach, because they passe the ordinary limits of common utterance, and be occupied of purpose to deceive the eare and also the minde, drawing it from plainnesse and simplicitie to a certaine doublenesse, whereby our talke is the more guilefull and abusing" (154). Paradoxically, that which is unnatural and deceitful is able to cure nature of its faults—in a specific context. Most of these vices, says Puttenham, can in poetry be transformed into virtues, and they occur as such in his lengthy list. Even some of the deviations that he lists unambiguously as vices can on some occasions become virtues, if they are handled in a particular manner by the poet.

What is it that defines the delicate—yet crucial—balance between virtue and vice? What is the source of the "discreet judgments" whereby nature is "corrected and reformed" by art and not further depraved? To answer these questions Puttenham invokes a completely independent standard, which he calls by a plethora of different names, their proliferation suggesting the importance of this moment within the argument as well as its elusiveness as a stable concept. Its titles include *decorum* (which I shall arbitrarily favor), *decency, discretion, seemliness, comeliness, agreeableness, seasonableness, well-temperedness, aptness, fittingness, good grace, conformity, proportion,* and *conveniency.*[11] And in a tight corner this notion is always available to be appealed to, by one or another of its names. If the argument seems to be heading toward a point where virtue and vice, good art and bad art, become

[11]Decorum in one guise or another has been a recurrent (and indispensable) element in the tradition of classical and postclassical literary criticism until this century. It is usually presented as a neutral critical term, referring to the proper matching of the various aspects of a text, so that its style is appropriate to the speaker, the theme, the time and place, the audience, and so forth; see, for instance, Smith, *Essays,* xli–xlvi; Rosemond Tuve, *Elizabethan and Metaphysical Imagery,* chap. 9 and passim; and Annabel M. Patterson, *Hermogenes and the Renaissance,* chap. 1. For a useful survey of the notion of decorum in classical, medieval, and Renaissance writing, see Thomas Kranidas, *The Fierce Equation,* chap. 1. Chapter 3 below deals with a Romantic transformation of the idea of decorum, and in this century Valéry remains wholly, and typically, within this tradition when, having defined the writer of literature as a "maker of *deviations,*" he adds that it is a question only of "the deviations that enrich" ("The Poet's Rights over Language," in *The Art of Poetry,* 172). Literary structuralism can be understood as an attempt to abolish the appeal to any such unformulatable principle by standing outside it and giving an objective account of it. I discuss in chapters 4-8 some of the difficulties entailed in the project of finding a position outside linguistic and literary systems.

indistinguishable—and the whole of Puttenham's enterprise threatens to collapse—decorum can step in to make the vital decision. In his comparison with the "great Madames of honour," Puttenham is comically forthright about the disastrous effects of attempting artful enhancement without the necessary control exercised by decorum. "If the same coulours in our arte of Poesie . . . be not well tempered, or not well layd, or be used in excesse, or never so little disordered or misplaced, they not onely give it no maner of grace at all, but rather do disfigure the stuffe and spill the whole workmanship taking away all bewtie and good liking from it, no lesse than if the crimson tainte, which should be laid upon a Ladies lips, or right in the center of her cheekes should by some oversight or mishap be applied to her forhead or chinne, it would make (ye would say) but a very ridiculous bewtie" (138). Decorum is the principle whereby any given poetic device can be judged, according to all the specific, perhaps unique, configurations of its individual situation. Clearly it is by far the most important rule in the poet's handbook; without it, he might as well not begin to write. Yet what emerges with surprising clarity from Puttenham's text is that *there is no such rule, and there could not possibly be one.* Decorum is precisely that aspect of the poet's art which is not reducible to rule. And human activity that is not reducible to rule is usually called "natural."

Puttenham does not shy away from this conclusion. When he begins his full and direct treatment of decorum in the third-to-last chapter (having availed himself somewhat surreptitiously of its aid throughout the treatise), he stresses both its central importance and its unamenability to rules: "In all things to use decencie, is it onely that giveth every thing his good grace and without which nothing in mans speach could seeme good or gracious, in so much as many times it makes a bewtifull figure fall into a deformitie, and on th'other side a vicious speach seeme pleasaunt and bewtifull: this decencie is therfore the line and levell for al good makers to do their busines by. But herein resteth the difficultie, to know what this good grace is, and wherein it consisteth, for peradventure it be easier to conceave than to expresse" (261). Puttenham's way of expressing it is by means of an analogy between mind and senses: as, for instance, a sound that is "too loude or too low or otherwise confuse" is displeasing to the ear, so a "mental object" (Puttenham's phrase), if it is disproportioned, can be displeasing to the mind. And whence is this immediate and appar-

ently instinctive response derived? "This lovely conformitie, or proportion, or conveniencie betweene the sence and the sensible hath
nature her selfe first most carefully observed in all her owne workes,
then also by kinde graft it in the appetites of every creature working
by intelligence to covet and desire: and in their actions to imitate and
performe: and of man chiefly before any other creature aswell in his
speaches as in every other part of his behaviour" (262). To counteract
the side effects of art's distance from nature—its potential viciousness, ridiculousness, and duplicity—a principle operating in the name
of nature must be reintroduced. That which the *pharmakon* is designed to cure must itself become a *pharmakon*. Thus in using the
analogy of the "Madame of honour" Puttenham refers to limbs clad
in their "*kindly* clothes and coulours" (137), those clothes and colors
which are in some way "fitting" or "natural" for the body.

It follows that the products of art and those of nature can be very
difficult to tell apart. In praising two of his favorite speakers in Parlia-
ment and the Star Chamber, Puttenham observes that it "maketh no
matter whether the same eloquence be naturall to them or artificiall
(though I thinke rather naturall) yet were they knowen to be learned
and not unskilfull of th'arte, when they were yonger men" (139-40).
He does not really know which it is—and it matters perhaps a little
more to him than he admits. Similarly, discussing the question of
style, he notes that a certain manner of writing is "many times naturall
to the writer, many times his peculier by election and arte, and such as
either he keepeth by skill, or holdeth on by ignorance, and will not or
peradventure cannot easily alter into any other" (148).

But the naturalness of art reaches even further, for an artful principle, it seems, is already present in nature. In discussing "feete of three
times," Puttenham notes that apart from the dactyl "they have not
hitherto bene made artificiall [that is, not been admitted into the art
of English poetry], yet nowe by more curious observation they might
be. Since all artes grew first by observation of natures proceedings
and custome" (128). And toward the end of the work Puttenham even
blurs the distinction to the extent of tracing the figures of rhetoric—
those "trespasses in speach"—back to nature itself: "All your figures
Poeticall or Rhethoricall, are but observations of strange speeches,
and such as without any arte at al we should use, and commonly do,
even by very nature without discipline" (298). Here he is perhaps
going too far, because art seems now to have disappeared entirely,

31

and he quickly adds, after noting that different people use these "strange speeches" to differing extents and in differing ways, "so as we may conclude, that nature her selfe suggesteth the figure in this or that forme: but arte aydeth the judgement of his use and application" (298). However, we know by now that the art in question, which makes judgments in specific situations—that is, the art of decorum— is in some way a natural rather than an artificial principle.

That art's difference from nature must be controlled by a natural principle is not an unfamiliar point of view, its most memorable expression in English perhaps being Shakespeare's lines on the subject in *The Winter's Tale*.[12] Perdita does not grow "carnations and streak'd gillyvors" in her rural garden, because of her belief in nature's perfection and in art's viciousness as the dangerous supplement to that perfection:

> I have heard it said
> There is an art which in their piedness shares
> With great creating Nature. (4.4. 86-88)

To which Polixenes replies, as might Puttenham (though the Shakespearean courtier does it a good deal more eloquently):

> Say there be;
> Yet Nature is made better by no mean
> But Nature makes that mean: so over that art
> Which you say adds to Nature, is an art
> That Nature makes. You see, sweet maid, we marry
> A gentler scion to the wildest stock,
> And make conceive a bark of baser kind
> By bud of nobler race. This is an art
> Which does mend Nature—change it rather, but
> The art itself is Nature.   (4.4. 88-97)

Only nature, then, can provide the art by which to make good its own deficiencies. As Derrida puts it, "the supplement comes *naturally* to put itself in Nature's place" (*Grammatology,* 149).

[12]Tayler points out that both Plato and Aristotle make similar comments and also quotes John of Salisbury to the same effect (135-36, 79). Coleridge, in the course of his disagreement with Wordsworth over the relationship of art and nature, cites the passage from *The Winter's Tale* (see chapter 3, n. 37 below).

The Politics of Nature

We need to scrutinize this return of nature a little more closely, however. As the sentence just quoted from Derrida might suggest, what has actually happened in the course of the argument is not that great creating nature, having been excluded by art, is allowed back in the form of decorum to control art; rather, a surrogate that is more acceptable to Puttenham and his courtly readers has taken over nature's role as a final determinant of art. Although the natural judgment of decorum is said to be equivalent to the ear's dislike of a harsh sound, it turns out not to be as universal a human capacity as aural sensitivity to unpleasant noise (it was universality that caused Puttenham trouble in Book One). The recurrent problem with decorum—and Puttenham sees this as clearly as anyone before or since—is that, because a final appeal to rule is by definition impossible, the "correctness" of the judgment to be made is ultimately a matter of the authority of the judge. "It may be a question," he notes, "who shal have the determination of such controversie as may arise whether this or that action or speach be decent or indecent: and verely it seemes to go all by discretion, not perchaunce of every one, but by a learned and experienced discretion, for otherwise seemes the *decorum* to a weake and ignorant judgment, than it doth to one of better knowledge and experience" (263).[13] Decorum, in other words, is what comes "naturally" not to all humanity but to an elite, and members of that elite can be identified by their "natural" sense of

[13]Decorum became notorious as a defense that writers (or their apologists) could take advantage of to justify an apparent lapse of taste by pointing to the unique demands of the particular text; Chaucer, for instance, is a past master at disarming criticism by appealing to the authority of decorum to allow low language in the depiction of lewd and villainous characters. Defined by the absence of a permanent or rational reference-point, the concept of decorum—like its modern equivalents—is empty of content, allowing whoever has authority over the discourse to fill it. It is not surprising that modern commentators, while recognizing its centrality, find it difficult to pin down as a critical tool; Kranidas, for instance, talks of its "ubiquity and instability" in Elizabethan criticism (39). He adverts to the source of decorum's power as a social weapon, though without realizing its significance, when he comments: "No matter how central decorum is to the work of art, no matter how long the tradition of its importance, it is applied anew to every piece of discourse, it adapts constantly to the environment" (18). It is because it is freshly invoked each time that it remains in the hands of those who have the power to enforce their own interpretation of it. The ethical equivalent is the virtue of prudence; see Victoria Kahn, *Rhetoric, Prudence, and Skepticism.*

decorum. Bourdieu, writing of the main twentieth-century descendant of decorous judgment, puts it thus: "Taste classifies, and it classifies the classifier. Social subjects, classified by their classifications, distinguish themselves by the distinctions they make, between the beautiful and the ugly, the distinguished and the vulgar" (*Distinction*, 6). What comes naturally to the majority, who are ignorant and inexperienced, is not *truly* natural.

This contradiction is something Puttenham simply does not notice, as is evident from his well-known discussion of the proper variety of language for the poet to use. He defines this linguistic paradigm extremely narrowly: "that which is spoken in the kings Court, or in the good townes and Cities within the land" (144). Even that geographical generosity shrinks, at least in the case of England, to "the shires lying about London within lx. myles, and not much above" (145). On what grounds is the poet to favor the language of a tiny minority of English speakers? It is, says Puttenham, "naturall, pure, and the most usuall of all his countrey" (144). "Usual," which is clearly nonsense in statistical terms, suggests that Puttenham is able to assimilate the notion of universality to a politically less troublesome notion of cultural superiority. So the appeal to "a learned and experienced discretion," which sounds like a democratic appeal to merit and effort, marks a prior exclusion of that class which has no access to learning or to the kind of courtly experience Puttenham has in mind.[14] Hence the "naturalness" of decorum is at a distant remove from universal human nature or instincts; it is an ideological product, a sixteenth-century equivalent of one of Barthes's modern myths, whereby a historically specific class attitude is promoted and perceived as "natural."[15] The social operation of decorum is well described by Bourdieu:

> The ideology of natural taste owes its plausibility and its efficacy to the fact that, like all the ideological strategies generated in the everyday class

[14]It would be possible to represent the dividedness within Puttenham's formulations as a tension between the humanist ideology (with its belief in human perfectibility and its program of education) and that of the courtier (with its strictly political criteria and its emphasis on advancement and power); G. K. Hunter has written well in "Humanism and Courtship" of this clash of attitudes. But both of these ideologies are inconsistent within themselves, claiming as each one does to be based on universal values but endorsing actions that serve narrower ends.

[15]See Roland Barthes, *Mythologies*, especially the essay "Myth Today."

struggle, it *naturalizes* real differences, converting differences in the mode of acquisition of culture into differences of nature; it only recognizes as legitimate the relation to culture (or language) which least bears the visible marks of its genesis, which has nothing "academic", "scholastic", "bookish", "affected" or "studied" about it, but manifests by its ease and naturalness that true culture is nature—a new mystery of immaculate conception. (*Distinction*, 68)

(Bourdieu is, of course, describing contemporary France, which makes the aptness of his description to the Elizabethan court particularly striking.) In maintaining its power, the ruling elite puts forward, and no doubt believes in, the idea of the "naturalness" of its own behavior and its "natural" self-sufficiency and primacy as a class, a matter as little open to question as nature's own self-defining identity. (Of course, to sustain this belief in the face of all the evidence to the contrary, the aristocracy has to have recourse to supplements to its own "natural" superiority—including a highly artificial mode of public display—which increasingly threaten to usurp the operation of that superiority.) As his metaphors imply, Polixenes' overarching nature that mends nature in the garden can also be appealed to as justification for selective intermarriage between the (male) nobility and chosen commoners, in the interests of a strong aristocracy.[16]

The problem for Puttenham at this point is that he is writing a *manual* whose only conceivable user is the individual who does *not* possess the natural decorum of the few: the would-be poet, who is eager to acquire the necessary learning and experience.[17] But if there are no rules to be adduced as to the essential distinction between

[16]Commentators have often pointed out the irony of Polixenes' argument in view of his opposition to his son's courting of an apparent commoner; perhaps a distinction should be made between looking favorably on a hastily engendered love-match and arranging a judiciously planned marriage between noble scion and common stock.

[17]Or the would-be courtier, as some studies of Puttenham have emphasized; see, for instance, Daniel Javitch, *Poetry and Courtliness;* Heinrich Plett, "Aesthetic Constituents"; and Louis Adrian Montrose, "Gentlemen and Shepherds." That the *Arte of English Poesie* can be read as a courtesy handbook does not, of course, diminish its importance as a poetic handbook; what it does do is to bring out the close relation between aesthetic and political questions. Montrose observes that—as "itself a courtly performance, an open bid for royal preferment"—"the most subtle irony of Puttenham's text is that it constitutes, in effect, a *meta*courtly discourse: it simultaneously exemplifies and anatomizes the art it purports to describe" (442). We should not, given our own institutional context, be too surprised that a scholarly book can at the same time be a bid for personal promotion, even if its subject is, in part, the art of getting promoted.

successful and unsuccessful poetry, how is Puttenham to pursue his aim as an instructor? His solution to the problem is a lengthy catalog of examples of decorum in action amounting to over a tenth of the book, drawn not from literature but from incidents in court life (264-98).[18] (Puttenham assumes, of course, that he belongs to the elite and that *his* judgment as to decorous speech or behavior—a courtier's excuse for a fart released before Henry VIII, for instance—is not open to question.) The neophyte poet is expected to acquire from these vividly depicted exempla a sense of decorum then to be applied to writing; Puttenham has no qualms about making a direct link between the modes of behavior which sustain political power and the graces of poetry. But his unwillingness to draw up rules of decorum, even though he has no hesitation in saying that rules can be deduced by the close observation of nature in its more general sense, points to a wider dilemma: if art—whether the art of poetry or the art of courtly conduct—were reconcilable to rule, it would be available to all who were willing to make the effort. As the existence of poetry, like the power of the court, is predicated upon exclusiveness, such a conclusion is unthinkable. Puttenham must therefore produce a manual designed to fail.[19]

We have not finished with the dangerous supplement of art, how-

---

[18]Puttenham also mentions a book of his, now lost, entitled *De decoro* (277), which no doubt contained many more exempla of this kind. On Puttenham's preference for examples over theory, see Victoria Kahn, "Humanism and the Resistance to Theory."

[19]These are, in fact, the terms used against Puttenham by Harington, who remarks cuttingly of the former's theory of poetry that "he doth prove nothing more plainly than that . . . it is a gift and not an art" because "he sheweth himselfe so slender a gift in it" (Smith, *Essays*, 2:197). Puttenham is not, for Sir John, a member of the natural elite, and therefore no amount of effort will allow him to succeed in his aim. Bourdieu describes essentially the same aim and the same difficulty as Puttenham's:

> Above all—and this is why aesthetes so abhor pedagogues and pedagogy—the rational teaching of art provides substitutes for direct experience, it offers short cuts on the long path of familiarization, it makes possible practices which are the product of concepts and rules instead of springing from the supposed spontaneity of taste, thereby offering a solution to those who hope to make up for lost time. . . . The embarrassment of academic minds, indebted and committed to acquisition, surfaces whenever it is a question of the adequate approach to a work of art and the right way to acquire it; and the contradiction is at the heart of all their aesthetic theories, not to mention their attempts to establish a pedagogy of art. The ideology of natural gifts is too potent, even within the educational system, for an expression of faith in the powers of a rational pedagogy aimed at reducing the practical schemes of familiarity to codified rules. (68, 74)

ever; it is not to be so easily controlled by being embedded in a social and political context and granted the status of a pseudo-nature. The threat of the supplement is that, because it belies its own secondariness in making good what is lacking in the nature that it supplements, it constantly endangers nature's primariness. If the natural body is weak—by nature—and needs the artificial assistance of the *pharmakon,* is not artificiality already presupposed in nature? Although the naturalness of decorum is determined by a minority culture, it must be believed to be identical with primary nature itself; and if art is allowed the role of supplier of nature's wants, that reference point loses its validity. (Renaissance writers were not afraid of the logic of this position and praised nature for its approximation to art. As Madeleine Doran puts it, "hairs become golden wires or threads, brooks are crystal, water dripping from an oar is a rope of liquid pearl, meadows are enameled or adorned with dainty gems, birds make sweet division" [*Endeavors of Art,* 69].)

The source of the problem becomes clearer if we ask what purposes the term "nature" in its most general sense is being asked to fulfill within the discursive system that makes possible Puttenham's writing. "Nature" is called upon to stand for a notion of self-sufficiency, wholeness, and plenitude, that which is, and is itself, without self-division or self-consciousness and without dependence on anything exterior to itself—like the past (in such forms as memory and history), the future (goals, for instance), and rules or codes that would preexist and predetermine it. This notion is powerfully operative even (or especially) within Puritan or Neoplatonic emphases on the fallenness or secondariness of the nature we experience: fallen nature is, precisely, fallen from its true self, from what it should have been.[20] But any attempt to ground this notion empirically, or even to give it theoretical or imaginative substance, necessarily fails, caught up as our existence, our language, our thought is in the operation of difference, loss, mediation, desire, secondariness, instability, deferral, and all the other features of our experience whose inescapability gives rise to our yearning for what we call (among other things) "nature." Art, which is a reaching after or an echo of that oneness and self-sufficiency which

[20]Compare Derrida's comment: "The speech that Rousseau raised above writing is speech as it should be or rather as it *should have been*" (*Grammatology,* 141). Empson writes interestingly on the particular melancholy induced by Milton's presentation of Edenic nature before the Fall, in *Some Versions of Pastoral,* 152-53.

37

is nature's alone by right, and which constitutes nature, is called upon at the same time to *produce* the oneness and self-sufficiency of nature by virtue of its own healing and perfecting powers. However, to accept fully that art has this central function, that the apparent supplement has a primary role and not a merely supplementary one, would be to allow the founding notion of nature, of a principle of plenitude and transcendence, to collapse, and with it much of the enabling intellectual (and political/religious) discourse of the time. In the *Apologie*, Sidney comes close to articulating this view by arguing that art is the only means of attaining, in a fallen world, a glimpse of prelapsarian perfection. He half withdraws the claim as soon as he has made it, however: "But these arguments will by fewe be understood, and by fewer granted" (157)—a strangely uncomfortable moment in the easy assurance of his rhetoric. (Were Sidney to follow this argument through, he would replace religion with poetry as the way back to God's grace, hardly an acceptable doctrine. Even within Christian doctrine, however, the structure of the supplement is ubiquitous: it is evident, for example, in the relationship of the Atonement to the Fall, in the operations of mercy and grace, and in the structure of the Trinity.) Spenser's superb meditations on the relationship of nature and art—in the description of the Bower of Bliss, for example[21]—are suffused with this fear, and it is the same fear that underlies Perdita's brusque rejection of Polixenes' position. Hers is at first sight a surprisingly negative response to an eloquent and persuasive argument, one that she seemingly stands to gain by:

> I'll not put
> The dibble in earth to set one slip of them;

[21]The Bower of Bliss is "A place pickt out by choice of best alive, / That natures worke by art can imitate" (*Faerie Queene*, 2.12 st. 42). There are natural vines with real grapes,

> And them amongst, some were of burnisht gold,
> So made by art, to beautifie the rest,
> Which did themselves amongst the leaves enfold,
> As lurking from the vew of covetous guest,
> That the weake bouwes, with so rich load opprest,
> Did bow adowne, as over-burdened. (st. 55)

Although the artificial grapes enhance the natural ones, their presence is clearly damaging to the whole vine; and the entire Bower of Bliss, while a supreme artistic achievement, is of course a place of destruction which must itself be destroyed. The division between Spenser's aesthetic and politico-religious beliefs is nowhere more dramatically presented than in this episode.

No more than were I painted I would wish
This youth should say 'twere well and only therefore
Desire to breed by me.   (4.4. 99-103)[22]

To allow art—however well disguised as a greater or subtler nature—
to replace nature in the garden would be the equivalent, for Perdita,
of allowing that most "natural" human response, sexual desire, to be
the product of a painted surface (or, we may paraphrase, thinking of
the end of the play, by which Shakespeare attempts a kind of
Hegelian *Aufhebung* of the art/nature contradiction, a painted
statue).[23]

The danger that art will supplant nature becomes most acute when
art ceases to be distinguishable by its distance from nature and takes
on the appearance of nature itself (as threatens to happen, for exam-

[22]Shakespeare's critics are sometimes more easily persuaded than Perdita. In a well-
known discussion of this passage, Harold S. Wilson asserts that Perdita "cheerfully
assents to the figure, if not to the application Polixenes intends" ("Nature and Art,"
151). To find "cheerfulness" in Perdita's brief "So it is" is already to have decided that
Shakespeare underwrites Polixenes' view of the distinction in question. Perdita's position in the argument is, of course, only apparently against her better interests; as one
who is nobly born, and therefore noble "by nature," she is unknowingly defending the
grounds both for Florizel's attraction to her and for her eventual triumph. The passage
is well discussed by Kermode in "The Final Plays," 244-46.

[23]Shakespeare's late plays are, of course, deeply concerned with the relation between
nature and art, and the endings seem to be utopian imaginings—characteristic of
romance—of a state in which the relation would be reciprocally enhancing, not supplementary. The most thoroughgoing exploration of the issue is *The Tempest* (which is
indebted to the discussion of nature and art in Montaigne's "Des Cannibales"), in which
the figure of Caliban represents some of the complexity of the Renaissance conception
of nature and Prospero the equally complex conception of art. (See Kermode's valuable
discussion in his Introduction to the Arden edition of the play [xxxiv–lix], and for a use
of the notion of supplementarity in relation to *The Tempest* somewhat different from
mine, see Julian Patrick's essay "The Tempest as Supplement.") Another Shakespearean play in which the various possibilities inherent in the term "nature" play a
central role is, of course, *King Lear;* see the rather oversimplified treatment in John F.
Danby, *Shakespeare's Doctrine of Nature.*

[24]The surface praise of the garden's inseparable blend of nature and art is sternly
qualified by such words as "wantonesse," "repine," and "undermine":

One would have thought, (so cunningly, the rude,
And scorned parts were mingled with the fine,)
That nature had for wantonesse ensude
Art, and that Art at nature did repine;
So striving each th'other to undermine,
Each did the others worke more beautifie. (2.12 st. 59)

ple, in the Bower of Bliss).[24] Puttenham has accepted that art can come naturally, as does Sidney in the famous passage in the *Apologie* about the "smally learned Courtier" who, "following that which by practise hee findeth fittest to nature, therein (though he know it not) doth according to Art, though not by Art" (203). But if art can come by nature, can nature come by art? The whole discussion of decorum tends in this direction, and is prevented from reaching this conclusion only by the insistence that decorum is not reducible to rules of art: *natural* art can come only by means of a natural principle. But at the end of his book, after a concluding summary of the whole treatise, Puttenham admits—in what can only be called a supplement—that art does have the power to disguise itself as nature. This assertion is, of course, as old as the notion of art itself; it appears as the classical *ars est celare artem* and the courtly accomplishment of *sprezzatura*, the ability to present the artificial *as* the natural, but it must always constitute an uneasy place in the discussion of the crucial distinction between art and nature.[25] Puttenham's belated treatment of it is no exception— that belatedness itself being one sign of its potential disruptiveness. In closing the final book, he says he will offer a "principall good lesson for al good makers to beare continually in mind," the lesson of the courtier, "which is in plaine termes, cunningly to be able to dissemble" (299). He states it in plain terms, because *he* is not going to dissemble in presenting us with this unpleasant fact, whose unpleasantness he stresses by going on to quote several unsavory examples of courtly duplicity. But the poet—or at least "our English maker"—is an honest man and not a hypocrite (Puttenham forgets that he has described *all* figurative language as deceitful) and is allowed only one form of deception: "When he is most artificiall, so to disguise and cloake it as it may not appeare, nor seeme to proceede from him by any studie or trade of rules, *but to be his naturall*" (302, my emphasis). At this point art, kept in check throughout the book by the operations of nature, breaks loose. If there is an *art* of behaving and writing naturally—and this more than anything else seems to constitute the arts of poetry and courtliness—the supplement has indeed put itself in nature's place.

[25]In "Interpretation at Court" Frank Whigham discusses the social importance in the Renaissance court of learning how to behave as if one had not learned how to behave (626). The belief—or the pretense—that courtly speech and behavior were a natural endowment was, of course, a denial of their institutional determination; to the extent that this *was* a belief (and part of a wider assumption about speech and human activity), it formed one constituent of an ideology that is still powerful today.

Puttenham makes one final attempt, in a kind of supplement to this supplement, to reassert the ultimate primacy of nature by setting out four kinds of relation between nature and art; but in so doing he succeeds only in articulating once more the instability and un-decidability of that relationship. First (I am not following Puttenham's order), art can *imitate* nature, as the painter or sculptor does, or the poet in reporting on the acts of Priam or Ulysses. Puttenham raises here the question of fiction, in which, unlike Sidney, he has little interest (though, as Derrida has shown, the domain of *mimesis* is also inhabited by the structures of supplementarity).[26] Second, art can use the stuff of nature but produce something quite different, as a carpenter does in making a table out of wood. This is what the poet is doing in constructing elaborate stanza-forms out of the material of language—the subject of Puttenham's second book, and again not of immediate relevance to our discussion.

The other two kinds of relation are directly concerned with the supplementarity of art. The first implies a deficient nature in need of repair: as a supplement, art can make up for the lack in nature; as the *pharmakon*, it can cure nature of its ills. Puttenham uses almost the same terms: "In some cases we say arte is an ayde and coadiutor to nature, and a furtherer of her actions to good effect, or peradventure a meane to supply her wants, by renforcing the causes wherein shee is impotent and defective, as doth the arte of phisicke . . . in a weake and unhealthie bodie. Or as the good gardiner seasons his soyle by sundrie sorts of compost . . . or perchaunce with more costly drugs" (303).[27] Art's other supplementary function, however, implies a transforming addition to an already self-sufficient nature, for it is "not only an aide and coadiutor to nature in all her actions, but an alterer of them, and in some sort a surmounter of her skill, so as by meanes of it her owne effects shall appeare more beautifull or

[26]See *Of Grammatology*, 203-16, and "The Double Session" in *Dissemination*, especially 185-93. Derrida has discussed the complicity between mimesis and metaphor, and their relation to a founding principle of nature, in "White Mythology," in *Margins of Philosophy* (see especially 237-38).

[27]Robert Herrick and Robert Burton are among the other Renaissance authors to use the word "supply" in describing art's addition to nature (Tayler, 14-15). Though these verbal coincidences are, in a sense, trivial, they do point to a recurrent problematic in discussions of this topic.

straunge and miraculous" (303). As the supplement art both repairs the deficiencies of nature and adds to a nature that is already complete; as the *pharmakon* it cures nature of its ills and also takes it into the realm of the unnatural or miraculous. Thus the physician not only cures the ailing patient but may "prolong the terme of his life many yeares over and above the stint of his first and naturall constitution" (303), while the gardener—in a passage Shakespeare might have read before he wrote *The Winter's Tale*—can produce blooms that nature cannot, including the double gilliflower (304).

But as we have seen, without the principle of decorum, that is to say, the principle of "naturalness," art is a vice that distorts nature and makes it ridiculous. Puttenham reiterates the reentry of nature into the argument at this point. Because the materials of the poet—"language and utterance, and discourse and persuasion, and argument"—are "little lesse naturall than his very sensuall actions," the best poetry, in spite of everything that has just been said in favor of art, is made by "naturall instinct" not "arte and precepts" (305). (This view goes, incidentally, with a preference for "long meditation" over "suddaine inspiration" [305-6]. Puttenham, like Wordsworth, is interested only in the spontaneity that comes as the final product of a long process of thought.) And in a final assertion of the overriding claims of nature, Puttenham proposes an idea that has so far not been fully articulated: "But for that in our maker or Poet, which restes onely in devise and issues from an excellent sharpe and quick invention, holpen by a cleare and bright phantasie and imagination" (when he is at his most creative, we might say), he is not imitating or perfecting or adding to the effects of nature, "but even as nature her selfe working by her owne peculiar vertue and proper instinct and not by example or meditation or exercise as all other artificers do" (307). Nature is that which, by definition, works without rules and art but simply by being itself, *natura naturans,* and it is after all possible—or it is necessary for Puttenham to believe that it is possible—for the poet to work in this way too. The analogy between nature's creativity and the artist's is of course a familiar and enduring one,[28] and it is a culmination of one thread that has run through Puttenham's whole argument. But the counterthread to this one is still visible too, woven inseparably with it into the text: the poet, repeats Puttenham in his

[28]Kant's use of this analogy is well-known; see Derrida's discussion of it in "Economimesis."

final sentence (apart from a last compliment to Queen Elizabeth), should be "more commended for his naturall eloquence than for his artificiall," but he has to add, "and more for his artificiall well desembled, than for the same overmuch affected and grossely or undiscretly bewrayed" (307). The ideal is to be natural, by being yourself as nature is. But if you cannot—and the entire manual is built on the premise that you cannot—you need to supplement your own natural inadequacies by the exercise of decorum, that "natural" art, so that you may artificially rise to the status of perfect and self-sufficient nature.

Because Puttenham's rhetorical and argumentative strategies are relatively open, it has been a fairly simple task to trace their contradictions and inner differences, but it is possible to follow the same shifts and rifts in many other Renaissance accounts of the distinction between nature and art (or terms with the same discursive responsibilities thrust upon them). The reason should by now be obvious: these contradictions arise not from the diversity of opinion or the vagueness of the words but from the precise demands made upon the distinction, the impossible expectations it has been brought into being to fulfill.[29] A principle of plenitude, self-sufficiency, self-presence is taken as the necessary condition for the production of truth or knowledge, and its inevitable failure in these terms results in the positing of a second principle, which is both perfecting and displacing. This structure of thought is far from being a mere historical curiosity: it continues to underlie most conceptions of ethics, education, religion, politics, law, and aesthetics. Thus ethical debate has to deal with the relation of the "good" and the "natural," and the degree to which the non-natural—in the realms of the medical or the penal, for instance—can serve the good; discussions of education are always structured around the question of what we should supply "natural" ability with to allow it to realize its full potential; the assessment of religious

[29]It is necessary, therefore, to revise Tayler's summary at several points: "When used together the terms represented an almost infinitely flexible and yet 'real' principle of classification that might be used to define the most fundamental relationships within the order of nature" (174). The terms represent a structure far from flexible which operates within the order of discourse, and the "reality" of the classification can be understood only as one of its effects. Renaissance accounts of "savage men," whether documentary or literary, and the genre of the pastoral, to both of which Tayler devotes considerable attention, demand a different analysis in the light of the relations of supplementarity within which, and with which, they operate.

doctrine and behavior hinges on the issue of man's supplementary actions in relation to an already self-sufficient divine being or realm; an interpretation of a law is a supplementary text that claims to reveal that law's "real" meaning; political systems are judged by their ability to guarantee "self-evident" and "inalienable" human rights through the imposition of rules; and any discussion of artistic conventions and effects is dominated by the question of the "natural" and the "artificial." In every case, difficulties arise when manifestations of the supplement—medical and educational practices, religious organizations and ceremonies, legal interpretations, political power structures, aesthetic conventions, and so on—are perceived, at least by some of those involved, as threatening the primary entity they are supposed to serve or bring forth in its pure state. Other places to look for the operation of the supplement are the history of gardening (as Perdita's words suggest), the relation between the Old and New testaments in Christian theology, and the practice of literary criticism and commentary. And attempts to define the distinctiveness of poetic language continue, long after Puttenham, to produce the problems inherent in the logic of supplementarity.

Is it possible to enunciate a consistent theory of literary language or of art in general which takes for granted a self-defined "natural" base (whether we call it "ordinary language," "the literal," "the real") against which the special practices of art define themselves? Or will such a theory always and inevitably find itself reintroducing the primary concept—or a disguised (and politically acceptable) version of it—as a way of controlling the otherwise uncontrollable secondary concept and at the same time discovering the secondary already inhabiting the primary? Roman Jakobson's account of the distinctiveness of literary language attempts to escape the problems of supplementarity by rejecting entirely the model employed by Puttenham and all those who share the same assumptions: "Poeticalness is not a supplementation of discourse with rhetorical adornment but a total re-evaluation of the discourse and of all its components whatsoever" ("Closing Statement," 377). Jakobson's discussions of poetry reveal, however, a structure very similar to the one he claims to be dismissing, in which the "referential" or "cognitive" function of language is treated as primary and the "poetic" function is one of several secondary (or supplementary) possibilities.[30]

[30]See Attridge, "Closing Statement," and chapter 4 below.

Literary theorists after Puttenham continue to reformulate and re-investigate the relationship between art and nature, and the definition of literature as linguistic difference, but few manifest so openly the instability of the system they are attempting to expound or reinterpret. Having begun with the *Arte of English Poesie,* we are now in a position to disentangle with greater success some of the threads that are more securely woven in later texts. Furthermore, we can appreciate that the difficulty of the enterprise these theorists are engaged in is an inherent and not a contingent one, a difficulty that faces anyone who would delimit and describe the peculiar language of literature.

Chapter 3

Romanticism and the Language
of Nature: The Project of
Wordsworth's Preface

Nature and Art: Neoclassic to Romantic

THE Renaissance emphasis on art's distance from nature gave rise, as we saw in the previous chapter, to an uncontainable oscillation between contradictory apprehensions of the meaning and ideological function of the concept of nature, as that which art is defined both by and against. To put it another way, an inherent instability in the set of ideological functions performed by the term "nature" resulted in a concept of art which both emphasized and denied its natural origins and subservience. All attempts to pin down the difference between nature and art, or more specifically between ordinary language and the language of poetry, produce further instabilities. Every characteristic of poetic language which is claimed as peculiar to it suffers the same double bind, because it is an instance either of a superior language, in which case the foundation of an ordinary language is discredited, or of an inferior language, in which case the defense of poetry as a special human achievement collapses.

The same irresolvable problematic can be traced through numerous endeavors during the seventeenth and eighteenth centuries to ground art in nature while continuing to define art by its differences from nature. Though the language of poetry changes, the insistence that poets should employ a special linguistic register remains powerful, and comments abound regarding the inappropriateness for poet-

46

ry of "idiomatic," "vulgar," or "low" language.[1] At the same time, however, that difference must be controlled by a strict principle whose immediate operation may be in accordance with statable rules but whose ultimate authority is nature—a court of appeal designed to mask the cultural and political exclusivity that is in fact being protected. Polixenes' reply to Perdita is echoed again and again: true art is art whose distance from nature is governed by nature itself. In Pope's words:

> Those RULES of old *discover'd,* not *devis'd,*
> Are *Nature* still, but *Nature Methodiz'd;*
> *Nature,* like *Liberty,* is but restrain'd
> By the same Laws which first *herself* ordain'd.
> (*Essay on Criticism,* 88-91)

Only in this way can nature's primary status be safeguarded against the dangerous supplement of art—and Pope's simile shows that he is also well aware that the argument has a political dimension. As a consequence, the imitation of the great exemplars of the past, which was Pope's ambition as it had been that of the sixteenth-century humanists, cannot be construed as the valuing of art over nature but must be presented as the discovery of nature in art. Pope imagines Virgil turning from "Nature's Fountains" to Homer:

> But when t'examine ev'ry Part he came,
> *Nature* and *Homer* were, he found, the *same.* (134-35)

But, as we saw with Puttenham, a conception of art based on the following of rules, even rules ultimately grounded in and guaranteed by nature, has to have a further ingredient which is not rule-governed to prevent that success from being available to all who master the appropriate technique. Sometimes still called "decorum," this necessary quality also goes under such names as "taste," "wit," "good sense," and "judgment," and like decorum and its equivalents in Puttenham it serves to guarantee the privileged position of those who

---

[1]Well-known examples include Addison's advice that "a Poet should take particular Care to guard himself against Idiomatick Ways of Speaking," *Spectator* no. 285, and Johnson's objection to Shakespeare's use of the word "dun" as "an epithet now seldom heard but in the stable," *Rambler* no. 168. See Wimsatt and Brooks, *Literary Criticism,* 340-43, for a discussion of these and other examples.

possess it.[2] Although the acquisition of this faculty is often presented as though it were merely a matter of industry and application on the part of the individual, it nevertheless combines a first-order discrimination on the basis of class (proper breeding is essential) with a finer discrimination on the basis of individual and inborn capacities (only a few of the dominant class will be favored by nature or, we might say, biology). There is always, therefore, a *je ne sais quoi* beyond the reach of rules and imitation, a something that cannot be taught and that protects the small caste of true poets. Pope, again, provides a classic formulation:

> Some Beauties yet, no Precepts can declare,
> For there's a *Happiness* as well as *Care.*
> *Musick* resembles *Poetry,* in each
> Are *nameless Graces* which no Methods teach,
> And which a *Master-Hand* alone can reach. (141-45)

Once we are aware of the important function of this element in the sociocultural system, its contradiction of the period's general tendency to endorse knowable and transmittable rules seems less surprising.[3]

What becomes much rarer is the open acceptance and admiration of artifice, which of course makes it easier to disguise the problem of the supplement, because art can now be presented as coming much closer to nature. But in an aesthetic still based on mimesis, that problem will not go away; the difference between the original and the imitation has to be specified, and must constitute the defining feature of art if art is to retain any value or any identity. Pope's attempt to

---

[2]These terms are not interchangeable to the degree that "decorum," "decency," "conveniency," "seemliness," and so on are for the Elizabethans, but they are all capable of being put to similar use. Their sociopolitical implications are seldom as openly stated as they are by Lord Kames in *Elements of Criticism,* where we learn that among those who are excluded from the "common" standard of taste are "those who depend for food on bodily labour" (quoted by M. H. Abrams, *The Mirror and the Lamp,* 109).

[3]See Abrams's useful summary of neoclassicism's tendency—apparently against its fundamental orientation—to posit an inexplicable and unpredictable "poetic grace," in *The Mirror and the Lamp,* 193-95. Abrams relates this notion of grace to two other metaphors favored in neoclassicism for the representation of the unlearnable element in artistic achievement: "inspiration" and "natural genius." Shakespeare remained, of course, the test case for all literary theorizing: his only entrée into the elite community of taste was his artistic achievement, the pure embodiment of his "genius," and that was a dangerous precedent which had to be firmly controlled.

48

navigate these treacherous waters is the most pithy and the most familiar statement of the commonplace:

> *True Wit* is *Nature* to Advantage drest,
> What oft was *Thought*, but ne'er so well *Exprest*. (297-98)

Pope is, of course, choosing his words with extreme care to avoid the implication that nature is in need of improvement: art's function is limited to showing nature at her best. However, the supplementary function of art can never be adduced, for reasons already given, without threatening to supplant that to which it adds. When Pope restates it, in the course of a contrast with the reprehensible masking effect of *"False Eloquence,"* the distinction he is drawing verges on dissolution:

> But true *Expression*, like th'unchanging *Sun*,
> *Clears*, and *improves* whate'er it shines upon,
> It *gilds* all Objects, but it *alters* none. (315-17)

To improve and gild the natural world without altering it: this is the recurring problem of both Renaissance and neoclassical art.[4]

The centuries-old continuity of this set of problems spawned by the equation of art with artifice (in however disguised a form) is broken, histories of literary criticism tell us, with Romanticism; and if one English work of literary theory had to be named as the watershed, the most popular candidate would undoubtedly be Wordsworth's Preface to *Lyrical Ballads* of 1800/1802. For the Romantics, a summary account of this change might state, the artist's task is not to gild nature but to remove the layer of gilt that has accumulated over the centuries and to show her forth in her nakedness and simplicity.[5] Art is not a

---

[4]In his "Life of Pope," Johnson falls back on a simple notion of mimesis in an attempt to abolish the problematic distance between art and nature altogether: "If by nature is meant, what is commonly called *nature* by the criticks, a just representation of things really existing, and actions really performed, nature cannot be properly opposed to *art;* nature being, in this sense, only the best effect of *art*" (*Lives*, 2:331). This is either to weaken art until it is entirely subservient to nature or to strengthen it until it totally dominates nature.

[5]I use the feminine personification in imitation of conventional discourse about nature, of course. That Nature names a female being is hardly surprising, given the similar double function of femininity in Western culture and politics: a principle that

supplement to nature, working to make good nature's limitations and remedy her defects. True art, rather, is nature herself at work, not in the sense of Polixenes' or Pope's overarching and all-mastering nature but in a new and narrower sense, nature as manifested in the nonhuman world and in the human being uncorrupted by civilization, unimpressed by rules, unfettered by the constraints of society and class. What had hitherto been seen as the defining feature of art, rendering it different from nature—from Puttenham's "artifice" to Pope's "rules"—becomes, by a sharp reversal of priorities, what unmistakably distinguishes false art from true art, the transient art of the fashion-bound versifier from the permanent art of nature's dedicated follower and favorite. As a result, the poet's method is no longer to observe and emulate rules enshrined in the great works of the past; it is to utter spontaneously the language that bursts forth in states of deeply felt emotion, recollected or imagined.[6]

---

can stand either for the pure, the instinctive, the undifferentiated, the non-rule-governed, the ahistorical, against which the self-conscious masculine principle defines itself, or for the imperfect, the culturally corrupted, the self-divided, the covention-bound, which the masculine is required to strengthen and perfect. Sherry B. Ortner has suggested that the universality of female subordination is due to the association of women with "nature," perceived as inferior to "culture" ("Is Female to Male"); one might add that even when the term "female" operates in (male) Western discourse as an idealized principle, it contributes to the subordination of women, because that ideal is not realized in (male) experience, giving rise to the need for (male) supplementation— in just the same way that nature is posited by the artist as an ideal and then found wanting, thus necessitating the perfecting operations of art. It is therefore possible to reverse the terms of the familiar argument that presents the female as the supplement, the *pharmakon*, the marked term, Adam's rib (see Jonathan Culler, *On Deconstruction*, 165-75, for a summary of such arguments). The stereotype of woman as nature is, of course, both exploited and exploded by Joyce in Molly Bloom's monologue in *Ulysses* and in the figure of ALP in *Finnegans Wake*. References to "the poet" as male in this chapter are also intended to reflect Romantic discourse, though much could be said about the role of gender in the determination of an appropriate poetic language.

[6]This sketch of a "new attitude" is, of course, as crude as such sketches always are and, given the complexity of the historical developments and the issues involved, cruder than most. It does not represent a view born with Romanticism (or "pre-Romanticism"), nor one that covers all English Romantics (let alone non-English writers of the time); but it will be recognizable as an important element in the approach of a number of major English writers at this period to the question of nature and art, and it had peculiarly widespread reinforcements and repercussions at the end of the eighteenth century. A corrective to any homogenizing account of Romanticism—including the privileging of a concept of "simple Nature"—is given by A. O. Lovejoy in his famous essay "On the Discrimination of Romanticisms," reprinted in *Essays in the History of Ideas*.

Thus the constantly recurring instability of the old crux is, it appears, finally overcome: the task of the literary artist is not painstakingly to learn the rules of his craft, study the best models, submit his work to the criticism of acknowledged masters, and hope against hope that the one crucial ingredient which cannot be acquired by skill, patience, and effort—call it "decorum" or "judgment"—will come unbidden. Rather, it is to allow nature to do its work upon him as an individual until fit words flow unforcedly from deep and refined feelings, in defiance of rules, models, and established criticism. The Preface to *Lyrical Ballads* argues this case, insofar as it *can* be argued without betraying its own principles, and *The Prelude* exemplifies it, tracing the slow growth of the true poetic faculty and at the same time demonstrating its powers in achieved poetry: the poem finds its real momentum only when the poet gives up the self-conscious search for a traditionally sanctioned theme and slips, in a mood of uncreative despair, into reminiscences of a childhood spent in nature's care. What Wordsworth has done is to acknowledge that the fugitive, unlearnable element in art is by far the most important, because this factor constitutes the distinction between good and bad art, the "line and level for all good makers to do their business by," as Puttenham calls it, the "nameless Graces" that only a master hand can achieve. Everything else can go by the board, for the genuine poet becomes a genuine poet through the gracious bestowing of nature, not through effort and application. What is more, the weapon that had safeguarded a cultural and sociopolitical elite by excluding all those outside it without hope of redress has now been turned against that very elite, and nature's gift is made not to the cultured denizens of the metropolis but to the lonely individual attuned to the life of the rural community. (It also remains a powerful personal weapon for the poet himself, who can still proclaim to his rivals: "My genius stems from the particular circumstances of my birth and breeding, and cannot, therefore, be matched by those without these advantages." One of the functions of *The Prelude,* for all its winning self-doubt, is to drive that message home.) Whereas studies of the art of poetry had hitherto been presented, in part at least, as manuals addressed to the would-be poet (however radically the simultaneous insistence upon the unlearnability of the vital ingredient undercut this teaching), Wordsworth's account of poetry (like those of Coleridge, Shelley, and Keats, in their different ways) proclaims as a central tenet the unthinkability of a manual of poetry. The Romantic poet is the child of nature, not its master; art—if it is true art and not a contrived imposter—is the finest expression of nature, not its supplement.

Even a brief survey of these changes has to acknowledge that Wordsworth's revolution was not a sudden break, of course, but the inevitable outcome of a gradual move away from the Renaissance valorization of artifice.[7] Once distinctiveness from nature ceases to be a major reason for valuing art, which happens as the natural world is progressively tamed and appreciated for its own qualities, that distinctiveness becomes more and more of an embarrassment for aesthetic theory. (This proposition is less true of artistic practice, which continues to rest securely on a clear difference between art and nature even while theory tries to elide it—though the history of landscape gardening might constitute an exception, as might some recent work in poetry and the visual arts which has taken the boundary between art and nature as its domain.) These tensions and tendencies grow in strength during the course of the eighteenth century, and Wordsworth may be seen as attempting a summation rather than effecting a breakthrough. The questions I want to address are these: Does this shift, whatever the exact configurations of its historical progress, constitute a solution to the perennial problem of poetic language and its relation to a norm, or do the same difficulties manifest themselves in different guises? And if the latter, what *has* changed, and what can we learn from the changes, both about the problem itself and about the Romantic response to it, which still has such a hold on aesthetic thought?

The only text I examine in detail in this chapter is the Preface to *Lyrical Ballads,* but this reading can serve as a commentary on many of the central features of Romantic literary theory. Similar readings of other theoretical and critical texts of the period, while bringing out the marked differences between writers, would not greatly alter the picture that emerges. I am not concerned here with the relationship between the theory of the Preface and the poems that follow it, as this

[7]Lovejoy's comment is apposite: "Aesthetic primitivism even in its later forms was thus not a direct reaction against neo-classicism but a natural development of one of the elements of that complex compound of aesthetic ideas" ("'Nature' as Aesthetic Norm," in *Essays in the History of Ideas,* 77). This short essay, first published in 1927, on the varied uses to which the term "nature" and the injunction "follow nature" have been put, especially in the eighteenth century, is richly suggestive. One might, incidentally, wish to scrutinize Lovejoy's own use of the term "natural" in the quoted sentence; such a scrutiny would lead to an appreciation of some of the differences between Lovejoy's project of reading Western texts ("the history of ideas") and Derrida's.

subject has been amply studied, and the importance of the Preface is not confined to its attempt to justify a particular poetic experiment. It should be clear too, that I am not seeking to pass judgment on Wordsworth; I am using his writing to explore one apparent escape from the dilemma we have been examining. If a judgment is implied, it is a strongly favorable one, because it is Wordsworth's refusal to rest with glib and outwardly coherent explanations that renders his texts so revealing and so profitable for our purposes. I refer for the most part to the text of the revised 1802 Preface, since this edition embodies two stages of Wordsworth's revisionary enterprise, not always consistent with each other but revealing most clearly the problems with which he was grappling.[8] My purpose is not to reconstruct Wordsworth's mental state at a given moment (an undertaking that always involves a large element of fantasy on the part of the critic) but to tease out some of the threads of argument coming and going between Wordsworth and Coleridge, and between them and others with whom they spoke or whose work they read, during those years of change and challenge—threads that interlace in the intricate web of the 1802 Preface. I seek to understand their unfixable oscillations not in terms of biography but in terms of the arguments themselves and their perhaps unconscious motivating impulses. The further shifts and qualifications in Wordsworth's later poetry and critical comments, though interesting and important, are not considered in any detail here; nor does Coleridge figure as largely as he might in a longer discussion of the intellectual and ideological texture of the period.[9]

Wordsworth and the Real Language of Men

Our major topic—and Wordsworth's—is the appropriate language of poetry (and by "language" we may understand him to be referring

[8]Owen and Smyser use as their main text of the Preface that of *Poetical Works* (1850), given in *Prose* 1:118-65 in parallel with the 1800 text and with variants from texts of intermediate dates. Otherwise unidentified page references in this chapter are to this text, which is very close to that of 1802; where there is a significant difference i have restored the earlier reading and so indicated in a note.

[9]Because I am not attempting to locate ideas in a single mind, the degree to which Coleridge contributed to the Preface is not an important issue here. Where I refer to "Coleridge," it is usually to the signatory of the critique of the Preface in *Biographia Literaria*, though that text too is the product of several minds and in some places of more than one pen.

as much to matters such as syntax, the use or avoidance of figures of sound and sense, and word order as to vocabulary and register). What we get first in the 1802 text is a statement of the basically mimetic theory adumbrated in the 1798 Advertisement and greatly expanded in 1800. The first volume of *Lyrical Ballads*, writes Wordsworth, had been published as an "experiment . . . to ascertain, how far, by fitting to metrical arrangement a selection of the real language of men in a state of vivid sensation, that sort of pleasure and that quantity of pleasure may be imparted, which a Poet may rationally endeavour to impart" (119). This in itself is not a new emphasis. We have already noted the admiration expressed by Sidney and Puttenham for the speech of the urbane courtier, and their approval of its status as a fit model for poetry—and we also saw that this move merely reduplicated the problem of the supplement, because the role of art in the courtier's *sprezzatura* remained unresolved. But Wordsworth is looking for a model of poetic language that bypasses the question of art altogether, a speech that can confidently be called nature's alone, which the poet can then annex without the intervention of art. Before he announces his conclusion, he prepares the ground by raising the question of the "present state of the public taste"—how far it is "healthy or depraved" (one is not left in much doubt as to Wordsworth's view)—and by predicting that readers of the poems that follow will have to "struggle with feelings of strangeness and awkwardness" (121, 123). The argument is clear, if obliquely stated: what passes for poetry in Wordsworth's time is not a reflection of the "real" language of men but an artificial confection which has become so dominant that the response to his very different poetry—from which that "real" language will shine out undimmed—will be bemusement and dismay.[10] Nevertheless, posterity will judge by different criteria, and if the experiment were to prove successful, "a class of Poetry would be produced, well adapted to interest mankind permanently" (121). The word "nature" has not been used, but it is clear that Wordsworth is appealing to something like nature, in the traditional

[10]At the same time he castigates "the triviality and meanness both of thought and language, which some of my contemporaries have occasionally introduced into their metrical compositions," a defect he finds more "dishonourable" but less "pernicious in the sum of its consequences" than the gaudiness that others employ (71-72). Wordsworth is having to traverse a narrow path between an older poeticality and a newer populism, both of which he finds distasteful; he is closer to the latter, however, and to some extent can be seen as providing a justification for a shift that has already occurred. See Mary Jacobus, *Tradition and Experiment*, chaps. 8-10, and John E. Jordan, *Why the "Lyrical Ballads"?* chaps. 3-6.

sense of an immutable and unquestionable ground: that which is "real," "healthy," and "permanent."

The well-known sentences in which Wordsworth enunciates and explains his choice of subject matter and at the same time his language (for his primary mode is narrative verse in which the language is a representation of the language of the characters) are an attempt to displace the traditional basis of poetic language. The attempt proceeds by taking seriously one aspect of the conception of "nature" which had been gaining strength in recent decades—nature as that which is untouched by humanity, an idea now free from the associations of savagery and uncouthness which had colored it for so long. The familiar passage is worth quoting at length:

> Low and rustic life was generally chosen, because, in that condition, the essential passions of the heart find a better soil in which they can attain their maturity, are less under restraint, and speak a plainer and more emphatic language; because in that condition of life our elementary feelings co-exist in a state of greater simplicity, and, consequently, may be more accurately contemplated, and more forcibly communicated; because the manners of rural life germinate from those elementary feelings, and, from the necessary character of rural occupations, are more easily comprehended, and are more durable; and, lastly, because in that condition the passions of men are incorporated with the beautiful and permanent forms of nature. The language, too, of these men has been adopted . . . because such men hourly communicate with the best objects from which the best part of language is originally derived; and because, from their rank in society and the sameness and narrow circle of their intercourse, being less under the influence of social vanity, they convey their feelings and notions in simple and unelaborated expressions. Accordingly, such a language, arising out of repeated experience and regular feelings, is a more permanent, and a far more philosophical language, than that which is frequently substituted for it by Poets, who think that they are conferring honour upon themselves and their art, in proportion as they separate themselves from the sympathies of men, and indulge in arbitrary and capricious habits of expression, in order to furnish food for fickle tastes, and fickle appetites, of their own creation.[11] (125)

---

[11]That Wordsworth is drawing on a tradition of eighteenth-century primitivism here—see *Prose* 1:168 for some instances—is important to keep in mind, not because it takes away from his "originality" but because it underlines the fact that the issues we are discussing arise from the shifting intellectual (and socioeconomic) complexion of the period, not from some unique personal intervention.

We shall return to some other details of this statement, but here our concern is Wordsworth's attempt to define a language that has the status of nature—not imperfect and contingent nature, in need of the healing and immortalizing power of art, but perfect nature, nature as essence or ideal which needs nothing but transposition onto the page to become the most lasting of all poetry.

If we recall the main purposes for which the term "nature" in its most general sense is used in rhetorical and discursive structures in the Western cultural tradition, we shall see that what Wordsworth is doing is looking for—one might say, inventing—a kind of language which is intended to function in exactly the same way. Just as nature stands for that which is self-sufficient, self-present, whole, perfect, unselfconscious, ahistorical, and noncontingent, so there must be a form of language which is not the product of custom and social change, not compromised by the depravity of the time, not subject to abuse or decay, not self-divided or ambiguous.[12] The dream of such a language is an old one, but its commonest form hitherto had been of an original, Adamic language scarcely visible since Babel. Wordsworth, writing after Rousseau and the French Revolution, and out of an antipathy for metropolitan culture, locates it around him in "low and rustic life" (a rather more radical definition than in the 1798 Advertisement, where the full force of a theory of language as nature has not yet struck Wordsworth: "the language of conversation in the middle and lower classes of society" [*Prose* 1:116]).[13] In this state of nature—and to call it this is not to misread Wordsworth's relation to

[12] "Nature" employed in this way brings together several of the senses catalogued by Lovejoy—as essence or Platonic idea, as generic type, as the system of necessary and self-evident truths concerning the properties and relations of essences, and as the universal and immutable in thought, feeling, and taste. Lovejoy is right to imply that even this primary sense of "nature" is not without its inconsistencies.

[13] James K. Chandler, in *Wordsworth's Second Nature,* argues powerfully for the affinities between Wordsworth's position after 1797 and that of Burke, and the conflicts we shall be tracing within the text support his contention to a large degree. His desire to find a Burkean impetus in almost everything Wordsworth writes leads him, however, to underrate the degree of internal tension in the work dating from the years after the poet's disillusionment with Godwinian rationalism and Painite radicalism. Wordsworth's idealization of "low and rustic" language and experience, and his attempt in the more experimental "lyrical ballads" to derive a poetic language from this idealized speech, has more in common with his Jacobin years behind than his Tory years ahead (though its actual connections with a radical politics have probably been exaggerated); and in terms of Wordsworth's contribution to the theoretical debate about a poetic language this endeavor is historically of much greater importance than his later, more traditional, enterprise.

the Rousseauist tradition, although Rousseau's own use of the concept is a good deal more complicated than that of those who adopted it—language and feeling are inseparable; indeed, for all his dislike of personification, Wordsworth has it that "passions . . . speak," not people. The old Adamic dream of words that perfectly name the essences of objects has been displaced by a Romantic dream of words that perfectly speak of the inner human world.

Given this view of an ideal language—or at least of an ideal poetic language, for poetry is understood precisely as this perfect expression of feeling—it is important, first, that the passions expressed are themselves "natural," in the full sense of the word, and second, that the language which expresses them is natural. Wordsworth finds both conditions satisfied in the same setting, in human beings untainted by the changeableness, complexity, ambiguity, indirectness, and arbitrariness of human social, political, and cultural formations. Like every concept of nature posited as an ultimate ground, this one cannot be found in the created world, and the best Wordsworth can do is to point, somewhat vaguely, to social groups in which these fallings off are relatively unmarked—where historical change is slow and an understanding of history limited, where speech is dominant over writing (the natural language envisaged by Wordsworth is always a spoken language),[14] where social relations are (apparently) simple and open, where human activities are repetitive and limited in scope, and so on.[15] Again and again we find Wordsworth imposing his imaginary

[14]Wordsworth's valorization of speech over writing, though it flies in the face of his vocation as a writer, is completely consistent with the other examples of this dichotomy analyzed by Derrida in *Of Grammatology* and "Plato's Pharmacy" (in *Dissemination*). It stems from the same association of speech with the unmediated expression of subjectivity and gives rise to the same unstable exclusion of language as a signifying system. Chandler fully documents this recurrent preference in Wordsworth's writing (140-55), though he makes no reference to Derrida.

[15]The vision of such a simple, openly self-expressive society before or outside the complexities of civilization is, of course, an eighteenth-century (and much older) primitivist commonplace—see *Prose* 1:168 for examples. But Wordsworth's combination of this vision with the equally traditional notion of a "permanent" and "universal" language is more original, and more politically radical, as Olivia Smith demonstrates (*Politics of Language*, 215-18). Earlier conceptions of a universal language, if they consider the language of the lower classes at all (and some, like Johnson's, explicitly exclude it), tend to stress what is shared by all classes. So Addison links the pleasure gained by a refined audience from "an ordinary Song or Ballad that is the Delight of the common People" to the pleasure gained by a common audience from Homer, Virgil, or Milton (*Spectator* no. 70, quoted by Wimsatt and Brooks, *Literary Criticism*, 361). Coleridge was to substitute the traditional idea of a *lingua communis* for Wordsworth's notion—see p. 77 below.

state of nature, with its attributes of simplicity, perfection, noncontingency, and permanence, on the rural community he is describing. It is there that humanity's *essential* and *elementary* passions find a *better soil* and attain their *maturity* (note how rural metaphors penetrate Wordsworth's own theoretical language) while coexisting in a state of greater *simplicity;* their language is *plainer, more emphatic, more forcible,* and is in touch with its *origins* (or rather those of the *best* part of language); it is *simple* and *unelaborated,* more *permanent* and more *philosophical.* (A truly philosophical language would be, in Joseph Priestley's words, "the most natural and perfect expression of human ideas and sentiments.")[16] The connection between the more abstract notion of nature and its newer use as a name for the world untouched by man is also clear: Wordsworth wants his ideal human society to be subsumed as far as possible in the nonhuman world (because it is by behaving *as* humans that humans fall away from the ideal of permanence and noncontingency). The conception is difficult and the language obscure, but a crossing of the human/nonhuman boundary is clearly at stake: "In that condition the passions of men are *incorporated* with the beautiful and permanent forms of nature"; "such men hourly *communicate* with the best objects."[17] (Compare Wordsworth's avowal later in the Preface of his "deep impression of certain inherent and indestructible qualities of the human mind, and likewise of certain powers in the great and permanent objects that act upon it, which are equally inherent and indestructible" [131].) Moreover, the language Wordsworth is seeking is the natural language of the passions, no longer the

---

[16]Quoted in *Prose* 1:169. For a discussion of Wordsworth's (and Hartley's) notion of a "philosophical language," see Jonathan Lamb, "Hartley and Wordsworth."

[17]The self-contradictory impulse that drives Wordsworth here is related to what Paul de Man, in "Intentional Structure of the Romantic Image," calls "the fundamental ambiguity that characterizes the poetics of romanticism": on the one hand, the attempt to bring language as near as possible to natural objects, and to the status of a natural object, and on the other the high valuation of the human imagination and its activities, including symbol and myth. In discussing Hölderlin's use of "flowers" as a simile for words, de Man comments: "By calling them *natural* objects, we mean that their origin is determined by nothing but their own being. Their becoming coincides at all times with the mode of their origination: it is as flowers that their history is what it is, totally defined by their identity. There is no wavering in the status of their existence: existence and essence coincide in them at all times" (4). Nature so conceived is necessarily outside all human experience, of course, hence the tension and irony, explicit or implicit, which always accompany such moments. We saw in the previous chapter that the word "flower" is not innocent of ambiguities as regards the distinction between nature and art.

"language of conversation" of the 1798 Advertisement, and this aspect becomes more important as his theory of the creative act is elaborated.[18] Finally, part of the definition is by negatives: what the true poetic language escapes is *arbitrariness* and *caprice* and what it refuses to encourage is *fickleness*—just the qualities against which self-sufficient, permanent nature is defined.[19]

Similar terms recur as a litany throughout the Preface. "Real" and "actual", for instance, serve to give rhetorical authority to Wordsworth's endorsement of a natural language as the basis for poetry, while what might be defined as "unreal" is left vague: so he writes of "language *really* used by men" (123), "the *very* language of men" (131), "the language *really* spoken by men" (137), "that which is uttered by men in *real* life, under the *actual* pressure of those passions" (138), "language . . . which the *real* passion *itself* suggests" (139), "the *real* language of nature" (142), "the *real* language of men" (143), "language closely resembling that of *real* life" (151), and "bring[ing] my language near to the *real* language of men" (151). The Appendix on poetic diction continues the refrain: "The earliest Poets of all nations generally wrote from passion excited by *real* events; they wrote naturally, and as men" (160) (here "as men" almost means "*not* as men*," at least as Wordsworth feels men are in his time); "expressions . . . dictated by *real* passion" (161); "the language of the earliest poets . . . was *really* spoken by men" (161) (my emphases throughout). The qualifier can even be dropped—"to bring my language near to the language of men" (131), and "poetry in which the language closely resembles that of life and nature" (153)—as if any other language would not be that of men, life, and nature but that of books or wayward individuals out of touch with the essence of humanity. This appeal to a "real" language more authentic than that of written texts has of course become a commonplace of criticism and does not necessarily underpin a radical position. T. S. Eliot's is a typical conservative use of it: "The poetry of a people takes its life

---

[18]The view that strong feelings produce peculiarly powerful or eloquent language is as old, at least, as Quintilian—see *Prose* 1:176—and clearly derives from a phonocentric equation of powerful feeling and powerful language.

[19]Wordsworth's hostility to "arbitrary" procedures in poetry is clearly related to his hostility at this time to "arbitrary" political power, as expressed in his *Letter to the Bishop of Llandaff* (see Will Christie, "Wordsworth and the Language of Nature," 40). For a suggestive discussion of the complex force of "arbitrary" as both a linguistic and a political term, see William Keach, *Shelley's Style*, chap. 6.

from the people's speech and in turn gives life to it" (*The Use of Poetry*, 15); and of numerous possible examples from the criticism of those associated with *Scrutiny* one strikingly Wordsworthian comment will suffice (made, significantly, in the course of an attack on Joyce's later writing): F. R. Leavis's reference to "the very spirit of the language— the spirit that was formed when the English people who formed it was predominantly rural" ("Joyce and 'The Revolution of the Word,'" 200). In a chapter entitled "The Real Language of Men", Heather Glen argues interestingly that the belief in a "fundamental community between men" upon which the Preface's view of natural language is premised contrasts sharply with the opaque otherness of individuals and their experience conveyed by the poems; she observes that "one after another, *Lyrical Ballads* suggest that 'men' are not thus generalizable: that each has his own individuality, his own perspective on and sense of the world. And in a divided society there can be no easy reconciliation of these perspectives into a comfortable general view. The assumption that there might be a single 'real language' which might embrace every man's experience is as contradictory as is the attempt, in 'The Old Cumberland Beggar', to affirm an unproblematic community" (*Vision and Disenchantment*, 85). Wordsworth is willing to push his argument to its logical conclusion, however problematic that may prove for his enterprise: "But, whatever portion of this faculty [of expression] we may suppose even the greatest Poet to possess, there cannot be a doubt but that the language which it will suggest to him, must, in liveliness and truth, fall far short of that which is uttered by men in real life" (138).[20] A depressing thought for the poet, but Wordsworth insists that it would be a sign of "unmanly despair" for him to endeavor "occasionally to surpass his original, in order to make some amends for the general inferiority to which he feels that he must submit" (139). The poet has to learn to live with his status as inferior echo of natural perfection.

There is also, of course, a historical dimension to Wordsworth's argument. Just as Puttenham looked back to "nature, antiquity, and universality," citing both the "ancient poets" who wrote in rhyme and the "Greeks and Latins," and as Pope urged the best classical models upon the poets of his time, so Wordsworth's poetry of "real language," if it eludes discovery in the present, can be located in the past,

---

[20]Thus in texts of 1802–36. In later texts this passage is somewhat weakened: "must" becomes "must often" and "far short" loses the intensifier.

before the onset of the current depravity. The analysis is very sketchy, but it contains hints of the same self-contradictions that haunted the humanist and Augustan uses of a historical model. "A multitude of causes, unknown to former times," writes Wordsworth, "are now acting with a combined force to blunt the discriminating powers of the mind, and, unfitting it for all voluntary exertion, to reduce it to a state of almost savage torpor" (129). Here is the problem that Puttenham wrestled with: if things get better as one goes further back, perfection must lie in precivilized life, and Wordsworth's somewhat surprising use of the word "savage" to refer to his contemporaries acknowledges the force of that conclusion while resisting it—it is civilization that is uncivilized, and the location of the ideal state of humanity in time, as in place, must remain unstated.[21] Wordsworth's continued emphasis on the permanence of natural forms and natural language, and of the best poetry, denies that history has a place in the discussion at all.

Wordsworth's theory of a language drawn directly from the speech of an ideal community has an obvious relevance to verse that uses dramatic speakers and narrators, but it offers no assistance to the poet who wishes to speak *in propria persona* unless the poet is, or manages to become, a full member of such a rustic community. There is plainly an attraction in this idea (the literary world's response to the presentation of Burns as a genuine rural poet is one indication of its appeal at this time),[22] and the "man speaking to men" tag is an index of it. Such a move would solve the problem of nature and art, and is a logical corollary of Wordsworth's primitivism, but it would introduce a host of new problems, among them the exclusion of virtually all poets from the canon, including Wordsworth himself. The daily life of the Wordsworths never approached that of an agricultural laborer's family, and Wordsworth was compelled to devise an account of the poet's activity which would allow him to tap the natural language of the primitive community without having to join it. What had to be kept at bay in this account was the old idea of the poet as craftsman, since every conscious decision about a word places a distance between the poet's language and the real language of men produced spon-

[21]One may compare Coleridge's line, "Through courts and cities the smooth savage roams" (*Religious Musings*, 151), which performs a similar metalepsis.

[22]Coleridge skeptically comments that there is "but *one* BURNS, among the shepherds of *Scotland,* and not a single poet of humble life among those of *English* lakes and mountains" (*BL* 2:132)—testifying to the appeal of the myth of naive poetic genius even as he tries to discount it.

taneously in states of passion. As poetry must itself be real language, not a simulacrum produced by art, the account of the poet's activity must correspondingly elide all matters of conscious composition and revision. (That his manuscripts and letters, and the comments of others, show Wordsworth to have been an inveterate reviser—D. D. Devlin offers a cento of quotations to illustrate Wordsworth's obsessiveness in this respect [*Wordsworth and the Poetry of Epitaphs*, 50-51]—only underlines the fact that his theory is dictated not by self-observation but by theoretical needs.) The 1800 Preface begins to sketch such an account in the famous "spontaneous overflow of powerful feelings" introduced to distinguish between Wordsworth's use of a simple style and that of some of his contemporaries (126) and repeated as part of the justification of meter (148), but it is in the 1802 additions, which we need not hesitate to call a "supplement," that the issue is fully tackled. Wordsworth there explicitly raises the question of those poems or parts of poems "where the Poet speaks to us in his own person and character" (144). His answer, which we can piece together from this and other passages, is in effect an alternative theory of natural language, taking its inspiration more from Hartley than from primitivistic or revolutionary ideals.[23]

The crux of the argument is that successful poetic creation depends not on accurately imitating the right kind of language but on being the right kind of person, one whose language will automatically be truly poetic. Only in this way can the poet be said to be composing *naturally*.[24] The issue of the difference between the poet's language and that of the ideal rustic community is subordinated to the issue of the poet's human qualities and past experience, an issue that gives rise to some of the Preface's most memorable passages. In describing such

[23]W. J. B. Owen discusses these alternatives in terms of a shift from a mimetic to an expressive theory (*Wordsworth as Critic*, 64-65), though it is perhaps more accurate to regard it as an attempt to supply what is lacking in the original formulation of the theory without contradicting that theory.

[24]Testimony to the success of Wordsworth's argument, and a powerful underwriting of it, occur in Arnold's influential packaging of Wordsworth's poetry for a late nineteenth-century audience. In the Preface to his selection *Poems of Wordsworth* he pronounces: "But Wordsworth's poetry, when he is at his best, is inevitable, as inevitable as Nature herself. It might seem that Nature not only gave him the matter for his poem, but wrote his poem for him. He has no style. . . . Nature herself seems, I say, to take the pen out of his hand, and to write for him with her own bare, sheer, penetrating power" (xxii–xxiv).

a person, however, Wordsworth finds himself facing the problem of difference in a new guise, for the poet must be at once like the ideal rustic, feeling deeply, communicating with the lasting presences of nature, free from "social vanity," and speaking a real language, and at the same time different—a difference that, however defined, will always be in danger of usurping the central position in the account of poetic creativity. Wordsworth does his best to avoid the working out of the supplementary logic in which he is involved by insisting, in a passage from which I quoted earlier, on what the poet has in common with others: "The Poet thinks and feels in the spirit of the passions of men. How, then, can his language differ in any material degree from that of all other men who feel vividly and see clearly? It might be *proved* that it is impossible."[25] If this were not the case, he goes on, "the Poet might then be allowed to use a peculiar language when expressing his feelings for his own gratification, or that of men like himself" (142-43). That last phrase hints at the separateness of poets as a breed, in spite of Wordsworth's wish to merge them with the generality of humankind, and in his account of the poet he cannot avoid specifying capabilities that do not appear to spring from rustic soil. Among other qualifications, the poet has "thought long and deeply" (127), he is "habitually compelled to create . . . volitions and passions . . . in the goings-on of the Universe," he has a "disposition to be affected more than other men by absent things as if they were present," an "ability of conjuring up in himself passions, which . . . resemble the passions produced by real events," and—only the last of a long list—"a greater readiness and power in expressing what he thinks and feels" (138). Hartleian associationist terminology readily serves Wordsworth's purpose here, with its emphasis on the *necessary* relation of ideas, feelings, and words; indeed, the attraction of Hartley can be seen as the attraction of a system that makes human psychology a matter of universal laws instead of changeable caprices, and hence an aspect of nature.

Thus Wordsworth can describe the act of poetic composition in terms far removed from the more conventional metaphors of struggling and searching: the poet "blindly and mechanically" (127) obeys the impulses of the habits he has built up through a long process of association of feelings and thoughts, and appropriate words emerge.

[25]Texts of 1836 and later substitute "human passions" for "the passions of men."

Hence, too, the concept of the "silent poet," as it occurs, for example, in lines 77–80 of "When, to the attractions of the busy world":

> Nature there
> Was with thee; she, who loved us both, she still
> Was with thee; and even so didst thou become
> A *silent* Poet.

The phrase is not as much of an oxymoron for Wordsworth as it may be for us; and he elaborates upon the idea in *The Excursion:*

> Oh! many are the Poets that are sown
> By Nature; men endowed with highest gifts,
> The vision and the faculty divine;
> Yet wanting the accomplishment of verse,
> . . .
> Nor having e'er, as life advanced, been led
> By circumstance to take unto the height
> The measure of themselves, these favoured Beings,
> All but a scattered few, live out their time,
> Husbanding that which they possess within,
> And go to the grave, unthought of.   (I. 77-91)

Here language is not an unimportant last stage in the creative process, as it occasionally seems to be in neoclassical criticism. (Thus Dryden can write in the Preface to his *Fables:* "Now the words are the colouring of the work, which, in the order of nature, is last to be considered. The design, the disposition, the manners, and the thoughts, are all before it" [275]. Classical rhetoric, of course, placed *elocutio* after *inventio* and *dispositio*.) On the contrary, for Wordsworth language is so intimately bound up with the poet's feelings and thoughts that in some sense it is there whether articulated or not. In the third *Essay upon Epitaphs* he very consciously provides a substitute for the traditional "dress" metaphor, with its implications of separable elements: the manuscripts show him replacing the phrase "clothed in a different manner" by "uttered after a different manner" (*Prose* 2:83), and soon afterward he refers to "those expressions which are not what the garb is to the body but what the body is to the soul, themselves a constituent part and power or function in the thought" (*Prose* 2:84) (One has here a hint that words have a reciprocal power of their own over thought, a hint which is echoed in the Note to "The

Thorn" and which suggests a more complex relationship that tends to undermine the main argument of Wordsworth's prose. The idea is more strongly articulated in the poetry, though that is a subject on which I can merely touch at the end of this chapter.) One might have expected Wordsworth's experience as a writer to have made him too conscious of the labor of manipulating language to allow any credence to such a notion, but it follows necessarily from the rejection of art as artifice; the alternative would be to locate the distinctiveness of poetic creation in linguistic composition, which would be once more to drive a wedge between nature and art.[26] The most Wordsworth can do is to insist on the difference between an emotional response and the same emotion recollected in tranquillity—and even this degree of separation between the thing itself and the language it evokes threatens to introduce a challenge to nature's primacy.

Prose versus Verse

There is one obvious difficulty in advancing a theory of poetry based on the foundation of a "natural" language, whether it be a language found in particular communities or a language produced automatically by a true poet—a difficulty that would have prevented most literary theorists from even starting down the road that Wordsworth traveled. Whatever other defining features it may have, poetry is indisputably marked by its *form:* "natural language" does not fall into regular rhythmic patterns, or use rhyme, or group itself into stanzas. Though modern readers may find puzzling the degree of attention Wordsworth gives to this issue, the point is crucial to his entire argument, and his handling of it is one of the boldest things in the Preface.

---

[26]See Stephen K. Land, "The Silent Poet," in which the relation between Wordsworth's views and the semantic organicism of Herder is discussed. Wordsworth's ideal language sounds close to Herder's conception of language as indistinguishable from the mental events it serves to communicate, but as Land points out, the former's view of language involves a good deal of suspicion, which links it also to the Lockean tradition with its emphasis on the arbitrariness of the linguistic sign. In any event, Wordsworth's inconsistent and shifting formulations about language cannot be accounted for by deriving them from a single intellectual tradition, as, for instance, Hans Aarsleff attempts to do (in this case, the tradition of Condillac) in "Wordsworth, Language, and Romanticism" (*From Locke to Saussure,* 372-81).

Romanticism and the Language of Nature

If poetry is not to be defined in terms of its difference from natural language, as it always had been, then the question of meter must be shown not to be the problem it appears to be. First of all the ground must be shifted slightly, from the distinction between the language of poetry and the language of men to the distinction between the language of poetry (or, as Wordsworth prefers to call it for the purposes of this distinction, "metrical composition") and the language of prose. In this way Wordsworth distances himself to some degree from the problems we have been discussing. The language of prose is allowed to do duty for the language of men, without the precise character of the relationship being spelled out (as W. J. B. Owen notes, "Wordsworth uses the phrase ['language of prose'] as if it denoted a definable essence of rhetoric, a stable idiom, 'pure' like the passions and language of the rustic, a permanently normative mode of expression" [*Wordsworth as Critic*, 23]), and the argument is brought within the confines of a much more traditional debate about poetic diction. Wordsworth can then pose the question baldly (in the 1800 Preface): "Is there then, it will be asked, no essential difference between the language of prose and metrical composition? I answer that there neither is nor can be any essential difference" (*Prose* 1:134). That one is organized into metrically regular lines, perhaps with rhymes and stanzas, is contingent for Wordsworth, a fact that has no bearing on the essential identity of (good) poetry and (good) prose.[27]

Wordsworth anticipates the obvious objection, and in 1800 proceeds straight to his answer (in the 1802 revision he interpolates, in mid-sentence, the long description of the poet which we have already discussed): "If it be affirmed that rhyme and metrical arrangement of themselves constitute a distinction which overturns what I have been saying on the strict affinity of metrical language with that of prose, and paves the way for other distinctions which the mind voluntarily admits, I answer that the distinction of rhyme and metre is regular and uniform, and not, like that which is produced by what is usually called poetic diction, arbitrary and subject to infinite caprices upon which no calculation whatever can be made" (*Prose* 1:136, 144). Rhyme and meter are acceptable because they can be stated in terms of regular and unchanging rules and are therefore on the side of

[27]This is not an idiosyncratic view; Wordsworth probably derived it from an article by William Enfield. See *Prose* 1:173, and Owen, *Wordsworth as Critic*, 18-20.

permanence, universality, and necessity, not on the side of changeableness, idiosyncrasy, and contingency; they are, that is, on the side
of nature. "No interference is made by them with the passion,"
Wordsworth goes on (and now we return to the 1802 revision), "but
such as the concurring testimony of ages has shown to heighten and
improve the pleasure which co-exists with it" (145). Just as the permanent forms of nature produce the most mature passions and the best
language, so the near-permanent forms of meter have a positive influence on poetry. It still remains to explain *how* meter has this effect—and Wordsworth's account is not without its contradictions—
but the foundations of the theory of poetic language as nature have
been preserved.[28]

The other traditional topic in discussions of the distinctiveness of
poetic language is the use of figures, and Wordsworth could not have
avoided it even if he had wished to. A poetics such as Puttenham's,
which welcomes figurative language, can adduce it as one of poetry's
chief glories, though as we have seen the story does not end there, for
the use of figures is simultaneously an "abuse" of ordinary language
which must be controlled by decorum, and turns out to be a feature of
ordinary language anyway. Wordsworth has two options: either true
poetry dispenses altogether with figures on the grounds that they are
products of poetic artifice, or figures are an aspect of the real language of men. Only the former would be consistent with the general
drift of the argument, because a figure is, by definition, an "unnatural" use of language; to go this far, however, would be to expose
the theory to attack on the grounds that it accounted for virtually no
poetry whatever (as well as to deprive Wordsworth of a major poetic

[28]Nevertheless, the acceptance of meter goes against the grain of the entire argument, and something of this strain emerges in the second *Essay upon Epitaphs,* where
Wordsworth restates the theory of poetry as the direct expression of feeling as a
warning against the temptations held out by meter: "A judicious Man will be less
disposed in this case [viz., the writing of an epitaph] than in any other to avail himself of
the liberty given by metre to adopt phrases of fancy, or to enter into the more remote
regions of illustrative imagery. For the occasion of writing an Epitaph is matter of fact
in its intensity, and forbids more authoritatively than any other species of composition
all modes of fiction, except those which the very strength of passion has created" (*Prose*
2:76). As late as 1827 Wordsworth adds to the Appendix to the *Lyrical Ballads* Preface a
final sentence reiterating the warning: "Metre is but adventitious to composition, and
the phraseology for which that passport is necessary, even where it is graceful at all, will
be little valued by the judicious" (164).

resource). Fortunately for Wordsworth, a well-established view existed that the first language, or at least the first poetry, was figurative,[29]
and that figurative language is the "natural expression" of strong
feelings.[30] He is consequently able to assert that the language of the
earliest poets, who wrote "from passion excited by real events" and
"naturally, and as men," was "daring, and figurative" (160), and to
allow personification in the language of men as "a figure of speech
occasionally prompted by passion" (131). At the same time his main
argument is directed against the use of figures, and we are prompted
to ask, as with Puttenham, by what criteria we are to judge a figure
acceptable or unacceptable. I take up this question shortly.

In the face of empirical evidence Wordsworth's account of the identity between the "language of men" and that of poetry breaks down
immediately, and Coleridge made this one of his main points of disagreement with the Preface. Rustic language, as a sociolinguistic reality, does not in fact provide a satisfactory model for the poetry that
circulates around a very different class, and it may appear that no
more needs to be said (though Coleridge manages to spin out his
objections at some length, seeing an incompatibility not between different sets of class expectations but between an imperfect local language and a universal language—the same universalizing gesture
performed by Puttenham when he identifies a minority language with
what is "usual" [see p. 34 above]). However, if we take seriously
Wordsworth's endeavor to find a "natural" language that could, without essential modification, form the basis of a poetic language, there
may be more to be said. The Preface is less a sociolinguistic report on

---

[29]See *Prose* 1:113-14 for a discussion of some of the English sources; a similar notion,
which reads back into history the experienced power of figurative language, can be
found in many eighteenth-century accounts of the origin of language, the best known
being by Vico, Herder, and Rousseau. Note the explicitness of Hugh Blair's identification of the supplementary function of artificial figures: such devices were introduced as
poets attempted to "supply the defect of native warmth" (cited in *Prose* 1:113).

[30]We have already seen that Puttenham uses this argument in order to adduce a
natural origin for the figures of rhetoric (31-32 above). Du Marsais, in *Des Tropes*,
objected to Quintilian's definition of figures as being "manners of speaking that are far
removed from the ordinary and natural manner," because "during one day at the
central market more figures are used than during several days of academic con-
ferences" (quoted by Group μ, *A General Rhetoric*, 10). The idea was something of an
eighteenth-century commonplace; see *Prose* 1:174-75 for examples. Wordsworth's development of this traditional view into a revaluation, with important political implications, of the role of figuration in both poetry and social experience is well discussed by
David Simpson in *Wordsworth and the Figurings of the Real*.

the language of rural English communities than an attempt to imagine or hypostatize such a language in its purest form, and Wordsworth's description of it is more a theoretical than an empirical statement. It may well have been more profitable in 1800—indeed, it may still be more profitable—to think not in terms of what the poet has to do to ordinary language in order to make it poetic but in terms of what kind of language might serve for a poetics of the ordinary, even if that language does not actually exist. It is true that such a language could be considered "real" only in a Platonic sense, but Wordsworth is perhaps less of an Aristotelian and more of a Platonist than he is sometimes made out to be.[31] Wordsworth's experimental poetry might be seen as an attempt to *create* the language of his theory, even if he continued to cling to the idea that such a language could really be found in the world around him.

The Principle of Selection: Imagination, Taste, and the Supplement

What, then, of the supplement? Has Wordsworth managed to evade its power, which seemed to threaten every endeavor to establish a conception of art based on a prior conception of a self-sufficient nature?[32] His strategy is certainly a powerful one: to deny the supplementarity of art—the best art—altogether, and to affirm instead an identity between nature and art when they present themselves in their most fully realized forms. The true poem is indistinguishable from the spontaneous utterance of the most fully mature human being under the pressure of the most significant emotions. Any observable

[31]Don H. Bialostosky argues this point in the opening chapter of *Making Tales*, though with the rather different aim of delineating a Wordsworthian "poetics of speech," which in my view underestimates the internal contradictions of Wordsworth's poetic program.

[32]Commentators have often taken the wish for the deed; thus Michael Ragussis claims that Wordsworth's critical essays, and Book 5 of *The Prelude*, "revive the problem of Nature versus Art, and solve it: a language of nature is what the greatest art speaks" (*The Subterfuge of Art*, 33). He concludes his chapter on Wordsworth with the assertion: "It is Wordsworth's genius to have reconciled the experience of nature with that of books" (34). We are likely to get a better sense of Wordsworth's achievement if we attend to the way in which such proclaimed "solutions" and "reconciliations"—which are as old as the controversy about nature and art itself—are doubted and tested in his writing.

disparity arises either because the utterance is not perfectly "natural" or because the poem is not a true copy of such an utterance. This reformulation by Wordsworth and, in related ways, by other Romantic writers of the relationship between art and nature has, of course, been extremely potent in the history of literature and literary theory; it has produced a totally different valorization of such terms as "artifice," "sincerity," "spontaneity," and "authenticity," and in the field of literary studies it has resulted in a displacement of questions of form by questions of content which shows no sign of being reversed. Indeed, recent trends in literary theory and criticism suggest something of a revival, with a distinct Romantic flavor, of antiformalism, in a period in which the long-enduring tendency to elide the role of language in literature had begun to be vigorously challenged. If we proceed to examine Wordsworth's text for signs that supplementarity has not after all been evaded, we do so not to score points against him but to demonstrate that the structures of Romantic and post-Romantic thought and feeling do not offer systems that are any more exhaustive in their explanations or consistent in their operations than those which characterize the Renaissance or classical periods.[33]

Wordsworth wants to present poetry as the pure transposition of natural language or the pure effusion of the poet in a state of heightened emotion, because any intervening stage reintroduces the notion of an art which is defined against nature and which therefore challenges nature's absolute authority. But there are two problems. One, already mentioned, is the empirical evidence: neither rural speech nor the utterances to which strong passion (even when recollected in tranquillity) spontaneously gives rise would provide the requisite pleasure to the reader if merely transcribed. This objection need not be fatal, however, although it obviously worried Wordsworth and has been pressed very hard by Coleridge and others since. The absence of a pure poetic language may, in theory, be the result not of a flaw in the argument but of the empirical absence of any purely natural societies or of any poet wholly qualified for his task by natural ability and appropriate experience. The other objection, not voiced by

---

[33]The operation of supplementarity also offers an approach that is more alert to the complexities of Wordsworth's position, in itself and within the history of literary theory, than a simple reversal of the privileging of "nature" over "art" usually ascribed to him, such as Stephen Maxfield Parrish attempts in *The Art of the "Lyrical Ballads."* At most, Parrish acknowledges an "ambivalence" or a "compromise" in the relation between nature and art in Wordsworth's theory (see, for instance, 4-5).

Wordsworth or any of his critics, is that the poet, *qua* poet, ceases to exist: he cannot claim for himself any particular aesthetic or linguistic talent (the art of writing in a metrical form being necessarily regarded as a wholly ancillary skill). However much he achieves as a poet of words, he is always subject to being surpassed by some "silent poet" who has not yet chosen or been compelled to give voice, and he is constantly aware that his special position as "poet," cut off from natural simplicity, renders him less rather than more capable of producing the highest kind of poetry. Although it is only the first of these objections that Wordsworth openly articulates, it is perhaps in part a screen for the second, which operates throughout the history of art to protect the artist from self-betrayal and self-obliteration. In Coleridge's theory of the primary and secondary imagination, for example, we can see an attempt—a highly successful one—to restore the place of the poet, indeed, to elevate it to a new height by absorbing the Wordsworthian emphasis on the poet as superior human being while finding new terms in which to describe particularly poetic capabilities.

To overcome both these objections, Wordsworth's theory requires a refinement: the introduction of a special activity on the part of the poet which will make the crucial difference between the language of poetry and natural language, an activity occurring not spontaneously but as a matter of conscious choice, thus overcoming the empirical problem by allowing for the rectification of what actually exists and simultaneously keeping the poet in existence. (Coleridge's account of the secondary imagination emphasizes the "conscious will," which occupies a similar place in the argument [*BL* 1:304].) Wordsworth, wishing to qualify his fundamental conception of the poet as little as possible, calls this activity "selection" or "purification," and its importance to him is suggested by the way these terms (especially the former) reverberate through the text (123, 125, 137, 139, 143).[34] Clearly Wordsworth, like many before him, is trying to find a way of defining the difference between "ordinary" and "poetic" language which will not imply that the former is in need of an enhancement that the latter provides. Thus the terms "selection" and "purification" imply only a

[34]In texts of 1802–32 Wordsworth calls the principle of selection "the principle upon which I have so much insisted," weakening this slightly in later texts to "the principle . . . which has already been insisted upon" (*Prose* 1:139). Owen notes that in the first version of the Preface the word "selection" occurs only once, an observation that seems to run counter to his characterization of the difference between the two versions as a move from a mimetic to an expressive theory (*Wordsworth as Critic*, 66-67).

subtraction from nature and not an addition to it, and Wordsworth would like to believe that this subtraction is sufficient to distance his theory from the traditional account of the artist as *improver* of nature. The poet, he writes, "will feel that there is no necessity to trick out or to elevate nature: and, the more industriously he applies this principle [of selection], the deeper will be his faith that no words, which *his* fancy or imagination can suggest, will be to be compared with those which are the emanations of reality and truth" (139). And, with a horror that is perhaps only partly ironic: "I forbear to speak of an incongruity which would shock the intelligent Reader, should the Poet interweave any foreign splendour of his own with that which the passion naturally suggests: it is sufficient to say that such addition is unnecessary" (137).[35]

The enemy throughout the Preface is the idiosyncratic, the idiolectal, the arbitrary. Wordsworth articulates two fears about his poems—that his "associations must have sometimes been particular instead of general," and that his "language may frequently have suffered from those arbitrary connections of feelings and ideas with particular words and phrases, from which no man can altogether protect himself" (153). If the poet once attempts to provide, in an act of self-conscious creativity, his "own" word or figure (which, by implication, will come from the stock authorized by the depraved taste of the time) instead of drawing exclusively from the language that arises unbidden from the feelings he experiences (through the processes of recollection or empathy), he falls into this danger. Such, at least, is the theory of selection. Wordsworth thus sustains the Renaissance and neoclassical demand for an art that excludes the particular in favor of the universal, but he locates the universal not in that which is most widely shared by mankind but that which is most purely born—however rare it might be. The natural word, as always, is uttered spontaneously and cannot be conjured up by the imagination (a faculty that does not yet carry the mystical baggage of semidivinity it was to

[35]There is a strong connection, as Owen points out (69), between Wordsworth's argument here and his attempts in the *Guide to the Lakes* to specify the proper relation between the works of nature and the works of man, attempts that are subject to the same problematic of the supplement. The following remark is particularly relevant to the discussion of poetic language (note the occurrence of the word "buildings" among the items of "natural" scenery): "This is, indeed, the main point; for, much as these scenes have been injured by what has been taken from them—buildings, trees, and woods, either through negligence, necessity, avarice, or caprice—it is not the removals, but the harsh *additions* that have been made, which are the worst grievance—a standing and unavoidable annoyance" (*Prose* 2:222).

acquire through Coleridge's intervention.)[36] Hence the act of purging nature of her defects is absolutely distinct from the act of adding to her creations. Hence, too, the only way the poet can write narrative or dramatic poetry is to "bring his feelings near to those of the persons whose feelings he describes, nay, for short spaces of time, perhaps, to let himself slip into an entire delusion, and even confound and identify his own feelings with theirs" (138); it is not enough to *imagine* them. The Keatsian note here need not surprise us, for as a Romantic theorist Wordsworth is far more partial to Negative Capability than to the Egotistical Sublime.

What Wordsworth, in his theory of selection, is doing his best to exclude from his account is any notion of *enhancement,* of poetic language as ordinary language suffused with some special quality that renders it memorable and pleasurable, in short, the traditional theory shared by Puttenham and Pope, and reformulated by Coleridge (in his reworking of late eighteenth-century German aesthetics) as a theory of the imagination.[37] The Preface is often read from a Coleridgean perspective, from within what Jerome McGann calls, in his book of that name, the "Romantic Ideology," and Wordsworth is condemned for failing to introduce the principle whose rejection forms the basis of his argument.[38] A focus on the question of the supplement and its

---

[36]Wordsworth's Preface to the 1815 edition of his *Poems* is largely devoted to an exposition of the distinction between "imagination" and "fancy," which seems likely to have been a Coleridgean hobbyhorse that Wordsworth reinterpreted for his own ends—before Coleridge himself had published a significant account of it.

[37]In the course of his presentation of an organic alternative to Wordsworth's theory of meter as a co-presence, "adventitious to composition," Coleridge quotes approvingly Polixenes' reply to Perdita on the matter of art and nature in the garden; the notion of an all-embracing "Nature" that can include the practices of art is closer to his mode of thought than to Wordsworth's (*BL* 2:66). I cannot agree with Laurence Lerner, who believes that Wordsworth viewed nature both as Perdita and (at his best—that is, in Lerner's eyes, at his most quietistic) as Polixenes ("What Did Wordsworth Mean by 'Nature'?").

[38]Thus James A. W. Heffernan, in *Wordsworth's Theory of Poetry,* having found fault with "the voice of reaction and revolt in the early essays," can applaud "the whispers of another tendency, of a new and positive approach to the role of feeling in the imaginative process" (53). Abrams, too, in *The Mirror and the Lamp,* tends to present Coleridge's apotheosizing of the Imagination as a triumph of poetic insight after Wordsworth's backward-looking account of the creative act. Abrams notes that "in Coleridge's criticism . . . the imaginative synthesis of discordant or antithetic aesthetic qualities replaces Wordsworth's 'nature' as the criterion of highest poetic value" (119), and that "in his critical writings, Wordsworth retained to a notable degree the terminology and modes of thinking of eighteenth-century associationism" (181-82), without observing the degree to which it is Coleridge who sets the clock back after Wordsworth's attempt at a radical account of creativity.

73

history makes it possible to appreciate how far the introduction into Romantic discourse of the term "imagination," in its Coleridgean sense, serves the same purposes as the term "decorum" and its successors. Although the term operates within a different discursive system ("reconciliation of opposites," "blending," "fusion," "synthesis," "wholeness," and so on), its central function within Romantic aesthetics derives from the fact that, although the decisive factor in the production of "true" poetry, it is not susceptible to rules, is not part of the craft of verse and so cannot be taught, and is a faculty dispensed as a kind of grace to certain favored individuals. Coleridge's exclusivism (dressed up, as in all such arguments, as universalism) is apparent in his response to Wordsworth:

> But if it be asked, by what principles the poet is to regulate his own style, if he do not adhere closely to the sort and order of words which he hears in the market, wake, high-road, or plough-field? I reply; by principles, the ignorance or neglect of which would convict him of being no *poet*, but a silly or presumptuous usurper of the name! By the principles of grammar, logic, psychology! In one word by such a knowledge of the facts, material and spiritual, that most appertain to his art, as if it have been governed and applied by *good sense*, and rendered instinctive by habit, becomes the representative and reward of our past conscious reasonings, insights, and conclusions, and acquires the name of TASTE. (*BL* 2:81)

The Wordsworth who wrote the Preface might have replied in terms similar to the ones he used in a well-known letter of 1802 to John Wilson, castigating those who treat class characteristics as universals:

> People in our rank in life are perpetually falling into one sad mistake, namely, that of supposing that human nature and the persons they associate with are one and the same thing. Whom do we generally associate with? Gentlemen, persons of fortune, professional men, ladies[,] persons who can afford to buy or can easily procure books of half a guinea price, hot-pressed, and printed upon superfine paper. These persons are, it is true, a part of human nature, but we err lamentably if we suppose them to be fair representatives of the vast mass of human existence. (*Letters* 1:355).[39]

[39]To be aware of the prevalence of the mistake is not the same thing, of course, as finding a way to escape from it—and if one's potential audience is not the vast mass of human existence but people like oneself, one may not wish to escape from it, however much one talks of "common humanity." Thus Wellek observes of Francis Jeffrey's

For Coleridge, however, the judgment of true poetry can be made only by a true poet; the closed circle of poets is self-justified and self-justifying; poetic genius is another version of the self-presence and plenitude of nature (and of course the repeated use of organic imagery to describe poems and the activity of poets is another version of the familiar appeal to nature—in Coleridge's case appearing also in the guise of the Divinity—as the shaper and guarantor of its own supplement): "For even as truth is its own light and evidence, discovering at once itself and falsehood, so is it the prerogative of poetic genius to distinguish by parental instinct its proper offspring from the changelings, which the gnomes of vanity or the fairies of fashion may have laid in its cradle or called by its names. Could a rule be given from *without*, poetry would cease to be poetry, and sink into a mechanical art" (*BL* 2:83). Coleridge's attempt to specify precisely the distinction between fancy and imagination provides neither a prescription for the poet nor a discovery procedure to apply to existing verse (though others, notably I. A. Richards in *Coleridge on Imagination*, have tried to make it perform these functions), and, as with all the terms that operate in this way, it is only by means of examples that the nature of the difference can be transmitted to the apprentice poet or the reader. The capacity to employ and recognize truly imaginative language is, as Coleridge's comments suggest, a version of taste, learned, as all tastes are, by exposure and not by precept, and hundreds of confident critical assertions as to the existence of one or other quality in specimens of poetry testify only to the conviction of later generations that they have absorbed the taste of the preeminent Romantics.[40] The most significant break with tradition that the Romantic concept of the imagination embodies is not its self-reinforcing rhetoric of blending and wholeness, of life as opposed to death, mo-

---

claims on behalf of a universal humanity: "In short, the common man is somebody like Jeffrey; and Jeffrey, as his wide audience shows, was the spokesman of a large middle class" (*A History of Modern Criticism,* 2:115). The social and political forces at issue in aesthetic debate are seldom as openly revealed as in the campaign waged by Jeffrey against Wordsworth, in spite of a large degree of overlap in their literary views (see Wellek, 111-20).

[40]The distinction Coleridge makes between an "imitation" and a "copy" is also cited as if it were an objective categorization rather than the reflection of a critical judgment of the same kind as that which governs the distinction between imagination and fancy. See for instance Emerson R. Marks, *Coleridge on the Language of Verse,* in which this distinction is made central to Coleridge's "correction" of Wordsworth and is regarded, somewhat surprisingly, as a foreshadowing of structuralist theory.

bility as opposed to fixity, but its relatively undefined social function (and here Wordsworth's projection of eighteenth-century primitivistic tendencies into the nineteenth century did prove effective): one did not, in theory, have to belong to a particular class to be blessed with a potent imaginative faculty.[41] (The strongest assertion of the imagination's revolutionary potential is, no doubt, Blake's.) In practice, however, an aesthetic category that escapes exact specification—and in this case is posited upon a hostility to the mechanical itself—is controlled by those who have acquired power within such critical institutions as nineteenth-century reviews (or twentieth-century universities). As Saussure observed with regard to language, one cannot *argue* that something should be changed if it is as it is solely by force of social consensus—though this does not mean, as Saussure thought, that it *cannot* be changed (see chapter 4 below, pp. 114-15).

Returning to Wordsworth, at a stage before he had followed Coleridge's lead in putting imagination into a central place—a stage at which he makes little distinction between fancy and imagination, regarding both as obstacles to the expression of reality and truth—we can see why a principle that allows for the removal of unsuitable matter suits the argument better than a principle that interposes a special poetic faculty to work on the primary material of nature. The defects of natural language which make selection necessary are described in such a way as to make them sound obvious, not to a particularly fine judgment but to anyone possessed of reasonable (and natural) sensitivity. In quoting the long passage describing ideal rustic language, I omitted the crucial qualification that occurs in parentheses: "The language, too, of these men has been adopted (purified indeed from what appear to be its real defects, from all lasting and rational causes of *dislike* or *disgust*)" (125; my emphases). In reiterating the importance of selection to the poet who identifies his feelings with those of his characters, Wordsworth comments: "He will depend upon [the principle of selection] for removing what would otherwise be *painful* or *disgusting* in the passion" (139; my emphases). "Lasting

[41]Coleridge's distinction between the "primary" and the "secondary" imagination, however, lends itself to a class-based distinction, since the former is the property of all mankind and the latter of the happy few. The secondary imagination is to be found, presumably, only in those who speak "the best part of human language," which excludes, for Coleridge, "uneducated man" (*BL* 2:54) The secondary imagination is, of course, a supplement, a derivative of the primary which is nevertheless needed to breathe life into it.

and rational causes"—the phrase constitutes, with something of a reversion to an eighteenth-century rhetorical mode, an appeal to universally agreed judgments, and terms such as "painful" and "disgusting" imply that no particularly sensitive discrimination is required.

It is easy to interpret Wordsworth's theory of selection in the way that Coleridge does, as the removal of all that renders rustic speech different from the norm: "A rustic's language, purified from all provincialism and grossness, and so far re-constructed as to be made consistent with the rules of grammar . . . will not differ from the language of any other man of common-sense, however learned or refined he may be" (*BL* 2:52). Such an interpretation ignores the fact that the presupposed common denominator of language being appealed to is itself as fictive as any idealized rustic speech: Coleridge has simply substituted an idealization he approves of for one he disapproves of (and the grounds for his disapproval are not far to seek) and has foisted his own conception upon his fellow-poet and theorist. He explicitly reformulates Wordsworth's "real language" as "ordinary" language or "*lingua communis*" (*BL* 2:56). Something of the political significance of this change is reflected in the approving comment made by the most recent editors of the *Biographia Literaria*, who assert that Coleridge's preferred norm for poetic language is "conservative in the best sense, cosmopolitan, antisubjective, antiparochial" (*BL* 1:cvii). But Wordsworth's model, as we have seen, is not (at least in 1800) a common or universal language but a "philosophical language," which, if it exists at all, exists at very few times in very few places. If Coleridge in the *Biographia* spends what seems to be an inordinately long time demonstrating the fairly obvious inappropriateness of the language of the poorer, inadequately educated English speaker for the acceptable poetry of the time, he does so probably because in the guise of an empirical correction he is taking issue with the theoretical drift and implications of Wordsworth's redefinition of the linguistic ideal. As Jerome Christensen puts it in his acute analysis of Coleridge's response to Wordsworth, Coleridge's "primary aim is not to attack Wordsworth's indecorous penchant for ascribing noble sentiments to low characters but to defend against the subversion of the principle of decorum involved in the poet's refusal to subscribe to the stabilizing function that class plays in ordaining limits of possibility and probability" (*Coleridge's Blessed Machine of Language,* 144).

There are more difficult questions to be put to the theory of selection, however. By what criteria are the judgments of suitability and unsuitability to be made? Is the poet operating in accordance with socially sanctioned standards of taste and decorum, and therefore remaining at the mercy of the culturally determined supplement that Wordsworth's theory is designed to escape, or in accordance with some natural, "spontaneous" principle, and therefore allowing to the poet as poet no special function as a producer of language? If selection is a self-conscious, deliberate procedure carried out by the skilled artist, with careful calculation as to its likely effects, it collapses back into traditional notions of artifice and craftsmanship; if it is an automatic response to evident blemishes (we may remember that Puttenham explains decorum by analogy with the ear's dislike of a harsh sound), the poet's occupation's gone. Wordsworth's account necessarily hovers between these two. He evinces both a desire to play down the principle of selection in order to reaffirm his faith in the language of nature and a desire to stress it in order to disarm criticism (and self-doubt). Thus he not only presents selection as the removal of a few obvious warts but also calls upon it as a champion against those who say that meter demands a special heightened language: "This selection . . . will of itself form a distinction far greater than would at first be imagined, and will entirely separate the composition from the vulgarity and meanness of ordinary life" (137). In 1802 he added a supplementary gloss to his phrase "selecting from the real language of men" which resulted in more responsibility for the poet but also more problems for the theory of selection: "or, which amounts to the same thing, composing accurately in the spirit of such selection" (143). To introduce the idea of a "spirit" of selection scarcely amounts to the same thing, because it renders the question of criteria even more insistent: Who is to judge what is consistent with this spirit? An older problem remains as well, which Wordsworth is prepared to acknowledge, for the poet has to remove not only blemishes that can be regarded as accretions upon a pure language of nature but some of the features inherent in that language itself—in particular, "the painful feeling always found intermingled with powerful descriptions of the deeper passions" (151). The remedy we have already touched upon. It is the addition of meter, or, we might say, a further principle of selection whereby the words chosen are those which fall into conventionally governed patterns of sound, producing a special type of pleasure which tempers the pain. Nature, by its very nature, is unpleasing; it is art that perfects and pleases. This is a familiar story, but one Wordsworth has set his face against—because if nature is inherently unpleasing, to whom is the poet to appeal for guidance?

Coleridge states the problem of criteria sharply when he observes that "the very power of making the selection implies the previous possession of the language selected" (*BL* 2:58). Wordsworth offers one kind of criterion which is consistent with his attempt to appeal to something more fundamental than the court of civilized taste when he describes the process of selection as "modifying only the language which is thus suggested to [the poet], by a consideration that he describes for a particular purpose, that of giving pleasure" (138). The fundamental principle guiding the poet, therefore, is "the grand elementary principle of pleasure, by which [man] knows, and feels, and lives, and moves" (140), a principle with whose guidance the poet is able to delete anything in the real language of men which might evoke dislike, disgust, or pain.[42] Now as long as the principle of verbal selection which distinguishes the language of art from the language of nature can be specified in purely mechanical terms, as in the case of meter, the theory remains intact, for it can still be said that there is no *essential* difference between the two. With the introduction of pleasure's controlling role, however, this notion begins to look somewhat doubtful: it could easily be argued that the essential difference between natural language and the language of poetry is the pleasure produced by the latter.

Wordsworth summons up his familiar rhetoric to assure us that all is well, employing terms like "*real* defects" and "*lasting* and rational causes of dislike" ("rational" is something of a surprise in this context, but we have already noted in discussing Puttenham's work how "reason" can function as another name for "nature"). With the bolstering of a materialist theory of psychology, the criterion of pleasure can perhaps pass as one that is applied "blindly and mechanically," though one whose rules could hardly be specified in advance. But when we inquire further into the qualities that entitle a poet to select in the name of pleasure, we hear echoes from earlier centuries (my italics throughout): "This selection, *wherever it is made with true taste and*

[42]The importance of poetry's end of producing pleasure, upon which Wordsworth lays at least as much stress as the neoclassical tradition he is criticizing, has not always been acknowledged: thus Abrams, in his drastically simplified but highly influential account of the Preface, "Wordsworth and Coleridge on Diction and Figures," can give the impression that Wordsworth rejects the neoclassical emphasis on the poet's obligation to produce pleasure.

feeling. . . . Passions the language of which, if selected *truly and judiciously,* must necessarily be dignified and variegated. . . . Those passages, which *with propriety* abound with metaphors and figures" (137). The critical decisions regarding what to leave out and what to put in cannot, it appears, be accounted for except by an appeal to the same inscrutable powers so often appealed to before: taste, judiciousness, propriety. (The equivalent power in the account of poetic creation given in the Preface to the 1815 *Poems* is "judgment," which operates in accordance with the familiar principle of decorum, including the determination of the "appropriate graces of every species of composition" [*Prose* 3:27].) It might be argued that Wordsworth is redefining these standards in his own terms, as modes of operation of nature, thus cutting poetry completely off from the social and institutional context that traditionally guarantees such standards; this, though an audacious step, would be consistent with the direction of the argument. He comes close to attempting it in the *Essays upon Epitaphs,* where the paradigmatic Wordsworthian poem—the natural utterance of strong feeling made permanent—is seen to be the epitaph. Here Wordsworth has to acknowledge that sincerely meant verse can be poetically meretricious, and the villain he identifies in such cases is "taste," that is, the prevailing style of the day, which can interfere with the purely natural expression of passion. He describes this interference explicitly as a struggle between nature and "the adversary of nature, (call that adversary Art or by what name you will)" (*Essay 3, Prose* 2:83). This characteristic displacement of poetic ability from questions of craftsmanship to questions of emotion and morality leads Wordsworth into further difficulty, however, because it follows from his assessment that the alert reader must be able to perceive genuine sincerity even through the artifice of mistakenly applied taste and to judge the poem accordingly—as having greater worth than those epitaphs, like Pope's, in which "the thoughts have their nature changed and moulded by the vicious expression in which they are entangled" (*Essay 2, Prose* 2:77). That the achievement of an *effect* of sincerity may depend both on the exercise of skill and on the prevailing taste as it conditions the reader's response is something Wordsworth cannot acknowledge, in spite of the difficulties that arise from any essentialist notion of sincerity as ground and guarantee of authentic poetry.

To identify taste or judgment totally with nature, therefore, would be just as damaging to the status of the poet as the denial of any modifying judgment at all, and Wordsworth does not take this route in the Preface. At most, he thinks in terms of the traditional notion of "second nature," habits of judgment that are both part of nature and not part of it—a typical manifestation of the supplement, with all its instability and doubleness.[43] Words such as "habit" and "custom," in particular, are very useful in bridging the domains of nature and art, because they can play a double role (we might call them *brisures*). They can be used as equivalents of nature, as that which has become so automatic as to have been absorbed into the domain of the natural, or as opposites of nature, as that which belongs to a particular time and place ("habit" when used in this way often acquires connotations from its sartorial sense). Wordsworth obviously regards the habits that the true poet acquires as transcending the particularity of the poet's situation and becoming at least quasi-natural, but habit in general he regards as the deadening influence that poetry should work to combat. Thus Wordsworth warns the reader somewhat sarcastically that his poems will fail to "gratify certain known habits of association" (123)— what he had called in the Advertisement of 1798 "that most dreadful enemy to our pleasures, our own pre-established codes of decision" (*Prose* 1:116)—whereas the poet who writes poems of such originality does so by obeying "habits of mind" he has acquired (127), must be an individual "habitually impelled" to create a spirit of life in the universe (138), and relies on the "habitual gratitude" that readers feel for the pleasure meter has given them (157). The contradictions implicit in the use of the term emerge most startlingly, perhaps, when we find him *attacking* poetry that works "by unsettling ordinary habits of thinking" (Appendix on poetic diction, 162).[44] Coleridge, in a well-

[43]See Chandler, *Wordsworth's Second Nature*, especially chap. 4, for a careful discussion of the importance of this notion—which Chandler traces back to Burke—and of its inevitable instability within the arguments about the revolutionary appeal to nature.

[44]The notion that habitual behavior (including linguistic behavior) is a kind of nature is discussed by Charles Altieri ("Wordsworth's 'Preface' as Literary Theory") as a feature that Wittgenstein's philosophy shares with Wordsworth's poetics; though both writers (as well as Altieri) ignore the specific cultural and political determinations at work. These are brought out clearly for the period before Wordsworth by John Barrell in *English Literature in History 1730–80*. Barrell's chapter "The Language Properly So-called: The Authority of Common Usage," in particular, demonstrates the ideological function of appeals to "custom"—"the wish," as Barrell puts it, "that the custom of the polite could indeed be represented as an unalterable nature, from which no appeal was possible" (169). See also Barbara Johnson's discussion of the Preface (which complements my own) in *A World of Difference*, chap. 9, especially her comments on the opposition "natural" and "mechanical."

known passage, praises Wordsworth's poetry for its attack on "the lethargy of custom" (*BL* 2:7) and its renewal of objects of which "custom had bedimmed all the lustre" (*BL* 1:80), but he can also explain Shakespeare's achievement by the fact that "knowledge become habitual and intuitive wedded itself to his habitual feelings" (*BL* 2:27). Associationist theory attempts to redeem habit, of course, hence its value to Coleridge (for a while) and Wordsworth. As we shall see, the word "taste" betrays precisely the same undecidable duality.

The principle of selection, then, turns out to be as troublesome as it is necessary. It saves the argument in favor of a language of nature from collapsing in the face of experience, but it brings in its train all the difficulties of the supplement, at once ancillary and indispensable, marginal and central. As with decorum, it functions both in the name of nature and in the name of art, and its oscillations can be controlled only by a force outside the domain of the literary.

The Poetic Context: Audience, Society, Books

Toward the end of the Preface the tensions within the argument come into the open as Wordsworth prepares to consign his poems to the public.[45] At this point he has to confront directly a problem that has been implicit throughout: if it requires a peculiarly untainted and complete human being to respond fully to nature as manifested in rustic life and language or in his own passions, it surely requires a special kind of reader to respond to the poems that such a person will write. Who is Wordsworth writing for? Not the ideal rustic, who has no need of poems, nor the "cultivated" man, whose taste is by definition perverted. (The question continued to weigh with Wordsworth when the experiment of *Lyrical Ballads* had been overlaid by a massive output of more conventional verse, and the 1815 edition of Wordsworth's *Poems* and all subsequent collected editions contained not only

---

[45]Devlin, in *Wordsworth and the Poetry of Epitaphs*, chap. 1, discusses the inconsistencies and shifts in Wordsworth's attempts to specify the appropriate audience for his poems. Thus "the 1802 preface moves in opposite directions; Wordsworth insists that the poet must be like all men, must speak to all men in the language of all men. . . . At the same time Wordsworth has an 'exalted notion' of the poet, who, if he is to cleanse our corruption and put on incorruption, will of necessity be a different kind of being" (15-16). This inconsistency is seen as the result of Wordsworth's transitional position between an old Renaissance tradition and a new Romantic view rather than as a symptom of a self-contradictory ideology shared by old and new.

a new Preface but the aptly named "Essay, Supplementary to the Preface," which addresses the question in some detail.) Wordsworth's first move is to request the reader who is passing judgment on the poems to "decide by his own feelings genuinely" (155), his faith being that if the reader is close enough to the "natural" ideal of maturity and sensitivity (or, in the Hartleian language of the 1800 Preface, preserved in the text until 1832, "in a healthful state of association" [126]) he will respond positively to the natural language of the poems. He seems to lose that Romantic faith in the next paragraph, however, where he chooses, against the drift of much of the argument, to entrust the judgment of his poems to the man of taste. Lest we think the word has been redefined, Wordsworth makes it clear that he is appealing not to some intuitive, "natural" taste but to the authoritative taste of the culturally dominant class, achieved by a lengthy apprenticeship, and no less a name than that of Sir Joshua Reynolds is there to underwrite it. The desire to have it both ways still makes itself felt, however, and the common reader is at once encouraged to make judgments and warned that those judgments will probably be mistaken:

> An *accurate* taste in poetry, and in all the other arts, as Sir Joshua Reynolds has observed, is an *acquired* talent, which can only be produced by thought and a long continued intercourse with the best models of composition. This is mentioned, not with so ridiculous a purpose as to prevent the most inexperienced Reader from judging for himself, (I have already said that I wish him to judge for himself;) but merely to temper the rashness of decision, and to suggest, that, if Poetry be a subject on which much time has not been bestowed, the judgment may be erroneous; and that, in many cases, it necessarily will be so. (157)

The appeal to Reynolds is not the product of a later, more conservative Wordsworth, reconsidering his early rashness; it is repeated almost verbatim from the Advertisement to the 1798 *Lyrical Ballads*.[46]

It is the disturbing thought of readers without such accredited taste presuming to condemn his poetry that evokes this explicit statement,

---

[46]As one would expect, the later Wordsworth frequently appeals to traditional notions of taste and judgment; Parrish gives examples in chap. 1 of *The Art of the "Lyrical Ballads,"* including a letter to R. P. Gillies of 1816 which includes the injunction "Do not let any Body persuade you that any quantity of good verses can ever be produced by mere felicity; or that an immortal *style* can be the growth of mere Genius" (7).

but as with Puttenham's invocation of decorum it can be seen as a necessary step in the argument: if poetry is to be valued as a pinnacle of human achievement, it cannot finally be consigned to the realm of the natural, where it would become indistinguishable from a multitude of human activities and would be out of the control of its self-appointed and self-legitimating guardians. The more Wordsworth emphasizes the lack of essential difference between the language of poetry and the language of men, and between the poet and other men, and the more the composition of poetry is presented as occurring "blindly and mechanically," the more certain it is that he will erect some safeguard in the form of a socially and culturally restrictive principle. Addressing the problem at length in the Essay of 1815, Wordsworth describes the ideal reader as combining natural and learned capacities (including the study of the "laws" of the poetic art) and admits that there is only a small number of "judges who can be confidently relied upon" (*Prose* 3:67). We have come a long way from the notion of the common language of poetry evincing its greatness by the breadth of its appeal; Wordsworth asserts in this essay that a *lack* of widespread success is one of the signs of great art. In an interesting passage not often discussed (but see Bialostosky, *Making Tales*, 4-7), he transfers part of the obligation to his readers, presenting "taste" as a metaphor that refers to "intellectual *acts* and *operations*" (*Prose* 3:81). The task of the poet is to "call forth and to communicate *power*" (82) from and to the reader in a reciprocal relationship clearly modeled on that between Wordsworthian nature and the poet—and just as truly imaginative poets are rare, so are readers capable of exerting a "corresponding energy" in their engagements with poetry. Even though taste is reinterpreted in this way, the argument remains circular: great art is defined in terms of its capacity to engage a small band of readers possessed of the proper imaginative receptivity, while the proper receptivity is defined as the ability to respond to great art.[47]

The principle upon which the judgment of true poetry is based will, therefore, of necessity be presented in contradictory terms: as innate (and therefore natural, not artificial) and learned (therefore available

[47]It may be, as Owen comments, that Wordsworth's argument in the Essay, Supplementary is "wrong-headed and tendentious" (229), but it is difficult to see how any account based on a notion of taste can escape circularity—at least without a consideration of the social and political forces at work.

84

only to the few who have earned it).[48] Many signs suggest that the criteria for the principle of selection are socially determined; as we have noted, Wordsworth uses value-laden terms such as "disgusting," "vulgarity," and "meanness" when trying to imagine a rustic ideal (he is also reported as saying that he dropped "vulgarisms or provincialisms" from rustic speech [*Prose* 1:169]) and appeals to "true taste and feeling" and "propriety" as the grounds for their removal. Taste may in theory be learned by anyone, but it operates in practice as a form of social discrimination. There are not many whose social and economic status is capable of supporting a long-continued intercourse with the finest works of art, and although Wordsworth might not have had exactly the background Pope or Reynolds would have expected of a man of taste, he was closer to them than to the men and women he professed to be imitating in *Lyrical Ballads*.[49] At the same time, of course, the social and political determination of good taste (unlike that of bad taste, which Wordsworth is quick to relate to the socioeconomic context) must be concealed as far as possible. Taste must appear to function as a surrogate or second nature (see Bourdieu's comments on the "ideology of natural taste" quoted above).

The experience of being caught between a theory of natural poetry and the actuality of the poet's craft and place in the world would

[48]Wellek summarizes the contradictoriness of the notion of taste in the eighteenth century as follows: "The 18th-century critics . . . defended the view that taste was both acquired and spontaneous, innate and cultivated, 'sentimental' and intellectual" (1:24). He goes on to observe the instability of this position, which the eighteenth-century notion of taste shared with the sixteenth-century notion of decorum, though his own perspective is that of Romantic organicism: "But these reconciliations of opposites raised a problem which proved dangerous to the basic assumptions of neoclassicism, which demanded, after all, an objective standard of value and beauty." The shift that occurs with Romanticism might be portrayed as a shift from a Renaissance and neoclassical position, which preserves the narrow domain of art by tempering a predominantly acquisitionist notion of taste with an element of innateness (so that it is not open to *all* who make the requisite effort), to a position that achieves the same end by tempering a predominantly innatist notion with an element of acquisition (so that it is not possible for individuals in *any* station to be favored). The most strenuous Romantic attempt to stabilize the oscillating condition of the concept of taste was, of course, Kant's Third Critique.

[49]It should not be forgotten that the Calvert legacy was as important to Wordsworth's successful poetic career as was communication with the permanent objects of nature, and anyone who has visited Alfoxden House will know that at the time when *Lyrical Ballads* was taking shape Wordsworth was living in the style not of the working population but of the comfortably endowed gentry.

undoubtedly have become particularly problematic for Wordsworth when he tried to evaluate the tradition of written literature and assess its importance to the poet (and, by implication, to the reader anxious to develop the proper faculty of poetic judgment). As one might expect, his attitude to existing literature is far from single-minded. To be fully consistent, he would have to argue that the poet should have no truck with writing: the pure and permanent language of rural life should be his only guide. Even if other poets have succeeded in capturing something of that language, why turn to inferior models when you have the thing itself around you? However, the fact of the written tradition and of its importance to any poet who seeks to join it is too insistent to allow this myth to survive unqualified, and Wordsworth cannot avoid allowing value to the literature of the past, however reluctantly he may do so. He refers, for instance, to "the invaluable works of our elder writers, I had almost said the works of Shakspeare and Milton" (129)—a heavy-handed piece of irony which reduces the English literary tradition to two authors. He observes in a note that "the affecting parts of Chaucer are almost always expressed in language pure and universally intelligible even to this day" (125), without indicating what proportion of Chaucer's work these parts might constitute. Popular ballads (such as "The Babes in the Wood") and the Bible receive favorable comment, but even their influence—which clearly was very great—has to be underplayed in the argument.

With this dilemma in mind we can perhaps appreciate more sharply some of the distinctive concerns and characteristics of Wordsworth's "lyrical ballads" themselves. Many of the poems in *Lyrical Ballads* are pitched against books, most obviously "To My Sister" (with its repeated injunction "and bring no book"), "Expostulation and Reply," and "The Tables Turned" ("Books! 'tis a dull and endless strife"). This attitude is a manifestation of a deeper current running through the poems which, taking to a more extreme point a tendency that the Preface itself has to hold in check, scrutinizes language itself and frequently finds it wanting.[50] There is a sense that all language, at

[50]In Wordsworth's 1800 note to "The Thorn" he observes, "an attempt is rarely made to communicate impassioned feelings without something of an accompanying consciousness of the inadequateness of our own powers, or the deficiencies of language" (*Lyrical Ballads*, 289). As Owen remarks, it is hard to see how this is to be reconciled with Wordsworth's assertions of the abundant adequacy of "the language of men" to the passion it expresses (64-65). Devlin also traces the inconsistencies in Wordsworth's comments on language (chap. 2 passim), attempting to find an organic resolu-

least all existing language, is compromised and tainted by the imperfections of those who use it—except perhaps those whose language exists on the fringes of social discourse. Thus we are presented with an idiot boy, whose language is in no danger of misrepresenting the world because it makes no attempt at accurate representation, and a young son whose answer to his father's question is all the more potent for being no answer—in any sense that a theory of discourse would recognize—at all. The narrator in "We Are Seven" laments that he is "throwing words away" because he gets no orthodox linguistic reply to his queries, merely formulaic repetition, but the poem endorses the greater insight of the "simple child." It is the crazed Martha Ray who has triumphed over the duplicity of language, not the loquacious narrator and his insistent interlocutor. These are not the naturally expressive and moving utterances of uncontaminated rustics; on the contrary, they are uses of language which question language itself.[51]

Whereas the first edition of *Lyrical Ballads* gives us survivors who demonstrate the wastefulness of words by expressing themselves—in what could almost be a parody of Wordsworth's arguments—through moaning, chattering, or burring, the second edition pays more attention to the silence of death; one thing about language that Wordsworth will trust is its effect when it stops. The "pauses of deep silence" when the owls make no response to the hallooing Boy of Winander (already operating beyond normal language), the unarticulated "difference" made by Lucy's death, the unrecoverable loss now that Matthew, singer of "witty rhymes," is "silent as a standing pool," and Matthew's own silence when confronted by an image of his loss— these are the moments of original power in the later "lyrical ballads," even though the language of the poems themselves is now less single-mindedly shorn of gaudy phraseology. It is above all in their refusals

---

tion in the *Essays upon Epitaphs;* the contradictions in the Preface are described as "a careful, subtle balancing (it is not yet a reconcilement) of opposites" (65). There does occur something of a shift in Wordsworth's thinking, as Owen and Devlin argue, but it should be clear by now that Wordsworth cannot escape a continual oscillation between faith in and mistrust of language.

[51]See Jonathan Ramsey, "Wordsworth and the Childhood of Language." This concern with the language of loss and absence is further reflected in Wordsworth's three *Essays upon Epitaphs;* see also Frances Ferguson, *Wordsworth: Language as Counter-Spirit.* An account of the language of the most experimental "lyrical ballads" would have to consider their use of cliché, which escapes from poetic idiosyncracy at the cost of emptying the language of semantic force, in an impersonal, formulaic utterance that is far removed from the vivid expression of deep passion.

to speak—the understatement of the "Lucy" and "Matthew" poems, the withholding of a "tale" of Simon Lee and of an account of the idiot boy's adventures, the low-key endings of "Old Man Travelling," "There Was a Boy," "The Brothers," and "Michael"—that the poems of *Lyrical Ballads* exemplify and underpin the Preface, testifying as they do to a power in the muting or absence of the language of our daily lives and perhaps opening a space for Wordsworth's unimaginable language of nature.

When Wordsworth came, in *The Prelude*, to write about the importance of books to the poet, it was in a section of the poem deeply at odds with itself. The uncertainties and self-contradictions of Book 5 have frequently been discussed and have in some cases been taken to be particularly revealing.[52] The only terms in which Wordsworth can give books credit are the terms he has developed for the praise of nature:

> Visionary power
> Attends upon the motions of the winds,
> Embodied in the mystery of words:
> There, darkness makes abode, and all the host
> Of shadowy things do work their changes there
> As in a mansion like their proper home. (1805, 5. 619-24)

Once again the traditional difference between nature and art is dissolved, and true art is praised as a manifestation of nature, not as an imitation or perfection of it. Wordsworth has just spoken of "the great Nature that exists in works / Of mighty Poets" (618-19)—which we should note, before we take this to be a simple repetition of Pope's dictum about Homer and Nature, vouchsafes its "enduring touches of deep joy" only to one who "with *living* Nature hath been intimate" (612-17, my emphasis). The nature to be found in books remains at best a derivative, supplementary version of the real thing.

In his poetry Wordsworth was able to transform the concerns of the Preface into new combinations and configurations of literary and linguistic conventions; in his theoretical writing he was constrained to a much greater extent by the terms and structures he and his readers inherited. For all the revolutionary thrust of its polemic, the endeavor

---

[52]See, for example, Cynthia Chase, "The Accidents of Disfiguration"; J. Hillis Miller, "The Stone and the Shell"; and chap. 5 of Chandler, *Wordsworth's Second Nature.*

to renegotiate the relationship between nature and art circles back in the end to the old distinction: art is grounded in the nature in which all participate, but its existence as art depends on its difference from nature, and that difference is in the hands of the minority who possess the leisure to cultivate, promote, and safeguard it. The taste that is able to make the crucial judgment cannot be a matter of rules— there Wordsworth is in complete agreement with his critical predecessors—but, it has finally to be acknowledged, it cannot be a matter of nature either.

Chapter 4

Language as History/History as Language: Saussure and the Romance of Etymology

Synchrony, Diachrony, and the Question of History

THOUGH the term "Saussurean revolution" is undoubtedly an oversimplificiation, there is some appropriateness in using it to refer to the extensive changes in ways of conceptualizing language, including literary language, which characterized the early part of this century and which still underlie a great deal of current thinking on the subject. For if the originality of Saussure's own work has sometimes been exaggerated and his influence on later linguists and theorists overemphasized, his account of the new science of linguistics nevertheless represents the clearest statement of the shifts in thought about language which marked the turn of the century, and, rightly or wrongly, his name is invoked more than any other in tracing the intellectual origins of the structuralist movement that transformed European literary and cultural analysis in the 1960s. After Saussure, the question of the distinctiveness of literary language no longer looks like the same question, because the linguistic framework in which it is posed has changed; in particular, linguistics is now constituted as a methodologically rigorous science of systems, focusing its attention on abstractable formal structures rather than patterns discoverable in large bodies of historical and comparative material. Literary language poses a new kind of challenge to the linguistics of ordinary language, therefore: it is troublesome insofar as it does not submit to the taxonomies and hierarchies elaborated by the linguist in order to ana-

90

tomize words and sentences in their primary task—as Saussurean linguistics sees it—of conveying meanings from speaker to listener. Yet a familiar logic is discernible. The properties of literary language that prevent exhaustive and objective analysis, making it overflow boundaries or resist classifications, can be shown to be not peculiar to literature; they are at work in all uses of language, interfering with the Saussurean goal of exhaustive and algorithmic explanation and destabilizing the mutually exclusive categorization of "literary" and "nonliterary."

Many areas of language and of linguistic analysis reveal the difficulty of excluding those complicating factors on which literature thrives. In the next chapter we shall consider the literary phenomenon of sound-symbolism, which has to be vigorously repulsed from the Saussurean paradigm of language, though it can never be completely expunged; other features of literary texts which exceed the linguistic taxonomies are metaphoric shifts of all kinds, patterning in sound and syntax, and functions of quotation and intertextuality whereby one piece of language becomes another while remaining itself.[1] This chapter examines another dimension of language which Saussure tried very hard, and for very good reasons, to control: its historical existence. Every reader of literature knows, habitually if not consciously, that the language of the literary text is never of an age. Words and phrasings that have the accumulated density of a long and varied existence jostle with others that reflect recent verbal fashions or come newly minted from their authors (think of the language of Anthony Burgess's *Clockwork Orange* or Russell Hoban's *Riddley Walker*). Spenser or Milton can play between the meanings of words in modern English and their classical etymological sources; Keats or Byron can sprinkle a poem with the dust of medieval diction; Beckett or Barthelme can burnish or brandish old words in ways that make them seem new.

Saussure's *Course in General Linguistics* is unlike Puttenham's *Arte of English Poesie* and Wordsworth's Preface to *Lyrical Ballads* in that it is

---

[1]The unfixable relation between grammatical and rhetorical functions of language has been most forcefully demonstrated by Paul de Man; see especially his *Allegories of Reading,* the introductory chapter of which constitutes the most concentrated exposition of the argument. Some aspects of the question of coincidences of sound in language are dealt with in chapter 7 below, as well as in this chapter; and for a valuable discussion of intertextuality and quotation, see André Topia, "The Matrix and the Echo."

not concerned overtly with literary language. Implicitly, however, literary language is present as a highly significant absence, excluded as an abnormal or derivative use of language. It is associated with writing, whose secondariness to speech Saussure insists on, with onomatopoeia, which cannot be allowed an important place in the linguistic model, and with crosshistorical influence, which contradicts the pure form of language operating always in a present moment. To a large extent twentieth-century linguistics has followed this lead, and attempts to integrate literary language into a linguistic account have so far—and for obvious reasons—not met with striking success.[2] Structuralism, making a different use of Saussurean linguistics (or, rather, Saussurean semiology), not to account for the language of literature but to make of literature a language in its own right, proved more fruitful, but it too suffered from the universalizing, totalizing, abstracting tendencies of its model. As a result, Saussure's influence on literary theory has been attacked in recent years as balefully ahistorical, for taking literature out of its cultural, social, and political context and treating it as an abstract and self-sufficient system. The various poststructuralist initiatives, with their critique of generalizing scientism and their reopening of the possibility of an informed and self-aware historical criticism, have also been branded with the same mark.[3] Above all, Saussure's separation of the synchronic and diachronic dimensions of language, and his apparent privileging of the former, is regarded as the source of the problem. Thus, to take a representative example, Frank Lentricchia refers in *After the New Criticism* to the "insistent charge that Saussure and his structuralist progeny suffer from a failure of historical consciousness that stems from the hierarchizing of synchrony and diachrony" (117), an accusation he finds in work by Fredric Jameson and Edward Said, notably the former's *Prison-House of Language* and the latter's "Abecedarium Culturae." And Lentricchia himself is in substantial agreement: "It is clear that the recent structuralist inability to come to terms with the

[2]One of the most brilliant and tireless tillers of this field, Roman Jakobson, produced no really healthy crops, though he made high claims for his use of the terminology and model of linguistic science to account for literary effects. His own resolute limitation of the domain within which literature was to be defined and analyzed—the formal properties of its language—remained inconsistent and open to those extratextual forces he tried to resist; for further discussion, see my essay "Closing Statement."

[3]Essays that demonstrate the importance, as well as the difficulty, of a fully theorized historical approach to literature are collected in Derek Attridge, Geoff Bennington, and Robert Young, *Post-structuralism and the Question of History.*

diachronic and executive dimensions of discourse has led to the Platonic pursuit of the taxonomy or model as transcendentals" (117). More recently, Terry Eagleton, in *Literary Theory* (110–11), has voiced a similar criticism, though without attempting to implicate Plato.

The question I wish to address is, in part, whether this is the whole story, because the answer to this question will take us to a consideration of the place of history, and indeed of stories, in the study of texts (including Saussure's own text) and will illustrate some of the effects of this century's linguistic reformation upon the "literary" dimension of language. Is it accurate, then, to portray Saussure's linguistic theory as profoundly and damagingly antihistorical, as Jameson and Lentricchia do? Such a view, and it is fairly widespread, has first of all to come to terms with Saussure's own interest (and reputation) in the field of historical linguistics, evident in his influential *Mémoire* on the Indo-European vowel-system and in the fact that the *Course in General Linguistics*, though one would never guess it from most commentaries, devotes more space to diachronic than to synchronic language study. That the priority the *Course* gives to synchronic linguistics is a methodological one should be clear enough to any conscientious reader: Saussure's point is simply that diachrony in strict terms does not exist for the ordinary language-user—the sense, so important in literary texts, that certain words are older than others is actually a synchronic fact which may or may not have diachronic underpinning. To analyze language as the knowledge and practice of the speaker and the community, therefore, diachronic facts must be ignored, however tempting they might be to the learned analyst. The continuing emphasis in the *Course* is on the need for a methodological *separation* of diachronic and synchronic approaches as different kinds of linguistics involving different procedures and different goals. And though this separation produces difficulties for diachronic (and indeed synchronic) linguistics which Saussure himself never overcomes and to which we shall return, it does not follow that he regards the historical study of language as uninteresting or unimportant.

Lentricchia is able to represent Saussure's careful distinction as the *rejection* of a diachronic linguistics by assimilating it to a quite different distinction, that between *langue* and *parole*. In making the latter distinction, Saussure is indeed separating something he considers susceptible of systematic study (a language as a shared system) from something he feels is not (individual acts of uttering and understanding speech), but he makes it absolutely clear, using a diagram to reinforce his point, that synchrony and diachrony are both aspects of *langue* and both worthy of the linguist's attention (139/98).[4] Lentricchia blurs the two distinctions by leaping over a hundred pages of the *Course* in mid-quotation and supplying his own causal connection: "'From the very outset we must put both feet on the ground of language (*langue*) and use language as the norm of all other manifestations of speech' [25/9] because language 'is a system whose parts can and must be considered in their synchronic solidarity' [124/87]" (116). In the first statement Saussure is fixing the object of study as *langue* rather than *langage* (the general phenomenon of human language, misleadingly rendered in the Baskin translation used by Lentricchia as "speech") precisely because *langue* is amenable to analysis, both synchronic and diachronic. In the second he is giving methodological priority to the synchronic approach, for the reasons I have already alluded to.[5]

Saussure's third famous distinction, between syntagmatic and associative (or paradigmatic) relations, is also frequently conflated with the distinction between diachrony and synchrony. "It is clear" states Jameson, "that Saussure's bias is for the synchronic, for the associative or paradigmatic, as against the diachronic or the syntagmatic" (*Prison-House*, 38). In fact it is not clear at all that there is any privileging one way or the other in the paradigmatic/syntagmatic distinction; Saussure argues, with obvious correctness, that the two kinds of relation

[4]In quoting from Saussure, I give page references first to the standard French edition of the *Cours,* which are unchanged in the Critical Edition (ed. Tullio de Mauro), then to the translation by Wade Baskin. The translations I cite are my own, but I have found the versions of both Baskin and Roy Harris useful. The name "Saussure" refers, of course, to the multiple authors of the published *Cours* rather than solely to the man on whose lectures it is based.

[5]The frequent conflation of the opposition synchrony/diachrony with the opposition system/systemlessness may derive from a misunderstanding (partly due to Jakobson's very different emphasis) of Saussure's claim that language change is the product of external, "blind," historical forces, unanalyzable and unpredictable (see 114 below). Saussure is here describing the nonlinguistic pressures that the language system suffers at particular points, but it must be stressed that *within* the system all change (occurring in response to this arbitrary external modification) is, of necessity, systematic and analyzable. Such changes first manifest themselves in the actual speech of a few people before spreading to become part of the system; hence Saussure observes that *"everything that is diachronic in language [langue] is only so through speech [parole]"* (138/98)—a remark that is sometimes wrongly taken to reinforce the misidentification of diachrony and *parole.* Even David Carroll's valuable reconsideration of the synchrony/diachrony distinction in *The Subject in Question,* chap. 6, tends to conflate these categories (141–44).

function with complete interdependence in discourse (177–80/128–31). Nor is there any particular link between synchronic and paradigmatic or between diachronic and syntagmatic. After all, it is the paradigmatic relations that connect the present utterance with the past via associations stored in the memory, and the syntagmatic relations that coexist, as Saussure puts it, *in praesentia*.[6] The notion that syntagmatic relations occur in a temporal dimension (between the utterance of a verb and the utterance of its object, say) and therefore belong exclusively to diachrony rests on mistaken conceptions of both syntagmatic relations and of diachrony. As rule-governed relationships enshrined in the language system, syntagmatic connections (which include morphological and syntactic rules) are as much part of the synchronic state as paradigmatic ones, and a diachronic description of language, far from being concerned with utterances as they are spoken in time, deals with changes in the system of paradigmatic and syntagmatic relations occurring *across* time (194–97/140–43).

Saussure's accusers combine all three distinctions to find him guilty of a bias toward the transcendental as against the historical. Thus Lentricchia summarizes, and endorses, Jameson's view that "the distinction between syntagm and paradigm is a disguised form of the enabling opposition between diachrony and synchrony, *parole* and *langue,* which generated Saussure's entire theory: the determinate syntagm is temporal whereas the indeterminate paradigm is transcendental" (*After the New Criticism,* 120). One doubts whether even the maligned structuralists would have jettisoned so much content to collapse a series of oppositions into one. (There is some justification, it is true, for the notion that syntagmatic relations have a connection with *parole,* in that Saussure regards the sentence as the free combination of units in the act of speaking; Noam Chomsky was the first fully to incorporate the sentence in the system of *langue* by means of rules that allow, especially through the property of recursivity, for cre-

---

[6]Jameson's use of a spatial metaphor is revealing: the diachronic, for him, is the "temporally successive, horizontal dimension," the synchronic "the simultaneous and systematically organized vertical one" (*Prison-House,* 37). Because this spatialization is entirely arbitrary, it suggests that the model Jameson has in mind is not the passage of history so much as the time elapsed in an utterance, which in the West tends to be symbolized as horizontal and left-to-right because of the influence of writing. But Saussure's spatialization is *vertical* for diachronic and *horizontal* for synchronic (see his diagrams in part 1, chap. 3, and the illustration of the cuts in a plant stem [125/88]). Jameson is followed in his conflation of Saussure's oppositions and in his spatialization by Terence Hawkes (*Structuralism and Semiotics,* 78).

ativeness on the part of the speaker. Saussure's discussion of syntagmatic relations [172–73/124–25], however, makes it clear that as systematic connections between units they are an aspect of *langue*.)[7] Lentricchia's conclusion could easily be reversed: one might argue that syntagmatic rules are transcendental in that they exist in a fixed form prior to and independent of the subject's employment of them, whereas the unlimited openness of the paradigm to individual associations and specific contexts—and thence to history, in one of its senses—is truly temporal. Indeed, such a reversal is implicit in Lentricchia's own citation of the New Critics' willingness to give Marvell's "vegetable love" a mid-twentieth century meaning (121): here the syntagmatic relations have remained relatively stable, while the associations of the word "vegetable" bear the imprint of three centuries of change.[8]

Although both Jameson and Lentricchia cast Saussure in the role of original sinner, both tend in practice to oscillate in their judgments, seeking a point of view from which his work can be redeemed as a necessary and positive stage in modern intellectual history. It is per-

---

[7]See also the Critical Edition of the *Cours*, ed. Tullio de Mauro, n.251; Robert Godel, "F. de Saussure's Theory of Language," 490–92; and Roland Barthes's discussion of syntagmatic relations in *Elements of Semiology*, 59–71. The conflation is even more total in Rosalind Coward and John Ellis, *Language and Materialism*, where one finds the assertion that "the analysis of *parole*" is "analysis of the syntagm, the diachronic analysis of that which unfolds through the passing of time" (14); conversely the analysis of *langue* is said to be analysis of the paradigm, or synchronic analysis. The terms become virtually interchangeable, so that structural linguistics can be accused of "an almost exclusive concentration on the paradigmatic mode of analysis" (14)—which makes little sense unless what is in fact meant is the *synchronic* mode, as it is the syntagmatic relations of syntax which have dominated linguistics for some time.

[8]Another misrepresentation of Saussure sometimes occurs in literary theory that sees itself as radical or progressively historical: the claim that in addition to the "signifier" (the "sound-image") and the "signified" (the "concept") Saussure proposes or implies a third term, the "referent" or the "real thing" (see Coward and Ellis, 22; Lentricchia, 118); he can then be accused of conceptual inconsistency. In the *Cours*, Saussure scrupulously and consistently avoids any such notion, which would fall outside the scope of the linguistic science he conceives; and he observes in a manuscript note that the language is shaped "without connection to any knowledge of a real, object-based relation. . . . If any object could be, at any point whatsoever, the term on which the sign is fixed, linguistics would immediately stop being what it is, from top to bottom" (Critical Edition, ed. Engler, fasc. 2, nos. 1089–1091, p. 148). The source of the error is perhaps Emile Benveniste's influential but misleading essay "The Nature of the Linguistic Sign" (*Problems in General Linguistics*, chap. 4), in which the notion of the referent is foisted upon Saussure. (Jakobson's difficulties with this notion are discussed in chapter 5 below, 129–32.)

haps not surprising, then, that Lentricchia is prepared to excuse Saussure, for all his faults, and shift some of the responsibility for our current malaise onto his "progeny," structuralists and poststructuralists (a characteristic strategy of the reformist historian, of course, and one that Lentricchia also applies to Derrida and *his* "progeny"). Thus he awards high marks to the notion of the arbitrariness of the sign, by which "Saussure's linguistics situates discourse, literary or otherwise, in its true home in human history," because "to designate the sign as arbitrary is simultaneously to call attention to it as a temporal and cultural production" (119). (Terry Eagleton makes a similar point about literary structuralism in *Literary Theory* [107–8], and for a realization of this potential in concrete analysis one need only turn to Barthes's *Mythologies*.) But Lentricchia's willingness to mitigate the harshness of the charge against Saussure does not obscure the negative thrust of his general argument, which colors his entire reading of recent intellectual events—that the very notion of system and structure, so potent in modern literary theory and so evidently derived from Saussurean linguistics, is fundamentally and inexcusably antihistorical. What I wish to argue, by examining one aspect of the conjunction of synchrony and diachrony as it is presented in the *Course,* is that Saussure's achievement lay not in clarifying (as he hoped to do) but in *problematizing* the notion of history and its relation to the present. Furthermore, if we want to escape the drift away from history which characterizes so much literary theory today—and the writings of Jameson, Lentricchia, Said, and Eagleton have been of the utmost importance in warning us of the dangers of that drift—we need to work through the problematic with which Saussure confronts us. After Saussure, there is no going back to a simple notion of the explanatory force of history in any domain constituted, like language (and like literature), by systems of equivalence or what Saussure terms "value."[9] In spite of his own explicit goals, therefore, his linguistic revolution has resulted in a new centrality for literary language, which, because it has never existed in a transparent relation to history, can serve as a testing ground for the linguist wishing, as many now do, to find ways of reintegrating synchrony and diachrony—not into the

[9]It should be noted that the extension of the Saussurean distinction between synchrony and diachrony beyond such systems of equivalence to wider domains of history and historical discourse (as in the work of Louis Althusser) removes much of the original point of Saussure's categorization, and involves a set of problems quite separate from those discussed here.

panchronic amalgam that Saussure rightly rejected but into a new set of approaches that recognize the complex and necessary interrelations between the two dimensions.

Etymology and the Nature of Authentic Meaning

Probably the most familiar area of diachronic linguistics to the nonspecialist is the history of words. Etymology is a field in which the productiveness of Saussure's sharp distinction between synchrony and diachrony can be clearly and convincingly shown, and he uses the distinction illustratively at several points. The first example he gives to demonstrate that the distinction is "absolute and does not admit of compromise" is the connection between two French phrases, *un mur décrépi* ("a peeling wall") and *un homme décrépit* ("a decrepit man") (119/83). For a contemporary speaker of French these homophones are related by more than mere coincidence of sound, and they actually come together in an expression such as *une façade décrépite* ("a dilapidated facade"). Yet their histories are quite distinct. *Décrépi*, etymologists tell us, comes from *dé* + *crépir*, *crépir* being to "rough-render," a descendant of Latin *crispus*, "wavy"; *décrépir* is therefore "to remove the plaster from" and *se décrépir* "to peel." *Décrépit*, on the other hand, is derived from the Latin adjective *decrepitus* ("worn out with age"). A comparable English example is the connection perceived by most speakers between the words *rage* and *outrage*, where the former comes from the French *rage* and the Latin *rabies* ("madness"), and the latter is a noun formed from *ultra* ("beyond") and the suffix *-age*, so that an *outrage* is a "going beyond the bounds" and has no historical connection with *rage*.[10]

Saussure's position here is, in its own terms, unassailable. If such coincidences of sound become meaningful parts of the linguistic system for the speakers of the language, they cannot be dismissed as "illegitimate" or "historically unfounded"; they simply become facts of language. The argument is a linguistic version of Nietzsche's more general argument in the *Genealogy of Morals* (1887):

> There is for historiography of any kind no more important proposition than the one it took such effort to establish but which really *ought to be*

[10]Other commonly associated pairs cited in etymological studies as having no historical connection are *isle/island*, *ear* (of corn)/*ear* (of body), *reign/sovereign*, *noise/noisome*, *school* (of pupils)/*school* (of fish).

established now: the cause of the origin of a thing and its eventual utility, its actual employment and place in a system of purposes, lie worlds apart; whatever exists, having somehow come into being, is again and again reinterpreted to new ends, taken over, transformed, and redirected by some power superior to it; all events in the organic world are a subduing, a *becoming master,* and all subduing and becoming master involves a fresh interpretation, an adaptation through which any previous "meaning" and "purpose" are necessarily obscured or even obliterated. (77)

"Outrage" and "rage" *are* synchronically related, no matter what counterpressures the etymological dictionary and the learned philologist bring to bear.

One thing under attack here is the common assumption that a speaker who has a knowledge of etymological history is in some sense a "better" speaker of English. Thus George H. McKnight writes in the Preface to his *English Words and Their Background,* "in order to operate an instrument efficiently one must be acquainted with the nature of its mechanism. In the same way in order to have an effective command of the resources of the English vocabulary, one must know about the materials of which the vocabulary is composed and the process by which its words have reached their present meanings" (v).[11] And Miss Jean Brodie's faith in etymology is as ill-founded as her belief in her own "prime" when she repeats to her girls the venerable argument: "The word 'education' comes from the root *e* from *ex,* out, and *duco,* I lead. It means a leading out."[12] Such a view of etymology implies the belief that the earlier a meaning the better, which must depend on a diagnosis of cultural decline (Miss Brodie, we remember, is an admirer of Franco, Mussolini, and Hitler) or a faith in a lost Golden Age of lexical purity and precision. The word *etymology* itself derives from such an assumption and offers its own self-confirmation, for its Greek root means "discourse on true meaning," while the Book of Genesis offers a different version of the same myth.

This view of etymology is one version of the widespread notion that words have *authentic meanings,* a notion instilled early in formal education and powerfully upheld by the ubiquity and status of the diction-

[11]A more convincing point is that such a speaker speaks a somewhat *different* language—see John Lyons, *Introduction to Theoretical Linguistics,* 407.

[12]Muriel Spark, *The Prime of Miss Jean Brodie,* 36. Richard Chevenix Trench, the popular Victorian linguist, appeals to this etymology in a characteristic way: "Education must educe, being from 'educare', which is but another form of 'educere'; and that is 'to draw out', not 'to put in'" (quoted in Hans Aarsleff, *From Locke to Saussure,* 38).

ary as a cultural institution.[13] Although it flirts with history, this is a deeply antihistorical attitude, replacing the social and historical determination of meaning (operating upon the arbitrary sign) by a transcendent "true" meaning. Just as some literary theorists cling to the notion of authentic meaning for a text, not because this notion is consistent with itself or with the facts of literary history but because they assume that to give it up is to invite unbridled relativism (and perhaps even revolution), so there is a common assumption that every word must have its authentic meaning or else meaning could not exist at all. And just as the literary theorist may turn to authorial intention or to the original readership as the only source (however inaccessible) of an authentic meaning, so the theorist of language turns to etymological origin. It is worth noting how often cheaper dictionaries dispense with obsolete meanings, which are of real value in reading the texts of the past, rather than with etymologies, which are of no practical use but appear to guarantee the identity and authenticity of the words they claim to "explain."

This unwillingness to conceive either of words or of literary texts as always embedded in a changing context, as always understood from a particular position, as always lacking in stable self-identity is of course only part of a wider intellectual and political refusal. Freud tells of an objection to his theory of masculine hysteria on the grounds that *hysteria* is etymologically descended from the Greek for "womb," and Derrida cites this anecdote in replying to conservative objections to *his* work (*Dissemination*, 182). Wordsworth, too, saw his theoretical advances being attacked from a conservative position that drew ammunition from etymology, and he makes this scathing comment on an attempt in Taylor's *British Synonyms Discriminated* to define the word "Imagination" in terms of its origins: "Is not this as if a man should undertake to supply an account of a building, and be so intent upon what he had discovered of the foundation, as to conclude his task without once looking up at the superstructure? Here, as in other instances throughout the volume, the judicious Author's mind is en-

---

[13]On the ideological function of the dictionary, see Roy Harris, *The Language Makers*, chap. 6; Richard Rand, "Geraldine," 295–99; and Allon White, "The Dismal Sacred Word." The myth of "authentic meaning" in the lexicon is, of course, a version of the myth of pure, whole, self-sufficient, self-determining nature in the wider universe, which we have already discussed. Like nature in this sense, it is never fully realized in experience. The work of the etymolgist is a supplementary labor, adding a history to a word to make up for its missing purity and wholeness of meaning.

thralled by Etymology; he takes up the original word as his guide and escort, and too often does not perceive how soon he becomes its prisoner, without liberty to tread in any path but that to which it confines him" (Preface of 1815, *Prose* 3:32).

A representative example from our own time comes from an *Observer* review (3 April 1983) of the *Penguin Book of Homosexual Verse*, edited by Stephen Coote. The reviewer complains that his dictionary does not give "homosexual" as a meaning for "gay," a meaning, he argues, that could exist only "if Dr. Coote presumes to conceive that all its old meanings have now been cancelled or forbidden, that from now on 'gay' will be applied only in a homosexual context, that the word has been somehow licitly sequestered by him and his for the exclusive celebration of homosexual personalities and tastes." The doctrine of "authentic meaning" (which is necessarily single meaning) requires that "gay" could mean "homosexual" only on condition that it stopped meaning anything else, and the smug tone of the passage is designed to gain "common-sense" agreement that this would be a betrayal of our linguistic heritage. The *linguistic* dogma is, of course, doing duty for a politico-sexual dogma of "authentic sexuality," which is as hostile to human diversity as its linguistic equivalent is to the diversity of speech (see Stephen Heath's elaborations of this point in *The Sexual Fix*). Saussure's insistence on the separation of synchrony and diachrony, replacing "authentic" meaning by the meanings possessed for a specific group at a specific time, opens the door to history, whereas a naive view of the historicity of language completely closes it.

The faith in authentic meaning, and in etymology as its key, is a popular survival of a theory that remained influential in Western thinking about language for a long period. It was propounded by the followers of Heraclitus, Plato's Cratylus among them, and was a central strand in medieval thought, as indicated by the extensive use made by Aquinas of the collection of bizarre etymologies by Isidore of Seville.[14] It played an important part in seventeenth-century attempts to arrive at the original, universal language,[15] but its heyday is probably to be located in the late eighteenth century when linguistic stu-

---

[14]For brief accounts see Etienne Gilson, *Les idées et les lettres*, 159–69; E. R. Curtius, "Etymology as a Category of Thought," in *European Literature and the Latin Middle Ages*, 495–500; William T. Noon, *Joyce and Aquinas*, 144–60. Curtius calls Isidore's *Etymologiarium libri* "the basic book of the entire Middle Ages" (496).

[15]See, for example, Aarsleff's chapter "The Study and Use of Etymology in Leibniz," in *From Locke to Saussure*, 84–100.

dents, spurred by the arguments of Condillac to trace in the forms of language the lineaments of the human mind, devoted a great deal of ingenuity and energy to the search for primary meanings, unhampered by the constraints of rigid principles or consistent methodology. The massive—and massively influential—work of such men as Charles de Brosses in France (*Traité de la formation méchanique des langues*, 1765) and John Horne Tooke in England (*The Diversions of Purley*, 1786–1805) made full use of the freedom offered by the etymological method, at times almost justifying Voltaire's famous gibe that "etymology is the science in which the vowels count for nothing and the consonants for very little." (Voltaire would be outdone a century or so later by Mark Twain's derivation of "Middletown" from "Moses" by dropping "-oses" and adding "-iddletown.")[16] One endearing example from Horne Tooke will suffice to illustrate the potential of the method: he argues that the word *shit* or *shite* comes from an Anglo-Saxon word *scyton*, "to throw, cast forth, throw out" (from, in turn, Latin *projicere, dejicere*), and that this derivation yields the clue to the true meaning of other, more seemly English words.[17] Thus a *shot* is something *cast* or *thrown* forth; a *shout* is a sound *thrown* forth from the mouth; to *shut* the door is to *throw* or *cast* it to; a weaver's *shuttle* is a small instrument *thrown* or *cast;* a *scout* is someone sent out, that is, *thrown* or *cast* (and this word is not a derivation from *écouter*, as some suppose, "merely," snorts Tooke, "because of a resemblance in the sound and letters"); a *skit* is a jeer or jibe or covered imputation *thrown* or *cast* upon anyone—and so on for fifteen entertaining pages (130–45).[18]

In the nineteenth century, however, the belief in authentic original meaning waned. (Who, after the publication of Darwin's *Origin of Species*—itself influenced by the study of etymology—could claim that

[16]There are useful discussions of the work of de Brosses in Gérard Genette, *Mimologiques*, 85–118, and of Horne Tooke in Aarsleff, *The Study of Language in England*, chaps. 2–3, and Olivia Smith, *The Politics of Language*, chap. 4.

[17]There is no such Anglo-Saxon word: Tooke has apparently conflated *scyttan*, to throw, and *scitan*, to shit.

[18]In Tooke's case, the impulse to etymologize can hardly be called conservative, whatever its results: his monumental labors began when he was in prison for sedition in 1778, meditating on the meaning of the word *that*, upon whose interpretation his conviction had turned (see M. C. Yarborough, *John Horne Tooke*, chap. 5). His discussion of *shite* is interrupted, Cobbett-like, by a magnificent passage of antigovernment invective.

the origin of an evolutionary process revealed the *true* nature of an existing specimen?) The speculative free-for-all that characterized late eighteenth-century etymology was countered by the introduction of rigid principles, primarily with reference to the laws of sound-change enunciated in the new positivistic science of philology. A derivation that involved a phonetic change could be accepted only if that change was in accordance with the established laws, which seemed to provide a new and trustworthy foundation for an objective science of etymology. In fact, it rested ultimately on nothing more stable than a vicious circle. As Saussure observes, to say that the identity of Latin *mare* and French *mer* is guaranteed by the fact that their relationship observes a recognized law is to put the cart before the horse, because such "identities" between words in different languages or periods have to be postulated before any law can be formulated (249/182). Nevertheless, etymology became accepted as a reliable and important branch of linguistics, and the work of scholars like Skeat, Partridge, Onions, and the compilers of the New (later Oxford) English Dictionary entrenched it firmly in the public's image of the language specialist, where it still holds pride of place.

What kind of history was represented in this new discipline, an etymology no longer conceived of as the search for authentic meaning in the sands of time? One characteristic example may be taken from the early twentieth century: Ernest Weekley's much reprinted collection of etymological divertissements first published in 1912, *The Romance of Words* (a companion volume to *The Romance of Names, Adjectives and Other Words, Words Ancient and Modern,* and *More Words Ancient and Modern*). In a section devoted to the names of high functionaries, to take a typical discussion, Weekley traces *chancellor* back to "a kind of door-keeper in charge of a *chancel,* a latticed barrier"; *constable* and *marshall* back to the names for servants who tended horses; and *steward* (as well as the Royal House of Stuart) to the *sty-ward* who "looked after his master's pigs" (87–90). But what does it mean to say that *steward* and *sty-ward* (or *stigweard*) are really the "same word," as etymology invites us to do? They can be so only from a completely transhistorical viewpoint, for as Jameson points out (*Prison-House,* 6), they were never the same word for a speaker in history. (Indeed, etymology gives the word "word" itself a wholly new sense, for *steward* and *sty-ward,* like many an etymologically connected pair, differ in both form and meaning.) It is evident that, far from reinforcing the presence and pressure of history, philological etymology drains it of its heterogeneity and materiality; substituting the myth of Progress for the myth of the Golden Age which inspired earlier etymological adventurers, it adopts a teleological orientation and takes as a guide through the welter of the past a present combination of signifier and signified, oblivious of the fact that the past had no knowledge of or use for the present unit. It assumes an unproblematic notion of "identity" across time, it claims to stand outside the history it relates, and it finds its rewards in "explanations" that are neat, ingenious, or ideologically satisfying—and therefore "convincing." The analogy with certain other kinds of history need not be spelled out.[19]

Not surprisingly, the rise of the more rigorous enterprise of modern structural linguistics put paid to the scientific pretensions of etymology—partly, no doubt, because the Saussurean divorce between synchrony and diachrony left no room for even the most attenuated hope that etymology could illuminate current meanings. Saussure's own comments on etymology in the *Course,* in a brief Appendix to the section on diachronic linguistics (259–60/189–90), are predictably dismissive. Etymology, he asserts, mixes descriptions of sound-change and meaning-change, it draws indiscriminately on phonetics, morphology, semantics, and other branches of linguistics, it lacks a coherent methodology, and it fails to scrutinize its own procedures. Textbooks on language and linguistics now seldom have sections on etymology, and although a fascination with the origins of words persists, it is more likely to manifest itself in the pages of the Sunday newspaper than in university seminar rooms. The occasional linguist who champions etymology today has to do so in defensive terms; thus we find Yakov Malkiel writing of etymology's "temporarily forfeited controlling position within linguistics" ("Etymology and General Linguistics," 219) as if it were a King Arthur whose time will come again. And Ernest Weekley is now less well remembered as the author of *The Romance of Words* than as the Nottingham professor who, in the year in which that volume was first published, introduced his wife Frieda to an ex-student of his named D. H. Lawrence.

[19]An example may be found close at hand, however: the history of language-study, as Murray Cohen complains, tends to regard as important only those studies which can be said to lead to the "true" linguistics of the nineteenth century (*Sensible Words,* xv; the whole introduction is valuable for its discussion of intellectual history). See also 120–21 below.

Word-History and Word-Play

Saussure's exposure of the fallacy of assimilating current meaning to etymological derivation is antihistorical only insofar as it attacks a simplistic view of history and its relation to present structures of signification. In his distinction between a synchronic and a diachronic approach, Saussure poses two meanings of "history" against each other: history as the complex of social and material forces that modify the individual and the community in a succession of experienced presents, and history as a supraindividual, supracommunal, transtemporal continuum, genetically or teleologically oriented. Jameson, although he portrays Saussure's distinction as a rejection of history, spells out very clearly the implications for historiography of the two kinds of linguistics, synchronic and diachronic: "The former lies in the immediate lived experience of the native speaker; the latter rests on a kind of intellectual construction, the result of comparisons between one moment of lived time and another by someone who stands outside, who has thus substituted a purely intellectual continuity for a lived one" (*Prison-House*, 6).[20] Thus in the act of freeing synchronic linguistics from the yoke of a naive and essentialist conception of history, Saussure places diachronic linguistics, and the mode of historiography it represents, in a very difficult position. In particular, the historian of value-systems (cultural, political, economic) who wishes to make the past bear fruitfully upon the present in terms of practical results is denied a simple notion of origin as explanation, a straightforward appeal to the way things were in order to understand (and to change) the way they are. To take a somewhat generalized example, the ideological system of values which helps maintain the class structure in Britain today is obviously the product of history, but it functions in the present, synchronically, in ignorance of history (or, more accurately, by virtue of a particular myth of history). Just as a word cannot be revealed in its authenticity by the production of an etymological origin, so this structure cannot be justified, as Burkean conservatism would seek to do, by referring to its history. By the same token, however, it cannot be discredited by its history either, any

[20]Saussure's notion of a synchronic state as a complete and homogeneous system cannot, in fact, be as easily derived from the individual language-user's experience as Saussure implies, and I shall argue later for a representation of that experience which does more justice to its heterogeneity. See also Roy Harris, *The Language Myth*, 49–53.

more than a linguistic usage we may wish to see disappear because of its sexist or racist connotations can be dislodged by an appeal to earlier forms.

In any attempt to escape the damaging effects of this distinction between past and present, with its enfeeblement of diachronic historiography, there seems to be little point in returning to the discredited notion of etymology. Yet there remains something we have not accounted for, something compelling in the revelation of an unexpected etymological origin which the Saussurean dismissal does not quite negate. Even Saussure's own discussion of *décrépi(t)* has an interest beyond its usefulness as an example, for we cannot simply disregard the connection between peeling walls and the impotence of old age once our attention has been drawn to it, and if we take Saussure's hint and trace the words further back, the tale grows even more interesting in its complex patterns and reversals. Latin *crispus*, the source of *crépir*, referred in fact to curly hair, which was an attribute not of age but of youth among the Romans. *Decrepitus* divides etymologically into *de* and *crepitus*, in which *de* could be either an intensifier of the symptoms of age suggested by *crepitus*—"rattling, clattering, chattering, or noisily breaking wind"—or an indication of a *reversal* of meaning, in which case *decrepitus* presents old people not as garrulous and flatulent but, in the words of the Latin lexicographers Lewis and Short (trying by a dab of poetic color to enforce their own choice of derivation), "creeping about like shadows." (One amateur etymologist fascinated by these tracings that yield opposite meanings within the same word was, of course, Freud.)[21] Saussure himself cannot escape the lure of etymology, however difficult it is to say what etymology illuminates: he asserts, surprisingly, that "the [diachronic] conditions which have produced a [synchronic] state throw light upon its true nature [*véritable nature*] and guard us from certain misconceptions" (128/90). Yet his argument has quite clearly been that there is no such thing as a synchronic misconception: *décrépi* and *décrépit are* related, however much the etymologist may protest, and a word's "true nature" is a matter not of history but of its present systematic relations. He even argues etymologically himself, justifying the usefulness of the idea of "language articulation" by a reference to the meaning of *articulus* in Latin (26/10) and, as Derrida has pointed out

[21]See Freud's review of Karl Abel's "The Antithetical Sense of Primal Words," in *On Creativity and the Unconscious*, 55–63.

in *Glas* (105–9, right-hand column), appealing to etymology to defend the arbitrariness of the sign against the apparently even more threatening encroachments of onomatopoeia (102/69). What is more, he becomes prescriptive in the way that is elsewhere the object of his attack when he compares the alternative pronunciations of the French word for "wager": *gažür* and *gažör*. "The real question," he insists, "is etymological: *gageure* was formed from *gager*, like *tournure* from *tourner*. . . . Only *gažür* can be justified" (53/31).

The temptation to turn for support to etymology is not peculiar to Saussure. Indeed, it occurs throughout the Western philosophical tradition, and for many writers it has provided an important mode of argument—among the more obvious examples are Plato's *Cratylus*, Nietzsche's *Genealogy of Morals*, Freud's essay "The Uncanny," and the many etymological tracings of Heidegger and Derrida. Sir Philip Sidney, in a gesture typical of Renaissance humanism, offers as a proof of poetry's importance the supposed derivation of Roman and Greek words for "poet"; Vico founds an epistemology and a historical method upon etymology; and poststructuralist writing seems to find the etymological turn irresistible. If this practice has no "truth" to offer about the language we speak, what is its function? Why is the appeal of etymology so powerful and enduring? What is the status of etymology after Saussure?

A brilliant short study by Jean Paulhan, *La preuve par l'étymologie*, is concerned with just this topic. Paulhan provides a forceful statement of the Saussurean position, remarking, for instance, that we may learn something about the history of cooking when we find that *foie* comes from Latin *ficus* because the Romans ate liver stuffed with figs, but we learn nothing about the current meaning of *foie* (47).[22] Indeed, Paulhan points out, etymology is more likely to mislead us as to current meaning; *sou* comes from *soldus*, piece of gold, and *chrétien* and *crétin* come from the same root (49). But having banished etymology from the realms of logic and science, he welcomes it instead

[22]My concern in this chapter is not with the use of etymology, or rather semantic change, as an index of social or ideological shifts; this is a mode of argument with its own difficulties and its own rewards. It has been employed in the service of many views of history—one might compare Raymond Williams's demonstration of the historical production of culture in *Keywords* with the following statement from the Preface to Ernest Klein's *Comprehensive Etymological Dictionary of the English Language:* "Language is a mirror in which the whole spiritual development of mankind reflects itself. Therefore, in tracing words to their origin, we are tracing simultaneously civilization and culture to their real roots" (x).

into a different realm, one that perhaps subsumes those of logic and science: the realm of rhetoric, where it has a subtle and scintillating role to play. Its rhetorical partner, from which it is sometimes indistinguishable, is the *calembour* or *paronomasia*, the play on words. In both devices the same process occurs: two similar-sounding but distinct signifiers are brought together, and the surface relationship between them is invested with meaning through the inventiveness and rhetorical skill of the writer.[23] If that meaning is in the form of a postulated connection between present and past, what we have is etymology; if it is in the form of a postulated connection within the present, the result is word-play. Sometimes jokes work by pretending to be etymologies, as in the (untranslatable) example discussed by Freud: *"Eifersucht* [jealousy] is a *Leidenschaft* [passion] which *mit Eifer sucht* [with eagerness seeks] what *Leiden schafft* [causes pain]" (*Jokes*, 68). Etymology is also closely related to the literary device of allusion, a topic brilliantly discussed by John Hollander in *The Figure of Echo*. Hollander remarks that "the relation of echo and source is like the curious dialectic of 'true' meanings of words: the etymon and the present common usage each can claim a different kind of authority. (The dialectic might be called the field of combat between synchrony and diachrony. That field is the domain of poetry as well.)" (62). Elsewhere he portrays etymology as it is experienced by the ordinary language-user and relates it to the operations of poetry: "Our common words originally came into the world as embodiments of our uses of them; the belated fables composed by etymologists are charming and compelling, but they come into the world so many ages after the fact of our experience. *Silly* means "silly", which we know well in childhood; the assertion that it once meant "innocent" and before that, "blessed" and "lucky", is the derivative, ironic epigram stretched

___

[23] A related argument is put forward by Tzvetan Todorov in *Symbolism and Interpretation*, 76–79; see also Umberto Eco's comments on Joyce's use of puns in *L'oeuvre ouverte*, 282. We may be reminded of similar uses of ingenuity in making connections between disparate domains: that of the stylistic critic who finds "appropriateness" in the relation of form to content, for example, and that of the psychoanalyst engaged in the interpretation of dreams. In both cases the "persuasiveness" of the connections drawn is not a simple matter of objective truth; it has, rather, to do with pragmatic effects on the reader or the analyzand. Indeed, with sufficient ingenuity, *any* two words could no doubt be connected, as Socrates' "etymologies" in the *Cratylus* tend to suggest. For a critique of stylistics which develops this point, see Stanley Fish, *Is There a Text in This Class?* chaps. 2 and 10. In interpreting dreams Freud moves between words by the same procedures that characterize the activity of the etymologist and the punning poet.

by a modern poet to cast a shadow across our sophistication" ("The Poetry of Everyday Life," 7–8).[24] The power of the current over the original meaning is related to the trope of "transumption" or "metalepsis" as employed by Harold Bloom: the history of a word is presented (in the layout of etymological dictionaries and in the chronology of language teaching, for example) as if the earlier meanings were derivatives of itself.

Word-play, in other words, is to etymology as synchrony is to diachrony. Thus it is an etymological move to write that *steward* and *styward* are related through the historical rise in status of the swineherd, but a play on words to write "I'll gild the faces of the grooms withal, / For it must seem their guilt" (*Macbeth*, 2.2.53–54). It is not hard to imagine the etymology and the paronomasia exchanged, and a poet exploiting the echo between *sty-ward* and *steward* while an etymologist derives *guilt* from *gild* and *gold* (no doubt finding a useful stepping-stone in German *Geld*). The *OED* in fact regards what for Weekley is etymology as no more than word-play, though not without a suspicion of relishing it in the act of discarding it: "There is no ground for the assumption that *stigweard* originally meant 'keeper of the pig-sties.'") Edmund in *King Lear* may seem to be playing the etymologist when he exclaims: "Why brand they us / With base? With baseness? bastardy?" (1.2.9–10), but he is in fact playing the poet, for etymologists tell us that the words *base* and *bastard* are historically unrelated. Saussure himself is on the way to enunciating the connection between etymology and word-play when he insists that "etymology is before everything the explanation of words by research into their connections with other words," and the example he gives of what he calls "the most important part of etymological research" is, in fact, not etymology at all in the normal sense but the synchronic investigation of verbal relationships (259). (Saussure's defense of the pronunciation of *gageure* with the same vowel as *tournure,* mentioned earlier, might have been put not as an etymological argument but as a matter of relationships within the synchronic system—which makes his appeal to etymology all the more surprising.)

That the etymologist is more of a poet than a scientist is by no means a new idea. Socrates, as he begins his etymological outpouring in the *Cratylus*, describes himself as one who is inspired and possessed,

[24]See also Hollander's entertaining discussion of proper names and etymology in "Originality," 27–30.

109

and the witty and ironic quality of his etymologies is certainly more literary than scientific; Sidney's glorification of the poet as godlike creator is a rhetorical rather than a logical formulation, and it loses nothing of its power when Paulhan tells us that *poetes* is better translated as *librettist* than maker (60); Vico's frequent use of etymology is related to his privileging of rhetoric, poetry, and the imagination over logic and reason. Modern etymologists seem quite prepared to accept the "poetic" aspect of their activity; thus Malkiel compares the etymologist to a pool-player "who, through a skillful and, above all, imaginative succession of shots, executed in a wide variety of directions and with numerous changes in his position, eventually succeeds in landing all the balls in the pockets" ("Each Word Has a History of Its Own," 148), and Raimo Anttila asserts that "the ingenuity of the etymologist and the power of his invention and combination cannot be replaced by mechanical rules" (*Introduction to Historical and Comparative Linguistics,* 331). It was principally the etymologists of the late nineteenth and early twentieth centuries who modeled their work on the natural sciences and vigorously rejected the imaginative element; thus W. W. Skeat, in the Preface to his *Etymological Dictionary,* deplores "those unscrupulous inventions with which English 'etymology' abounds, and which many people admire because they are 'so clever'" (xxviii). He adds that "the number of those who literally prefer a story about a word to a more prosaic account of it, is only too large." But, we may ask, what are etymologies if not stories? What is the model for the history of the word if not the biographical narrative? And what are Weekley's accounts of the fortunes of *steward, chancellor, constable,* and *marshall* if not versions of the Cinderella myth, that comforting fiction in a society where real sty-wards tend to remain sty-wards?[25] He himself refers to his etymologies on more than one occasion as "short stories"[26]—and it is not for nothing that his book is called *The Romance of Words.*

[25]When Max Müller, in his enormously influential *Lectures on the Science of Language,* wishes to give picturesque examples of etymology to his audience, he chooses a set of words of exactly the same type— *palace, court, government, minister, lord, lady, earl, king*— and shows how each one has "risen in rank" (251–56). Trench, however, manages to draw an ethical and religious lesson from both rises *and* falls in English words, the former revealing "the influences of a Divine faith working in the world," the latter being something "which men have dragged downwards with themselves" (*On the Study of Words* 72–79; see also 160–61).

[26]See the prefaces to *Words Ancient and Modern* (1926) and *More Words Ancient and Modern* (1927).

If the etymologist is neither a tracker-down of authentic meanings buried in history nor a detached scientist presenting an objective truth about the past, but a manipulator of words, a story teller, a rhetorician, is etymology to be relegated once and for all to the realms of the secondary and the superfluous? Must we exclude etymology from serious study, in contrast to the truth-revealing synchronic analysis of the language system or the diachronic account confined modestly to observable material changes in sound and spelling, as having no importance for the present? And by analogy, is the historian of literature (or literary theory, or any aspect of the world of human discourse and signification) a mere entertainer, telling us stories that have no bearing on the present, a present given to us as a self-sufficient system whose origins are as unknowable as they are irrelevant? If this were so, it would substantiate entirely (though for different reasons) the charge that the Saussurean linguistic model leads to a rejection of history, and there would seem to be no way of retrieving history without reintroducing the confusions that Saussure so effectively exposed. Although the notion of the arbitrary sign within a synchronic system of differences valuably demonstrates that language is a product of historical forces, as Lentricchia and others have observed, the very same notion seems effectively to prevent us from making anything of that history.

Folk Etymology and Feedback

The question we are posing itself hints at the possibility of a different way of reading Saussure's *Course* which may lead to more positive answers than those we have been able to give so far, a reading that treats the *Course* not as a scientific study (couched, *faute de mieux*, in words) to be judged correct or incorrect, consistent or inconsistent, but as a verbal text, a discursive production, perhaps even as a story. In such a reading we would need to ask where the narrative falters, where the tone betrays a struggle, where the rhetoric protests too much, because at such points the strains of Saussure's enterprise, and therefore the possibilities of moving beyond it (and beyond the structuralist tradition that stems from it), will be most evident.

There *are* times—we have already noted one of them—when the serene descriptive surface of the *Course* is ruffled by the kind of prescriptive attitude that Saussure, and with him the whole tradition of modern scientific linguistics, professes to abhor. Derrida has subjected one of these moments to a revealing analysis in his well-known discussion of writing and speech in the *Course,* but by isolating it he has given only a partial picture of the tensions at work in Saussure's text (*Grammatology,* 41–42). If we return to the example of *décrépi(t),* we may observe—indeed, it is implicit in Saussure's account—that the meanings of the two words (as of the words *rage* and *outrage* in English) have in fact been *modified* by the false (and unconscious) etymological theorizing of native speakers, who assume connections between signifiers on the basis of a similarity in sound. The synchronic state of the language is thus affected not by a "blind" external force, on which Saussure places all his emphasis, but by the community's own interpretation of its language's history. Pronunciation, too, can be affected by such native-speaker theorizing; most of us probably pronounce the noun *outrage* with the same vowel sound as *rage* and not, as the "correct" etymology suggests, and as the *OED* actually stipulates, with the same vowel sound as *bondage* or *breakage.* This phenomenon of language change is known as "folk" or "popular" etymology, and it provides many a colorful passage in the annals of lexical history. (Some linguists make a distinction between "popular etymology," denoting widespread but erroneous assumptions about the history of words, and "folk etymology" [*Volksetymologie*], denoting language changes brought about by such assumptions.) Thus we are told that the word *renegade,* one who *renegues,* became, as a result of the vivid image of a refugee in flight, *runagate;* and the Dutch phrase *verloren hoop,* the "lost heap" of soldiers in the vanguard of an attack, became naturalized—and generalized—as *forlorn hope.* The "scientific" etymologist is often to be found taking quiet pleasure in some quaint misunderstanding by the ill-educated but imaginative "folk" which has resulted in the introduction of a new pronunciation, meaning, word, or phrase into the language. Ernest Weekley, as one might imagine, has a field-day with folk etymology.

Such changes form part of the readily observable diachronic mutation of language, and Saussure accordingly devotes a brief chapter of the section "Diachronic Linguistics" to what he terms "étymologie populaire." But instead of merely recording the operation of folk etymology, for which his separation of synchrony from diachrony seems to provide the perfect framework, he reveals an unexpected animus against it. Folk etymology begins when we "mangle" words (*estropier* can mean to "cripple" or "mutilate"), producing "bizarre innovations," and it results in what Saussure calls *des coq-à-l'âne* (238/173–74) (which his translators render as "absurdities" or "howlers"; it means arbitrary changes of direction, literally "from cock to ass"). It "maltreats" words (240/174) and, like onomatopoeia (a kind of folk etymology which relates words to nonlinguistic sounds) and words created *ex nihilo* by individuals (another example of the language-user's intervention in language change), it "is not to be taken seriously into account" and has "only minimal importance or none at all" (242/176). In a sentence excluded by the editors from the final version of the *Course*, Saussure uses the terms *vicieux* ("erroneous," but with a hint of "perverse") and *"pathologiques"* ("pathological") to describe the effects of folk etymology on the language.[27]

The other kind of change that Saussure resists, and on which Derrida has commented in *Of Grammatology* (41–42), is known as "spelling pronunciation." Here a phonetic alteration occurs because speakers are influenced by the way a word is spelled; so, for example, in English it is becoming normal to give spelling pronunciations to *often* and *forehead* instead of saying *offen* and *forrid*. Saussure's hostility to this perfectly ordinary process is again palpable, revealing itself at times in exactly the same terms he uses for, or rather against, folk etymology: "The visual image leads to the creation of erroneous pronunciations

[27]See the Critical Edition of the *Cours*, ed. de Mauro, 473 n.286. Historical linguists still tend to present the operation of folk etymology in language change as a marginal phenomenon, though it is always good for an entertaining example or two, often delivered in a suitably patronizing tone. Thus Jean Aitchison gives examples from the "less educated classes" and refers to "lower class folk etymologies." She concedes that what she calls "errors of ignorance" (as if language-users *ought* to be etymological scholars) "can set off changes in isolated vocabulary items" but states that they are otherwise irrelevant to the study of language change (*Language Change*, 187–90). A greater awareness of the centrality in language change of the processes that underlie folk etymology is shown by Samuel Jay Keyser and Alan Prince in an essay that focuses on one of its major mechanisms, the subdivision of an unfamiliar word into parts that can be given meanings ("Folk Etymology"). They remark: "The analysis of words into component parts is a fundamental linguistic operation; folk etymology may be viewed as extending this process in order to make unfamiliar words more transparent" (67n.). One has only to reflect on the number of "unfamiliar words" encountered by speakers at all stages of language knowledge, and within the larger processes of interreacting languages and dialects, to appreciate how important "folk etymology" is as a linguistic phenomenon. Keyser and Prince yoke their account of literary uses of this phenomenon to an odd notion of "language enacting the world"; what is actually at stake is a process of *secondary* motivation (what Saussure calls "relative motivation" [180–84/131–34])—unfamiliar words are made to relate to familiar ones, and the "world" does not come into it.

(*prononciations vicieuses*); this is in a strict sense a pathological phenomenon" (53–31). Spelling pronunciations are "monstrosities" (*des
cas tératologiques*), which the linguist should "place under observation
in a special compartment" (54/32). The threat of the spelling pronunciation of *gageure*, it will be recalled, is so great that, as in the case of
claims for onomatopoeic derivation, Saussure is prepared to call upon
the discredited testimony of etymology to reinforce his attack.

What is it that produces this highly emotive and ethically colored
language so at odds with the claim to be neutrally concerned with
scientific observation? Why are folk etymology and spelling pronunciation not merely registered among the common types of language
change whose effects are observable in the synchronic state of the
system? (The argument that Saussure's hostility is primarily toward
writing seems less convincing when we include folk etymology, because here it is precisely speech unsupported by writing that is often
the culprit.) Before we attempt an answer, we can add to these two
kinds of change the effects of prescriptive intervention, whose existence Saussure simply denies: "Not only would an individual who
wished to do so be unable to modify in any way a choice that has been
made [within the language], but the community itself cannot exercise
control over a single word: it is bound to the language as it exists"
(104/71). Again he uses emotionally tinged language: "We can conceive of a change only through the intervention of specialists, gram-
marians, logicians, etc.; but experience shows us that all such meddlings [*ingérences*] have failed" (107/73). Such antiprescriptivism is a
regular feature of both nineteenth-century philology and twentieth-
century linguistics; it is part and parcel of the claim to an objective,
descriptive, scientific status for language study, which must not be
suspected of interfering with ethics, or politics, or value-judgments of
any kind. Saussure insists that language change can come only from
outside the system and is in that sense "blind" (127/89; 209/152).
Moreover, he asserts, it is the *social* character of language, its existence
within the domain of material human history, that makes it vulnera-
ble to these historical forces (112–13/77–78). (The illusion of purposeful change results from the diacritical nature of the system, so
that an alteration at one point can have widespread and regular effects.) The impossibility of prescriptively induced change is presented
as a result of the arbitrariness of the sign, that is, no *linguistic* reasons
can be adduced for preferring one form to another. (Other reasons,
such as moral or political ones, can be adduced and can be effective,

as in the endeavor to eliminate implications of racism and sexism from a language, but for Saussure, wishing to constitute an object for study as close as possible to the objects of natural science, these reasons would be external to the language system as such. They would be the operations of human art and artificiality upon the wholeness and self-consistency of nature, to put the argument in the terms at issue earlier in this book). It is rare to find a linguist who accepts that changes in language, or resistances to change, which result from prescriptivism, of however misguided a variety, are as much part of the evolution of language as any other change, and who accepts that to think otherwise is to introduce prescriptivism into linguistics itself; one exception is Dwight Bolinger, who discusses "the conservative forces that nip many incipient changes in the bud, which the linguist should be willing to recognize—and to describe, as just another linguistic phenomenon" (*Forms of English*, 241–51). On the other hand, Bolinger's position—though in one sense more consistent than that of linguists who wax prescriptive about prescriptivism—involves a tension between the assumption that a neutral, descriptive linguistics is possible and a desire to emphasize and legitimate the effects upon language of all linguistic theorizing.

In fact, plenty of evidence exists to suggest that languages *do* change as a result of prescriptive intervention. One example is the existence of spellings and often pronunciations that reflect "reforms" carried out in the name of classical etymology. Thus the deliberately introduced "b" in *debt* or "d" in *adventure* are as firmly entrenched as their more "natural" brethren. Saussure himself cites a French example, the *d* in *poids* inserted because of a "false etymology" (50/28). He also argues fiercely against the spelling pronunciations he hears around him, clearly hoping that he will produce an effect on the language in contradition of his own rule against the effectiveness of such "meddlings."[28] Here the learned etymologist plays a role exactly equivalent to that of his popular namesake. When the former derives *aventure* from *ad-venire* and the latter derives *renegade* from *run-a-gate*, they are not doing anything essentially dissimilar—both are engaged in the kind of word-play we have discussed, both are telling stories about their language. The "correctness" or "incorrectness" of the derivation is not at issue; what unsettles Saussure is a change in lan-

---

[28] In fact, the rule proved the stronger: no one today would share Saussure's horror at the pronunciation of the *t* in *sept femmes*.

guage that arises directly from the intrusion of a diachronic interpretation into the synchronic system.

It could be called a problem of *feedback:* the rigid insulation of synchrony from diachrony is threatened by a short circuit whereby history is reinscribed in the present—not as a series of "real events" (which, having passed, can no longer intrude) but as the only way in which history *can* intervene in the present, as a theory or story of the past.[29] The chapter on *étymologie populaire* in the *Course* is largely devoted to differentiating between folk etymology and *analogy,* the process whereby language-users create new forms on the models of familiar ones (as when the plural *cows* came to displace the old plural *kine* by analogy with most other English plurals). Although this is also a process whereby the language-user reinterprets the language according to an "incorrect" theory, Saussure is perfectly happy with it, regarding it as part of what he calls the "normal functioning of language." The crucial difference, he insists, is that analogy results from the "forgetting" of the language's history, whereas folk etymology, a "diametrically opposed process," results from a "confused memory" of that history (240–41/175–76). The effacement of the past is "natural," the reactivation of the past as memory, story, or history is "pathological."[30] Saussure's hostility toward spelling pronunciation now appears in a light somewhat different from that shed on it by Derrida's reading: it is not just the hostility of the phonocentrist toward writing but a reluctance to accept that a word's spelling, a record (accurate or not) of its past, should modify its present state. Derrida's

---

[29]Barry Hindess and Paul Q. Hirst state most forcefully the impotence of history understood as what existed in the past: "The study of history is not only scientifically but also politically valueless. The object of history, the past, no matter how it is conceived, cannot affect present conditions. Historical events do not exist and can have no material effectivity in the present" (*Pre-capitalist Modes of Production,* 312). This is not to say, however, that history understood as a *representation in the present* of past events (or of past representations of events), however unscientific, is ineffectual; its power is only too evident.

[30]Other etymologists see no important distinction between popular etymology and analogy. McKnight, for example, ends his chapter on folk etymology thus: "The process of folk-etymology is, then, only a popular form of a tendency, prevailing among the lettered as well as the unlettered, to attempt to bring about uniformity and system into speech. . . . Strange appearing words, native as well as foreign, are recast in familiar molds. Attempt is made, on the part of scholars, to restore distorted forms of classical derivations to their original form" (*English Words,* 190). For a somewhat more recent assertion that popular etymology is a normal and significant part of language change, see John Orr, "L'étymologie populaire," 3–15.

demonstration of the consistent privileging of speech over writing in Western philosophy therefore needs to be balanced by an awareness of the reverse structure of priorities produced in many areas of thought by the fixity and permanence of writing—especially when, as with Latin for several centuries, a common orthography contrasted with national variations in pronunciation (see Attridge, *Well-weighed Syllables*, 54–57). Saussure's hostility toward writing is in part directed against this privileging of a fixed form of language, and he argues always for a view of language as inherently and unpredictably changeable, infinitely open to the accidents of history (though entirely closed to the intentions of man). "It is impossible," he writes of sound changes, "to foresee where they will stop. It is childish to think that a word can change only up to a certain point, as if it had something in it which could prevent it" (208/151). It ought to be noted, however, that in a spelling pronunciation it is not strictly spelling as an immutable form untouched by history which inhibits or reverses changes in speech but *interpretation* of that spelling according to current practice, which may have little relation to any actual pronunciation of the past.

For Saussure, spelling pronunciation is in league with folk etymology and learned prescriptivism as means whereby the language user and the language community intervene, consciously or unconsciously, to alter the language system, on the basis of a diachronic model completely at odds with his own. Saussure's emphasis, we recall, is entirely on language's openness to external modification by material and humanly uncontrollable forces (and it is in this sense that it situates discourse, to use Lentricchia's phrase, "in its true home in human history"). What Saussure regards as secondary is history as intellectual construct, the history of the etymologist and the theorist of language (academic or popular); and when history in this sense interferes, it threatens the whole distinction between synchrony and diachrony, and therefore the stability and self-consistency of the system, and has to be excluded.[31] The stories we tell about the past are all very well in their place, but they have no right to change the way we live. Saussure's failed attempts to control folk etymology, spelling

---

[31]Saussure is here following in the footsteps of those who in the nineteenth century founded the study of language as a science on the model of natural history; thus Max Müller, in his popular lectures on language, emphasized that though language is constantly changing, "it is not in the power of any man either to produce or change it." As a result "language is independent of political history" (see Aarsleff, *From Locke to Saussure*, 36).

pronunciation, and prescriptive modification point the way toward a different view of history, one that will not simply reverse his privileging of synchrony over diachrony but encourage what Saussure tried to forbid, the entry of diachrony *into* synchrony—the entry of history into our current experience and current struggles.

History and Narrative

One could, no doubt, trace similar uneasy spots produced by the phenomenon of feedback in much structuralist literary theory, moments when the claim to theorize from a point outside the history of texts and readers comes up against the effects that precisely such theorizing has upon that history, or when the denial of the validity of authorial intention or historical meaning confronts the fact that reading is inescapably affected by conceptions of authorial intention or historical meaning (just as language is affected by its users' belief in etymological and onomatopoeic motivation, however "erroneous"). Bearing in mind the wider implications of our linguistic model, let us ask how we might build into a theory of language the effects of popular and learned etymology, and of spelling and prescriptive arguments, instead of attempting, like Saussure, to exclude them. How might we acknowledge the feedback of history into the here and now, how acknowledge the determination of language not by "blind" forces but by human, social, and political agency, both conscious and unconscious? To do so would require us to regard language as *inherently* unstable, internally (and eternally) shifting between synchrony and diachrony—not that the past can itself reach forward and affect the present but that the present is always inhabited and modified by theories (or stories) of the past, popular and scholarly. Synchrony is an impossible fiction, not because language is always changing—Saussure knew that better than most—but because even as a methodological hypostatization a synchronic state is never consistent with itself.[32] Folk etymology and spelling pronunciation are no more than

[32]Roman Jakobson, who shared many of Saussure's basic assumptions and adopted many of his tools, made a strong point of rejecting the separation of synchrony and diachrony, but he did not fundamentally depart from Saussure's methodology in this regard; indeed, his insistence on the systematic nature of language change is more Saussurean than Saussure ever was. A linguist who, almost in spite of himself, has shown more clearly the instability between the two axes is Bolinger: in his papers "On

points at which language's difference from itself becomes obvious. If the way I pronounce *outrage* implies an etymological theory, is the same not true with every word I utter, using *this* rather than *that* pronunciation? Am I not, as a literate English speaker, *always* suspended between written and spoken forms, modifying each by its relation to, and difference from, the other? Does not my knowledge (whether accurate or not) of past forms of the language necessarily affect my present use and understanding of it? And are the coincidences of sound upon which word-play is based not continually subverting the dictionary's attempt to keep words (and meanings) in separate compartments?[33] Language and theories about language, popular even more than academic, must be seen as constantly in a condition of mutual interchange, and for this reason a neutral descriptive linguistics is impossible. The same is true for literature and theories about literature. The way people speak has been modified in this century by supposedly nonprescriptive linguists; the way people read has been modified by supposedly metacritical literary structuralists; the way people act has been modified by supposedly objective historians.[34] And, more than that, those self-proclaimed "objective" theories have always been formuated in the service of certain goals, usually concealed but occasionally emerging with disarming clarity, as they do in a sentence from Weekley's preface to the third edition, published in 1917, of the book already mentioned: "In the interval since the last edition of *The Romance of Words* the greatest *Romance of Deeds* in our story has been written in the blood of our noblest and best" (ix).

Weekley's comment is interesting not just because of the overt political rhetoric but because he succeeds in accommodating even World War I to the same narrative model that serves him so well in his etymological derivations. We are brought back to the question of etymology's status as imaginative story telling (and, by implication, the

---

Defining the Morpheme" and "Rime, Assonance, and Morpheme Analysis" he demonstrates that the identification of morphemes (and his account could be extended to wider semantic domains), notwithstanding its claim to be a wholly synchronic procedure, has to rely on etymology, and that to eschew diachronic information entirely would be to produce an absurd proliferation of morphemic units (*Forms of English*, 183–89, 203–26).

[33]This subversion operates even on the boundaries between proper and common nouns; see Derrida's *Signéponge*, passim.

[34]Note also the way in which the psychoanalyst's interpretation can affect the analyzand's dreams; Freud, *The Interpretation of Dreams*, 516.

similar status of all historical writing). It is from their success as stories with good plots and ingenious word-play that folk etymologies (and for that matter learned etymologies) derive their power to change the language, not from their accuracy.[35] Greek *alcuon,* "kingfisher," for example, became Latin (and English) *halcyon* through the charming but mistaken belief that the Greek word was made up of *hals* (sea) and *kyon* (conceiving), a reference to the fable that the halcyon broods on her nest floating on the calm sea. Similarly, the power possessed by history, whether that of the professional historian, the journalist, or the person-in-the-street, to sustain or to alter prevailing value-systems depends on the success of the stories it tells. (Etymology and word-play tell us, in fact, a story about the interchangeability of *history* and *story,* even more striking in the doubleness of *histoire* and *Geschichte.*) Hayden White has argued for the importance of narrative models in historiography, Fredric Jameson has elaborated a theory of the "political unconscious" which rests on the centrality of narrative in human consciousness, and Jonathan Culler has portrayed theories of reading as themselves stories.[36] As I tried to show in the first part of this chapter, the version of Saussure's theory produced by Jameson and Lentricchia conforms less to the "objective reality" of Saussure's text than to the demands of the story they wish to tell about twentieth-century literary theory. Nor is the history of the study of etymology, and of linguistics more generally, exempt from the need for narrative. Chomsky tells a story in *Cartesian Linguistics* about the importance of Descartes and the Port-Royal grammar which is unabashedly designed to establish an ancestry for his own linguistic theory, while Aarsleff counters with a story about the importance of Locke and

[35]John Orr, in "L'étymologie populaire," argues that there is a kind of "unconscious poetry" in folk etymology, which he relates to rhyme and punning—and which, he asserts, "ne diffère pas essentiellement de sa soeur savante, l'étymologie des philologues" (14).

[36]White, *Metahistory* and *Tropics of Discourse;* Jameson, *The Political Unconscious;* Culler, *On Deconstruction.* White makes the interesting point that the historian, by turning a chronicle of events (in mere succession) into a story, transforms them "into a *completed* diachronic process, about which one can ask questions as if he were dealing with a *synchronic structure* of relationships" (*Metahistory,* 6). See also White's "The Value of Narrativity in the Representation of Reality" and "The Narrativization of Real Events." John Frow's "Annus Mirabilis" is a valuable discussion of the literary historian's dilemma, while Jean-François Lyotard, in *The Postmodern Condition,* extends the category of "narrative" to cover a variety of nonscientific modes of knowledge. There is an interesting meditation on the question of narrative in Marxist history in Eagleton, *Walter Benjamin,* 63–74.

Condillac in *From Locke to Saussure;* both are challenging an older story about the negligibility of language study before 1800, and neither acknowledges the degree to which "importance" is retroactively constituted by just such narratives as their own and their success in meeting the needs of their time.[37]

Not only do historical and theoretical narratives, if they are convincing enough, change the way we think and act, but theories *about* them can do the same. The story that the etymologists tell about the "folk" and their picturesque wit, their resourceful ingenuity, their quaint misapprehensions, has itself had an effect on our understanding of language change thanks to its conformity to a certain romantic class stereotype.[38] (The *OED* itself half admits that its etymology for *halcyon* is only a fable about a fable: "The spelling *halcyon*," it begins, "is *supposed* to have arisen out of the fancy that . . ." [my emphasis].) One of the most compelling stories about history, which is also told about literary theory and about linguistics, concerns the importance and achievability of strict objectivity—of history *without* story—and Saussure remains one of the most persuasive tellers of it. (The vigorous rhetoric of *After the New Criticism* relates the same story, and, in this respect at least, Lentricchia himself must be numbered among Saussure's "progeny.")[39] We may agree that the point, as always, is not to interpret the world but to change it; the problem, however, is that to interpret the world convincingly *is* to change it—and there are few more powerful stances from which to effect such a change than one that entails disclaiming any intent or even any capacity to do so.[40]

[37]For a more complex notion of "anticipation" in the history of linguistics, see Derrida, "The Linguistic Circle of Geneva," *Margins,* 137–53.

[38]This is exemplified, for instance, in the Rev. A. Smythe Palmer's massive *Folk-Etymology: A Dictionary of Verbal Corruptions or Words Perverted in Form or Meaning, by False Derivation or Mistaken Analogy* and its companion volume, *The Folk and Their Word-Lore: An Essay on Popular Etymologies.*

[39]A necessary characteristic of the rhetoric that promotes "objectivity" is blindness to its own rhetoricity. Thus Lentricchia can comment, apparently without any awareness of the irony of making the statement in so rhetorically crafted a text as *After the New Criticism,* "the irony of many of these texts is that they attempt to demonstrate their theories not so much by the power of their arguments, but by the posture of their various rhetorics" (216).

[40]Curiously, one of the charges brought against any argument that seeks to undermine the notion of an attainable objective truth is that it is a *dangerous* argument—an appeal to pragmatic effects of precisely the kind that undermines the notion of objectivity. On the ideological function of claims to historical objectivity see Hayden White, "The Politics of Historical Interpretation."

The really effective story is the one that is understood as anything but a story.

To challenge this position without simply replacing it by another authoritarian assertion of "objective truth," it is necessary to have recourse to other kinds of reading and writing, which follow through the traces of narrative, of rhetoric, of ideological pressure, in supposedly neutral theory or history (as we have done with Saussure) but which remain aware of their own fictionality and provisionality. One of the methods of achieving this kind of reading is to exploit the power of etymology. Etymology *can* be used, as we have seen, to confirm a dominant ideology, to deny the possibility of purposeful change, to reinforce the myth of objective and transcendent truth; but it can also be used to unsettle ideology, to uncover opportunities for change, to undermine absolutes and authority—and to do so without setting up an alternative and equally challengeable truth-claim.[41] For example, something can be done to expose and destabilize the hierarchy of gender by advertising the etymology of the word *sex;* it comes from Latin *sexus* or *secus,* and this, Eric Partridge tells us in *Origins,* "has suggested kinship with Latin *secare,* to cut: originally, with reference to female sex, a division." Implicit in the word's history, therefore, is the patriarchal assumption that sex, as determined by a phallocentric culture, is not only a division between man and woman but also woman's self-division, her difference from herself, and that this is symbolized by the division or cut in the female body.[42] An etymologically related word is *insect,* from Latin *insecta* (and *insecare*), "cut into"—an insect is an animal whose body is cut into, or divided, and therefore incomplete.[43] As in the case of the female gender, the impropriety, and inferiority, of this division of the animal world seems to derive from its lack of wholeness, its self-division. Joseph T.

[41]The use of etymology for ideological ends is nothing new. Noon notes of Aquinas's use of Isidore: "In general one might say that Aquinas appeals to the etymological argument whenever it favors his own, and that he disputes it whenever his own argument has anything to lose thereby" (*Joyce and Aquinas,* 146). It is, of course, its unprovability that makes etymology such a versatile ideological weapon.

[42]On cultural definitions of woman as difference and self-difference, see Barbara Johnson, *The Critical Difference,* and Shoshana Felman, "Rereading Feminity." During one period of its history, the word "sex," in the phrase "the sex," could mean "female sex," as if the dividedness of humanity could be associated with one of its divisions.

[43]In *Finnegans Wake,* by a literal metathesis, *insect* is a disguised form of *incest,* thus substituting a division where there should be union for a union where there should be division.

Shipley even manages to introduce a tone of mild disgust into the etymological note on *insect* in his *Dictionary of Word Origins:* "Look at a few *bugs;* the first thing you notice is that they are all notched or cut in, towards the middle." Lift up the stone of language, and hidden networks of meaning, suggestive of age-old practices of exclusion and exploitation, become visible.

The etymological content of such a discourse may be erroneous, but its effectiveness does not depend on correctness. ("Correctness" is not, in any case, a concept that can be rigorously used in etymology; the question mark that Partridge scrupulously adds to his derivation should, strictly speaking, be placed in front of all derivations, because they are all finally untestable.) It depends on the way in which words we regularly encounter, and treat as solid, simple wholes (representing solid, simple concepts), can be made to break apart, melt into one another, reveal themselves as divided and lacking in self-identity, with no clear boundaries and no evident center. When Vico informs us that " 'logic' derives from the word *logos*, which first and properly meant *favola* [fable] which became the Italian *favella* [language]"; when Nietzsche traces words for "good" back to words associated with a conquering race; when Freud explores the history of *heimlich* in Grimm's dictionary; when Heidegger argues that the common source of *bauen* ("build) and *bin* ("am") reveals their true meaning as "dwell"; when Barthes makes much of the derivation of *text* from *textus* ("woven"); when Derrida turns to Littré to show that *hymen* and *hymn* might be etymologically related, none of these authors is simply deploying the etymological argument favored by Miss Brodie and ruled out of court by Saussure.[44] Rather, they are turning the etymological dictionary against itself, using the power of etymology to undermine the easy mastery of language implied in much of our literary and philosophical tradition and to shake our assurance in fixed and immediately knowable meanings. Derrida's practice is well described by Culler: "What we call a 'literary technique' or a literary moment, when a pun like *différance* produces a conjunction of non-synthesizable meanings, is in fact also a philosophical moment *par excellence:* a breaching of the rationality of logocentrism by inserting, as the lynch-

---

[44]Vico, *The New Science*, 85–86 (para. 401); Nietzsche, *On the Genealogy of Morals*, 27–31; Freud, "The Uncanny"; Heidegger, "Building Dwelling Thinking," in *Poetry, Language, Thought*, 146–47; Barthes, "From Work to Text," in *Image-Music-Text*, 159, and his "Theory of the Text," 32, and "Textual Analysis of Poe's 'Valdemar,' " 157; Derrida, "The Double Session," in *Dissemination*, 213.

pin of a system, a construct which is not a concept in that it is contradictory" ("Jacques Derrida," 179). Derrida himself stresses the
usefulness of etymology as a philosophical tool in the course of a long
footnote in *Edmund Husserl's "Origin of Geometry."* Husserl is taken to
task for a failure of attentiveness to the "fact" of language; what is
needed is "a certain renewed and rigorous philological or 'etymological' thematic, which would precede the discourse of phe-
nomenology" (69). In the same book Derrida compares two possible
endeavors in the face of the equivocity of language: Husserl's own
attempt to "reduce or impoverish empirical language methodically to
the point where its univocal and translatable elements are actually
transparent, in order to reach back and grasp again at its pure source
a historicity or traditionality that no de facto historical totality will
yield of itself," and an alternative, in which etymologizing would
clearly have an important part to play, "to repeat and take responsibility for all equivocation itself, utilizing a language that could equal-
ize the greatest possible synchrony with the greatest potential for
buried, accumulated, and interwoven intentions within each linguistic
atom, each vocable, each word, each simple proposition, in all wordly
cultures and their most ingenious forms (mythology, religion, sciences, arts, literature, politics, philosophy, and so forth)" (102–3). It
need hardly be said that the second endeavor is that of James Joyce,
and *Finnegans Wake* its chief example.

Writers such as these are also, it seems to me, denying that the
speaker and the community are simply helpless in the face of a language system that is always already in position. For Saussure has his
own highly influential myth of authentic and single meaning, not
based on etymological origin but determined and guaranteed by the
synchronic system, held in joint ownership by the linguistic community, codified and enforced by the dictionary and the grammar of current usage—and impervious to the self-reflexivity of folk etymology
or linguistic theorizing. To initiate a science of linguistics, he needs to
constitute a stable and knowable object of this sort, and he has to
resist, as we have seen, the language-user's reintroduction of the history he has so deliberately excluded.[45] The writers I have mentioned
have no such aim, and offer no such resistance. Because they recognize the impossibility of a detached and objective science of language,

[45]For an excellent discussion of Saussure's problems with the object of his study, see
Samuel Weber, "Saussure and the Apparition of Language."

which observes and describes without altering the object of its attention, in a metalanguage wholly independent of the language it is discussing, they intervene—they offer their own folk etymologies—to make manifest the instability of language, to demonstrate the diachronic density within any synchronic state, to present language as always open to reinterpretation and change. They vary, of course, in the degree to which they openly invite such a reading: Vico and Heidegger may sound more like de Brosses and Tooke in their earnest search for "authentic" meanings, whereas Plato's and Derrida's ironies play freely through their writing. (Derrida observes of his own procedure, at one point, "we turn again to Littré, from whom we have never, of course, been asking for the *truth*."[46] In Plato's case the irony is at the expense not of the notion of an absolute and transcendent truth but of the notion of language as a guide to that truth.) But in every case the use of etymology fissures the synchronic surface of the text, introducing diachronic shadows and echoes, opening the language to shifts of meaning that can never be closed off. Even when the etymological argument is explicitly offered in the service of the doctrine of original authentic meaning, as in Horne Tooke's account of *shit* and its assonant relations, or in the service of a bourgeois ideological position, as in the case of Weekley's discussion of *steward,* it sets going a movement that cannot be arrested at a single point of truth or origin.[47]

In thus employing etymology, these writers are, in their different ways, exploiting its affinity with word-play—or, what amounts to the same thing, we are exploiting this affinity in thus reading etymological accounts. And the connection between etymology and word-play can be generalized to a connection between etymology and literature. Literature too can be read for or against absolutes, transcendence, closure, authentic and original meaning: and it too varies in the degree to which it invites a reading that opens rather than closes. (The whole of this chapter, to paraphrase a notorious footnote of Derrida's, is, as will have become evident, nothing but a reading of

---

[46]"The Double Session," *Dissemination*, 271. Derrida criticizes the naive use of etymology as a key to true meaning (which he calls "etymologism") in "White Mythology," *Margins*, 253–55.

[47]Nancy Struever gives a good account of etymology's imbrication with ideology, power, and social history, in "Fables of Power"; less convincing is her claim that "modernist" uses of etymology (among which she includes Heidegger's and Derrida's) avoid these areas.

Finnegans Wake.[48] In the chapters that follow we shall be examining some of Joyce's texts with an eye to those aspects of them which, like their play with linguistic history, question the assimilation of literary language to positivistic models.) But where etymology uses the tools of the tradition whose hierarchies it deconstructs—the tools of logic, empiricism, scientific method—and is thereby granted by our culture the right to be read in, and against, that tradition, the word-play of literature is all too easily partitioned off as another pathological development of the language to be kept under observation. This is one reason why the deconstructive etymological argument, and poststructuralist theory more generally, has an important role to play in the cultural and political arena, where the notions of "authentic meaning" and "true history," and the stories in which they are embedded, exercise a powerful ideological function, and where any challenge literature and its readers might mount against these notions is disabled by the prior marginalization of the literary.

Saussure, as I have tried to show, can be read in support of both sides in this struggle: as spokesman for and illustration of an essentialist and conservative account of human cultural productions, and as a story teller whose narrative opens possibilities for cultural—and political—praxis precisely at the points where it betrays its own rhetoricity. And the very existence of these two antithetical readings invalidates the view of history and of reading implied in one of them. That, at least, is *my* story.

[48]See "Plato's Pharmacy," *Dissemination*, 88 n.20. (The translation of this note implies that the reference is to an essay by Bataille; for confirmation that it is Derrida's own essay which is in question, see his "Two Words for Joyce," 150.) Joyce, it goes without saying, was fascinated by etymology. Hugh Kenner points out that the infant Joyce and Skeat's *Etymological Dictionary* appeared in the same year, 1882, and that Stephen Dedalus reads it "by the hour" ("Joyce and the 19th Century Linguistics Explosion," 45). See also Kenner's essay "The Invention of Language," in *The Pound Era*, 94–120, and Noon, chap. 8, "The Root Language of Shem." Fritz Senn supplies a nice example from *Ulysses:* "Desolation", a weighty word forming a whole paragraph (*U:* 63), has nothing to do with Latin *sol*, sun, but with *solus*, alone. Yet this is the moment when that remarkable cloud begins to 'cover the sun slowly wholly' and Bloom's morning becomes in fact de-sunned for a while. *Finnegans Wake* will later purposefully take such accidental concurrences of etymology in its semantic stride" ("Righting Ulysses," 19). For a reading of *Finnegans Wake* that gives the etymological principle its due, see John Bishop, *Joyce's Book of the Dark.*

The vagaries of the signifier even succeed in transforming an early French review of *Dubliners* by Edmond Jaloux, who regards the stories as the acme of realism, into an appreciation of Joyce's etymological punning: the *Critical Heritage* translation has it that Joyce's narration is "the minute and pure application of a botanist or of an entymologist [*sic*]" (1:70).

Chapter 5

Literature as Imitation: Jakobson, Joyce, and the Art of Onomatopoeia

Hermogenes or Cratylus?

A<small>T</small> about the same time that Saussure's *Course in General Linguistics* was being put together from students' notes, the twentieth century's most thoroughgoing endeavor to specify an objective distinction between literary and other uses of language was initiated in Russia. The Moscow Linguistic Circle was founded in 1915 and, in Petersburg, the Society for the Study of Poetic Language (OPOJAZ) was formed the following year. After the mid-1920s the movement weakened in Russia, partly because of official opposition, but the Prague Linguistic Circle, founded in 1926, pursued many of the same goals for another two decades.[1] The major link between what became known respectively as Russian Formalism and Prague Structuralism was the figure of Roman Jakobson who, having played a leading role in the Moscow Linguistic Circle, moved to Czechoslovakia in 1920. Although within and between these groups and movements there

---

[1]The most comprehensive study of Russian Formalism remains Victor Erlich's *Russian Formalism*, first published in 1955. Useful collections of essays are those assembled by Lee T. Lemon and Marion J. Reis, *Russian Formalist Criticism;* Ladislav Matejka and Krystyna Pomorska, *Readings in Russian Poetics;* and Tzvetan Todorov, *Théorie de la littérature*. Two valuable critical engagements with Russian Formalism are Fredric Jameson, *The Prison-House of Language*, and Tony Bennett, *Formalism and Marxism;* while a recent reconsideration is Peter Steiner, *Russian Formalism*. A representative selection of work from the Prague school has been edited and translated by Paul L. Garvin as *A Prague School Reader;* the most influential member of the group, apart from Jakobson, was Jan Mukařovský, many of whose works have been translated into English.

were wide differences, both among individuals and over time, the theorists concerned were held together by a consistent concern with the question of "literariness," the features or functions that could be said to distinguish literature as a special form of language. Jakobson continued to stress this question, and refine his position on it, throughout his long career. Between 1941 and his death in 1982 he lived and taught in the United States, where he played an important part not only in the development of linguistic (especially phonological) theory but in the growth of stylistics as a discipline.[2]

His most influential pronouncement on the subject of the distinctiveness of literary language (which for Jakobson, as for Puttenham, primarily meant poetic language)[3] was the paper "Linguistics and Poetics," given as a closing statement to a conference on stylistics in 1958.[4] Here Jakobson asserted that the "poetic function" entails a set (or "*Einstellung*") not toward what he called the *context* of a message, not toward the *addresser* or *addressee*, not toward the *code* shared by the addresser and addressee or the *contact* that enables them to stay in communication, but toward the *message as such*. The poetic function is not peculiar to poetry, but in poetry it becomes dominant, constituting the defining feature, just as the other orientations, when they dominate, produce respectively the *referential*, *emotive*, *conative*, *metalingual*, and *phatic* functions (353–57).[5]

Interpreting Jakobson's gnomic formulation "the set toward the message as such" necessitates careful consideration of the contrast he

[2]A sympathetic summary of Jakobson's linguistic theory, together with a bibliography of his output to 1976, can be found in Linda R. Waugh, *Roman Jakobson's Science of Language*. A somewhat more detached view is taken in Elmar Holenstein, *Roman Jakobson's Approach to Language*.

[3]The inadequacy of Jakobson's treatment of prose literature—which he regards as a "transitional linguistic area" between poetic and referential language—has often been commented upon; see, for instance, David Lodge, *The Modes of Modern Writing*, 91–92, and Mary Louise Pratt, *Toward a Speech Act Theory*, 33–35. Pratt's study is a valuable contribution to the debate about the distinctiveness of literary language; see especially chap. 1, "The 'Poetic Language' Fallacy."

[4]For a reading of this paper from the perspective of the mid-1980s, see Attridge, "Closing Statement."

[5]In this theory, which Jakobson first put forward in his presidential address to the Annual Meeting of the Linguistic Society of America in 1956 (see "Metalanguage as a Linguistic Problem"), he is of course drawing heavily on the arguments developed by him and others in the contexts of Russian Formalism and Prague Structuralism. For a useful summary of earlier formulations of the theory of linguistic functions, see Peter Steiner, "The Conceptual Basis of Prague Structuralism," 359–69 and 381 n.48.

makes between what he calls the "context" (the orientation toward which is the "referential" function) and the "message." In the 1920s he used the Husserlian term "expression" instead of "message" in similar formulations, in what appears to be an attempt to isolate meaning that is present as an inherent part of the sign in contradistinction to a more strictly referential meaning.[6] The "message" thus includes not only the chain of material signifiers, aural or visual, organized into grammatical relations with one another but also their meanings as given by the linguistic system, though without reference to the world beyond language. This is not an easy distinction to sustain, and it becomes especially problematic as Jakobson moves from the acceptance of a rigorous separation of meaning and reference to the view that the only relevance "reference" can have in a discussion of the language system is as an aspect of linguistic meaning; the "real world" to which words refer is a linguistically constituted feature of human experience (see Holenstein, *Jakobson's Approach,* 87–89, and Waugh, *Jakobson's Science,* 28–31)—hence Jakobson's preference for the term "context" over what he calls the "somewhat ambiguous" term "referent." (It is difficult to deny the force of this argument, and I use terms such as "referent" and "reality" in something like Jakobson's later sense, as aspects of experience and products of perception, not as independently existing entities. They are hence not sharply distinguishable from such terms as "concept," "meaning," and "signified.") If the "message" is taken to include the semantic aspect of linguistic signs, therefore, very little is left for the referential function to do: the "set toward the message" that characterizes poetry would embrace all language's business with meaning and communication. Jakobson clearly does not hold this position, and he reinforces the centrality of the referential function to the daily operation of language by equating it with what others call "ideation" and the "denotative" or "cognitive" function (353). On *this* reading, however, the poetic function is left with very little in the way of meaning within its domain.

There is clearly a tension here, as a result of which Jakobson's argument can be associated with two very different conceptions of

[6]See, for instance, the 1919 "Fragments de 'La nouvelle poésie russe'": "La poésie . . . n'est rien d'autre qu'un *énoncé visant à l'expression.*" Jakobson continues, "la fonction communicative, propre à la fois au langage quotidien et au langage émotionnel, est réduite ici au minimum" (15–16). The debt to Husserl is discussed by Steiner in *Russian Formalism,* 208–31.

poetic language, both of which we have considered earlier. If meaning is largely the preserve of utilitarian discourse, poetry may be said to be a linguistic practice that specially emphasizes the material properties of language in certain organized forms and the capacity of these forms to provide pleasure and significance independently of cognitive content—a position with which a Renaissance theorist like Puttenham would have had some sympathy. If, on the other hand, the task of poetry is to heighten attention to the meanings of words and sentences, the distinctiveness of poetic language must lie in the particular forcefulness with which it presents its semantic content—a view much closer to that of the Romantic poets and given forceful expression in Wordsworth's Preface to *Lyrical Ballads*.[7] We see here the familiar structure of supplementarity which has characterized discourse on the distinctiveness of literary language since classical times. If the linguistic norm of referential language is its "natural" condition, the poetic function must represent an "artificial" supplement that merely adds something, such as an enhanced attention to the material properties of language, to an already complete and self-sufficient entity. But at the same time, if the poetic function produces a superior kind of language, it must make good some lack in the "normal" operation of referential discourse, such as its failure to represent meanings with the full intensity of which language is capable.[8]

At times Jakobson's formulations seem to emphasize the distance between the kind of attention poetic language invites to itself and the focus on meanings in the world typical of most nonpoetic language. Thus he follows up his definition of the poetic function with the comment that "this function, by promoting the palpability of signs, deepens the fundamental dichotomy of signs and objects" (356). Some twenty years earlier he had addressed the same question in the paper "What Is Poetry?" and produced a comparable formulation:

[7]The history of discussions of rhythm and versification as features of poetic language reveals the same dual emphasis: metrical and rhythmic organization is presented both as the source of formal patterns that provide their own aesthetic satisfaction and as a means to heighten the vividness with which objects, sounds, or emotions are evoked—without much recognition that these involve contradictory positions with regard to the foregrounding or translucence of poetic language. In *The Rhythms of English Poetry*, I termed these two approaches to the sign in poetry "nonsemantic" and "semantic" functions respectively (286–87); I made no attempt, however, to deal with the tension between them.

[8]Stanley Fish presents a version of this argument in "How Ordinary Is Ordinary Language?" in *Is There a Text in This Class?* 97–111.

"But how does poeticity manifest itself? Poeticity is present when the word is felt as a word and not a mere representation of the object being named or an outburst of emotion, when words and their composition, their meaning, their external and inner form acquire a weight and value of their own instead of referring indifferently to reality" (750). (Note that among the internal properties of words to which poeticity draws attention Jakobson includes "their meaning," thus keeping alive the alternative conception of poetry as semantic heightening, though what meaning consists of if it does not include representation of objects or emotions is not very clear.) With this kind of emphasis, and in many of his analyses of intricate patterns of phonological and syntactic categories in poems in a number of languages, Jakobson seems to align himself with a conception of the distinctiveness of poetic language which has proved highly attractive in this century. The more extreme manifestations of this approach include the foregrounded sound-pattern of the Russian Formalists, the "self-valuable word" and "transrational language" of the Futurists, the autonomous signifier of some poststructuralist theorizing, and the materiality of the sign in certain Marxist approaches to poetry.[9] The notion is also evident in less theoretical, frequently heard claims about the pleasure to be derived from the "sheer sound" of the words of poetry.

At other times, however, Jakobson appears to move in the direction of a semantically oriented theory of poetic language, notably when he is discussing a topic that held a lasting fascination for him, sound-symbolism.[10] If one of the resources of poetic language is the creation

[9]Not surprisingly, readers have often assumed that Jakobson's formula "set toward the message" refers to a focus of attention on the properties of the signifier alone quite separately from meaning. Thus Roger Fowler glosses "message" as "the palpable surface structure of the communication (e.g. phonetic substance)" (*Literature as Social Discourse*, 83), and Terence Hawkes believes that Jakobson's poetic function "systematically undermines the sense of any 'natural' or 'transparent' connection between signifier and signified" (*Structuralism and Semiotics*, 86). A theory of the separateness of phonetic properties and thematic content in poetry which offers an alternative approach to Jakobson's is proposed by Veronica Forrest-Thomson, *Poetic Artifice;* see also Brian McHale, "Against Interpretation."

[10]The switching of emphasis in Jakobson's discussion has seldom been commented on, although an important exception is Gérard Genette, who devotes several pages of *Mimologiques* to a discussion of this self-contradiction, relating it to a long history of conflict between "formalist" or "Hermogenist" and "mimeticist" or "Cratylist" assumptions (302–12 and passim). See also Stephanie Merrim's review of Genette, "Cratylus' Kingdom," and Genette's earlier essay, "Poetic Language, Poetics of Language," re-

of sequences of sound and rhythm which imitate sounds or other qualities in the world beyond the poem, referentiality becomes a crucial element in its operation. Thus in "Linguistics and Poetics" Jakobson states that "poetry is not the only area where sound symbolism makes itself felt, but it is a province where the internal nexus between sound and meaning changes from latent to patent and manifests itself most palpably and intensely" (373). Far from being seen as held apart, signifier and signified (to use currently more familiar equivalents of Jakobson's *signans* and *signatum*) are seen as unusually united in poetry; the "palpability" of poetic language has been transferred from the independence of signs from their referents to the inherent connection between sound and meaning.[11] Although this position makes sense only if "signified" and "referent," or *signatum* and *denotatum*, are clearly distinct, we have seen that Jakobson does not—and for good reason—wish to make this distinction. The sound that is imitated in a poem is a sound as perceived by a human auditor, which is to say that it is already part of a signifying system.

The idea that the distinctiveness (and special pleasurability) of poetic language lies in its capacity to heal, at least momentarily, the breach between signified and signifier, to produce a revitalized language that is not arbitrary and conventional but motivated and natural, echoes through discussions of poetry down the ages and receives both learned and popular expression. Barthes refers to it as "that great secular myth which desires that language should imitate ideas and that, contrary to the specifications of linguistic science, signs should be motivated" ("Proust et les noms," 158). Valéry's comment, "A poem . . . should create the illusion of an indissoluble compound of *sound* and *sense*"

---

printed in his *Figures of Literary Discourse* (75–102). Todorov, in a somewhat hagiographical essay, "Jakobson's Poetics" (*Theories of the Symbol*, 271–84), reproduces Jakobson's ambiguous stance; he acknowledges in a note Genette's "painstaking analysis" of this ambiguity but "is left with the impression" that Genette exaggerates the importance of the facts he has established (280 n.8).

[11] Jakobson believes this to be a tendency in all languages; see "Quest for the Essence of Language," and Jakobson and Waugh, *The Sound Shape of Language*, chap. 4, "The Spell of Speech Sounds." Ivan Fónagy, in *La vive voix*, assembles evidence for the expressiveness of particular sounds; Jakobson contributes a laudatory preface. Although the search for iconic universals in language may be interesting from the point of view of the speculative linguist-philosopher on the lookout for clues to the origin or essence of language, it is not particularly productive for the literary critic. To the degree that language is regarded as originally and essentially imitative or iconic (a recurrent tendency in the history of linguistics), the iconic force of poetic language loses its distinctiveness.

(*Oeuvres* 1:210–11), could be matched in a hundred places from the writing of poets and their readers.[12] The common feeling that the words of a favorite literary passage have an unusually strong purchase on reality, a peculiarly intimate bond with the nonlinguistic phenomena to which they refer, is often accounted for—in conversation, classrooms, and critical explication—by finding ways in which it can be said that the properties of the objects or events in question are represented, independently of the conventional semantic system, by the physical properties of the language, its sounds and their sequential arrangement. This direct evocation of the meaning that the linguistic system as a conventional code can only indirectly signal is seen as the explanation of the "vividness," "rightness," or "exactness" of the successful passage; language is felt to be working here with superefficiency, every aspect pointing beyond itself to what it means. And it is frequently assumed that the relationship between the signifier and its referent in such language is one of *resemblance*—literary criticism abounds in phrases such as "mimetic syntax," "appropriate sound-patterns," "rhythmic enactment," "aural embodiment," and other related terms. As an entirely typical passage from a recent handbook on style in the novel indicates, moreover, the scope of this assumption stretches well beyond verse: "The iconic force in language produces an ENACTMENT of the fictional reality through the form of the text. This brings realistic illusion to life in a new dimension: as readers we do not merely receive a report of the fictional world; we enter into it iconically, as a dramatic performance, through the experience of reading" (Leech and Short, *Style in Fiction*, 236).

We seem to be confronted, then, both in Jakobson's own theory and in the traditional ways, whether academic or popular, of talking about literature, with two conflicting accounts of the role of speech sounds in the reader's experience of poetic language as distinctive and gratifying. According to one, the sounds of language draw attention to themselves and their configuration, independently of their referen-

[12]See also Genette, "Valéry and the Poetics of Language"; in *Mimologiques*, too, Genette gives abundant evidence of the attractiveness of the "Cratylist" position in Western thought. Todorov, in *Theories of the Symbol*, chap. 5, discusses eighteenth-century examples. Even Saussure's emphasis on the arbitrariness of the sign is undercut within his own writing—see Derrida's discussion of the *Course* in *Glas* (104–12, right-hand column). More recently, Julia Kristeva's theory of poetic language, in *La révolution du langage poétique*, makes use of Fónagy's account of a "natural" connection between certain sounds and meanings, understood as unconscious drives (209–63).

tial function; according to the other, they tend to disappear in an enhanced experience of referentiality.[13] In his survey of semantic theory Stephen Ullmann distinguishes between two kinds of words, the "opaque" word, "without any connexion between sound and sense," and the "transparent" word, which possesses at least some degree of motivation.[14] Each of these views takes poetic language to be an enhancement and extension of one of these categories. The divergence of views is, of course, a version of the old battle between formalism and realism, a restatement of the fundamental disagreement between Hermogenes and Cratylus.

The answer to the problem might seem to be that there are (at least) two kinds of distinctive poetic language, each using sounds in its own way. It is characteristic of Jakobson, however, that his goal is an account of "poeticity" which will combine these apparently conflicting positions, and in his writing after 1958 one finds several attempts to bring both positions together in a single formulation. The following date from 1979 and 1980 respectively:

> The sounds of poetry indispensably carry a distinctly more autonomous task, and their bonds with poetic semantics are not reducible to the ordinary role required from them within these conventional units by the humdrum use of language. In poetry speech sounds spontaneously and immediately display their proper semantic function. (Jakobson and Waugh, *Sound Shape,* 222)

> [The poetic function] entails an introverted attitude toward verbal signs in their union of the *signans* and the *signatum*, and it acquires a dominant position in poetic language. ("A Postcript," 22)

---

[13]Thus F. R. Leavis praises a passage from Milton's *Comus* as follows: "The texture of actual sounds, the run of vowels and consonants, with the variety of action and effort, rich in subtle analogical suggestion, demanded in pronouncing them, plays an essential part, though this is not to be analysed in abstraction from the meaning. The total effect is as if words as words withdrew themselves from the focus of our attention and we were directly aware of a tissue of feelings and perceptions" ("Milton's Verse," in *Revaluation,* 48–49).

[14]Ullmann, *Semantics,* 81. It is indicative of the problems we are dealing with that the Group μ, in *A General Rhetoric,* apply the terms "transparent" and "opaque" in precisely the opposite way (12). The uncertainty is productive when Todorov paraphrases Jakobson's definition of the poetic function as "a language that tends to become opaque"; given the ambiguity of Jakobson's position, the term could have either meaning in this context (*Theories of the Symbol,* 279).

The greater autonomy of the sounds of poetry is now the autonomy of sounds not so much from the realm of referentiality as from the operations of the conventional language system; what is fore-grounded is not the signifier but its union with the signified. Yet Jakobson writes at the same time of "a dynamised tension between *signans* and *signatum*" in poetry, which seems to point in the other direction. He follows this with another gesture toward unification in which the two positions remain distinguishable: "That spell of the 'sheer sound of words' [admired by Sapir] which bursts out in ex-pressive, sorcerous, and mythopoeic tasks of language, and to the utmost extent in poetry, supplements and counterbalances the specif-ic linguistic device of 'double articulation' and supersedes this dis-unity by endowing the distinctive features themselves with the power of *immediate* signification" (Jakobson and Waugh, *Sound Shape*, 230, 231).[15]

I do not wish to suggest that the notion of a single defining feature of poetic language is a necessary or an adequate one—we are dealing with an experience much more shifting and various than Jakobson's crusading positivism will acknowledge—but I do share Jakobson's sense that a characteristic response associated with the reading of poetry, at least in postmedieval Western culture, is a feeling of inten-sified referentiality combined with (and inseparable from) a height-ened awareness of the aural qualities of language. What prevents Jakobson from producing a satisfactory account of this response (and keeps apart the divergent schools of literary theory and criticism which espouse these two positions) is an attachment to an unexam-ined concept of art as *imitation,* whose pedigree may be impressive but whose effect on literary discussion has often been distorting and in-hibiting. Rather than examine once more the history of mimetic theo-

---

[15]This running together in a single sentence of contrary views sometimes carries over to commentators on Jakobson. Joseph Graham, for example, summarizes Jakobson's argument as follows: "The poetic function, defined as a focus on the message for its own sake, renders meaning almost palpable by precipitating those features of language especially appropriate for its representation. Becoming the dominant function, it char-acterizes poetry as the most iconic or mimetic form of language" ("Flip, Flap, Flop," 33). Waugh, in summarizing Jakobson's work on poetic language, does justice to both views and produces the same inconsistencies: thus we learn that "a poem may be said to be perceptible and palpable 'form' as against 'content' (= 'objects', 'referents', 'ideas', etc.)" and that in poetry "the *inner relation* between *signans* and *signatum* . . . is focused upon and strengthened" ("The Poetic Function," 153, 154).

135

ries of poetic language—a subject ably dealt with by Genette in *Mimologiques* and Todorov in *Theories of the Symbol*—I shall prepare the way for an account that does justice to the reading experience itself by focusing on a concrete example of what appears to be language functioning unproblematically as direct imitation of the real world. The word available to literary criticism for centuries to refer to directly imitative devices, especially where sound is concerned, has been "onomatopoeia," and the imprecision with which this term is used may be a good reason for continuing to use it. Terms such as "iconism" and "echoism" are often employed in discussions that aspire to a taxonomic precision which is not my present purpose; what I want to look at are the traditional claims for onomatopoeia, and the degree to which one literary text lives up to these claims, or, rather, in both senses of the phrase, makes fun of them.

"Fff! Oo!": Nonlexical Onomatopoeia

Joyce's dexterity in handling the sounds and patterns of English is evident on every page of his published work, but one episode of *Ulysses* is explicitly concerned with music and imitative sound, the chapter known from the Odyssean scheme as "Sirens." We can expect to find here not only Joyce's customary linguistic agility and ingenuity but also some consideration—if only by example—of the whole question of language's capacity to imitate directly the world of the senses. In the well-known closing passage of the chapter, we find a very rudimentary type of onomatopoeia: the use of the phonetic characteristics of the language to imitate a sound without attempting to produce recognizable verbal structures, even those of traditional "onomatopoeic" words. I shall call this type *nonlexical onomatopoeia*. Indeed, the device is perhaps too simple to be called "onomatopoeia," which means in Greek "word-making" and usually implies reliance on the imitative potential of the accepted lexicon. In its naked ambition to mimic the sounds of the real world, however, nonlexical onomatopoeia exposes sharply some important but easily overlooked features of more sophisticated imitative figures.

Leopold Bloom, having imbibed a glass of burgundy at lunch and a bottle of cider at four o'clock, is walking along the Liffey quay uncomfortably aware that the aftereffects of this indulgence will be embarrassing for him should they be heard by any passer-by. In particular, he wants to avoid being noticed by an approaching prostitute, and he therefore gazes strategically into a shop window that happens to contain a print of Robert Emmet together with Emmet's famous last words on Irish nationhood. Just at that moment a tram passes, providing an acoustic cover under which he can achieve the desired release without fear of detection:

> Seabloom, greaseabloom viewed last words. Softly. *When my country takes her place among.*
> Prrprr.
> Must be the bur.
> Fff! Oo. Rrpr.
> *Nations of the earth.* No-one behind. She's passed. *Then and not till then.* Tram kran kran kran. Good oppor. Coming. Krandlkrankran. I'm sure it's the burgund. Yes. One, two. *Let my epitaph be.* Kraaaaaa. *Written. I have.*
> Pprrpffrrppffff.
> *Done.* (11.1284)[16]

Several nonlexical onomatopoeic sequences occur here, proffering with a vivid and comic directness the sounds and sensations of tram and fart and contributing to the undoubted memorability of the writing:

> Prrprr.
> Fff! Oo. Rrpr.
> . . . kran kran kran.
> Krandlkrankran.
> Kraaaaaa.
> Pprrpffrrppffff.

But how simple, obvious, or direct *is* the onomatopoeic imitation of sound here? Several factors complicate the picture, and I shall isolate eight of them. The first four are concerned with the assumption that onomatopoeia involves an unusually *direct* or *unmediated* link between language and its referent, the next four with the complementary assumption that onomatopoeia involves an unusually *precise* representation in language of the physical world.

---

[16]References to *Ulysses* are to the corrected text, ed. Hans Walter Gabler et al., and indicate episode and line numbers. In quotations of more than one line, only the first line number is given.

(1) The most elementary question to be asked is how these black marks on the page represent sound at all, and the answer is, of course, that they rely as much on the reader's knowledge of the phonological system of spoken English and the graphological system of written English as does lexical onomatopoeia or, for that matter, any English text. Onomatopoeia does not lead us into a realm of direct and concrete significance, where many writers have dreamed of going; we remain firmly held within an already existing system of rules and conventions, and whatever mimetic capability the sequences have they owe entirely to this fact. Putting it another way, although these are not words and sentences, they mimic words and sentences—and it is this mimickry that permits us to pronounce them at all. In reading "Fff! Oo. Rrpr," for instance, we give a specific phonetic interpretation to the sequence exclamation mark (or full stop)/space/capital letter and treat it quite differently from the rhythmic repetitions of "Tram kran kran kran," with its absence of punctuation and its lower case, or the continuous "Krandlkrankran," which has the graphic form of a single word. Even if the normal phonological restrictions are breached, as in the climactic string of letters ("Pprrpffrrppffff"), the resulting articulatory awkwardness helps draw attention to the sounds themselves, an effect that is equally dependent on the reader's prior familiarity with rules of graphology and phonology. Elsewhere in *Ulysses* Joyce goes even further in the direction of unpronounceability within the conventions of English: the Blooms' cat goes "Mkgnao!" "Mrkgnao!", and "Mrkrgnao!" (4.16, 25, 32), and in "Circe" the "dummymummy" produces the sound "Bbbbblllllblblblblobschb!" as it falls into Dublin Bay (15.3381). The difficulty of pronunciation is obviously part of the comic point (when Bloom imitates the cat in reply he goes, conventionally, "Miaow!" [4.462]).[17]

---

[17]Fredric Jameson also emphasizes the unpronounceability of the letters representing the cat's noise but offers a somewhat different (and to me slightly mystifying) explanation: "With Mr Kenner, I also admire Joyce's evocation of the cat's mew . . . ; but is it not clear that the elegance of this transcription—"Mkgnao! Mrkgnao!"—is of a wholly different structure from that of the *mot juste?* It is precisely *not* a perfect rendering of the cat's mew, at least not as I can hear it or read it. It is a perfect rendering *for other people*, and as a reader, I see this new alphabetical object, not as a transparency (through which Joyce's intention, the banal sound he wishes me to recall, is clear and even banal on account of its very clarity), but rather as an opaque object, as it were, intercepted by 'the other' readers, and by Joyce himself as an Other. I take the letters as a sign that for someone else a cat's mew has been adequately set down on paper" ("Seriality in Modern Literature," 78).

(2) The sequences we are looking at do not constitute lexical items, but they do not function purely as phonetic chains either, without reference to the morphological system of the language and its semantic accompaniment. (It would be difficult to find a string of letters that had *no* semantic coloring, given a specific fictional setting and the eagerness of readers to find meanings in what they read.) The letter "f" hints at the word "fart," and "kran" is not very far from "tram." There are also links with words accepted in the lexicon as representations of sound: "Prr-" suggests "purr" (another long-drawn-out sound made by the expulsion of air through a restricted passage), and "kran" has elements of two of the words used elsewhere in the novel to represent the sound of trams, "clang" (7.10) and "crack" (15.190). "Krandl-" evokes phonetically related verbs of movement and noise such as "trundle," "rumble," "grumble," "shamble," "scramble"— what has been called a "phonesthetic constellation."[18] Mechanical associations, moreover, are evoked by its closeness to "handle" and by the presence of "-krank-" later in the string. We might also note that the most salient word in the quotation from Emmet is "epitaph"; its [p] and [f] echo the onomatopoeic fart, deflating the heroic gesture as it is made. This link is all the stronger because Joyce has implanted it in the reader's mind in the chapter's prelude, where it occurs in the initially uninterpretable "My eppripfftaph" (11.61). The reader might also be induced to make a connection with another sign system, that of musical dynamics, where "ppffff" would signal "very soft" and "very loud indeed." (When Molly breaks wind in "Penelope," and also does her best to be quiet about it, she addresses the words "piano" and "pianissimo" to herself at the critical moment [18.907, 908].)

The onomatopoeic effect also relies on an *avoidance* of certain morphological associations where these would be irrelevant or distracting: this is one reason—we shall look at others in a moment—why the spelling *cran* with a *c*, though it would indicate exactly the same pronunciation as *kran* with a *k*, would seem less appropriate, as it would

---

[18]This phrase is taken from Dwight L. Bolinger who, in a series of important and entertaining articles reprinted in *Forms of English* (191–239), discusses the ways in which "an 'arbitrary' form [a morpheme or word], once integrated into the system, assumes all the affective and associative privileges enjoyed by the most obvious onomatopoeia" (231). The term "phonestheme" comes originally from J. R. Firth and was adopted by Fred W. Householder ("On the Problem of Sound and Meaning"). The subject has frequently been discussed; see, for example, Leonard Bloomfield, *Language*, 244–46; I. A. Richards, *The Philosophy of Rhetoric*, 57–65; David I. Masson, "Vowel and Consonant Patterns in Poetry"; and Joseph Graham, "Flip, Flap, Flop."

produce associations with cranberries or craniums or Stephen's erstwhile companion Cranly.[19] And what if the tram went "bramble" or "gran, gran, gran . . . ?"

(3) The passage relies on our knowledge not only of the conventions of graphology, phonology, and morphology, however, but also of those of the rhetorical device of onomatopoeia itself. To take one example, the convention that a repeated letter automatically represents a lengthened sound is not to be found among the rules of the English language; the spelling of *gaffer,* for instance, does not imply that the medial consonant is pronounced at greater length than that of *loafer.* The rules cannot handle a succession of *more* than two repeated letters at all. But we have no difficulty with Joyce's triple *Fff,* which we interpret as an indication of marked duration, and such breaches of the graphological rules function, in fact, as strong indicators that we are in the presence of an onomatopoeic device.

The conventions of onomatopoeia relate not just to spelling, however, but also to the associations evoked by sounds and letters. Within the tradition of English poetry, the onomatopoeic associations of /s/ and /ʃ/ are more appealing than those of /f/, though there is nothing intrinsically beautiful about the former or ugly about the latter. A succession of *f*s is therefore relatively uncommon in traditional onomatopoeia, which is one reason why it *is* effective in a comic context in a way that "ssss" or "sh-sh-sh" would not be. The difference between "kran" with a *k* and "cran" with a *c* is also partly a matter of onomatopoeic conventions, *k* traditionally representing a "harsher" sound than *c* (a distinction that does not make much sense within the science of phonetics). This difference is no doubt related to the existence in the language of an alternative, "soft" pronunciation of *c* and to the "hardening" effect of adding a *k* to a *c* as found, for instance, in

[19]Bolinger wishes to exclude the syllable *cran* (as in *cranberry*) from the set of English morphemes on the ground that it has no semantic force ("On Defining the Morpheme," in *Forms of English,* 187); yet it is still capable of eliciting echoes of other words. As Bolinger himself recognizes, fixed dividing lines between meaningful and meaningless elements in language, and between one word and another, are impossible, given the multiple overlapping of sound-sequences in the language; see also his "Rime, Assonance, and Morpheme Analysis," *Forms of English,* 203–26. The phenomenon of "folk etymology" discussed in chapter 4 above is one way in which these echoes affect the language as a historical process and as a synchronic system.

the distinction between *lacing* and *lacking*.[20] The foregrounding of
the *k* in our example is increased by the fact that its appearance
contravenes the spelling conventions of English, which demand a *c* in
initial position before an *r*. Going further, one could speculate on the
association of *k* with Northern European and *c* with Southern European languages, and the familiar opposition between stereotypes of
North and South, cold and warm, Gothic and Mediterranean, barba-
rism and culture—an association traceable, for instance, in the differing connotations for English readers of *Kaiser* and *Caesar* or in the
spelling of *Amerika* with a *k* used in satiric magazines during the Viet-
nam war and in a 1987 television film about a Soviet occupation of the
United States.

More generally, to respond to onomatopoeia of any kind it is necessary to have learned how to do so, because it means overriding the
normal procedures of language comprehension whereby the sound
functions, in Saussure's vocabulary, entirely as a differential entity
and not as a positive term. (To achieve this mode of reading may
however, entail unlearning something that constituted a crucial
breakthrough in one's early acquisition of language; see Fónagy,
"Motivation et remotivation.") In sum, onomatopoeia requires *interpretation* as much as any other system of signs does; it is a convention among conventions. Like any aspect of style to which readers
respond in a relatively consistent way, onomatopoeia must be seen as
a matter of *langue* as well as *parole:* any specific instances can be
understood only in relation to a shared system.[21] Reading a literary
text is not a "natural" activity, a simple transference to the field of
literature of the linguistic ability to read grammatical sentences; it is a

[20]Morris Halle has suggested that the letter *k* may be used regularly in English
orthography as a marked alternative to the unmarked *c*, in cases where the rule for
velar softening (which turns /k/ into /s/) does not apply (personal communication).

[21]These conventions are to a large extent language-specific. Thus Jean Paulhan cites
as examples of "words which seem to us to imitate a natural sound" *glas* (knell), *fouet*
(whip), *rire* (laugh), *cingler* (to lash) (*La preuve par l'étymologie*, 41); but the onomatopoeic
appropriateness here may not be so obvious to an anglophone ear. It may even be the
case that the sounds we hear are already colored by the conventions of the language we
speak: the native English speaker, for whom the bell tolls, perhaps perceives on Sunday
mornings a different sound from the French speaker hearing "le glas d'une cloche"—
and both find a degree of onomatopoeic precision in their language as a result. For a
full discussion of the conventional determination of "iconic" signs, see Umberto Eco, *A
Theory of Semiotics*, 191–217.

learned skill, and it has a history, which is part of the history of our culture, and a future, which we cannot predict.

(4) Although we have been discussing onomatopoeia as if it were a purely aural device, it is evident that the effect of these sequences is partly *visual*. If one can imagine *Ulysses* broadcast as a radio serial, the contrast between *c* and *k* would be wasted on even the most attentive listener. A further contrast lies in the visual appearance of the letters themselves, between the sharp angularity of *k* and the smooth curve of *c*, again making the former more suitable—within the conventions in force—for the depiction of a harsh sound.[22] A mere glance at the passage, in fact, signals to the eye the presence of sequences of letters which go beyond the normal configurations of written English, and the visual patterns contribute to the mimetic impressions received by the reader—the short, visually contrasted segments of "Fff! Oo. Rrpr"; the identical repetitions of "kran kran kran"; the undifferentiated extension of "Kraaaaaa," with a run of letters all the same height; and the more varied continuities (and presumably sonorities) of "Pprrpffrrppffff," where the graphic shapes not only differ from one another but protrude above and below the line. (The reader familiar with musical scores might even respond subliminally to this up-and-down movement as a representation of pitch changes.) The unpronounceable examples mentioned earlier rely even more on apprehension by means of the eye: they remain resolutely visual, rendering any attempt to convert them into sound arbitrary and inadequate. One does not have to go to *Finnegans Wake* to find a text in which neither eye nor ear is sufficient on its own; indeed, one does not even have to go to Joyce or to "experimental" writing.

(5) Turning now to the common notion that onomatopoeia constitutes an unusually precise representation of the physical qualities of the external world, we may ask how successful we would be in identifying the sounds referred to by these strings of letters outside the specific context of this passage from *Ulysses*. Joyce in fact poses this question at the beginning of the chapter, as if to underline the point

[22]Compare John Orr's observation that "there are people who find a thrill in the useless and unetymological *h* of *ghost*, and a seventeenth-century Frenchman is said to have found a pictorial value in the *h* of *houlette*, 'a shepherd's crook' " (*Words and Sounds*, 26–27). Bolinger discusses the semantic force of the appearance of words in "Visual Morphemes," *Forms of English*, 267–76.

in advance. Among the brief fragments that open "Sirens" are the following, without any accompanying explanation:

Fff! Oo! (11.58)
Rrrpr. Kraa. Kraandl. (11.60)

These enigmatic scraps, like all the items in the list, convey very little in terms of the fictional setting and can be interpreted only retrospectively. Appearing where they do, they highlight the dependence of linguistic formations—onomatopoeic and otherwise—on their immediate context. Thus our "hearing" of the tram in the final passage of "Sirens" depends entirely on a clue not given in the prelude, the word "tram" itself, without which we could make no sense of the onomatopoeic sequence. And the fart has already been carefully prepared for earlier in the chapter, without, it is true, anything so gross as the word "fart" crossing Bloom's mind or the text's surface. (Molly, in a similar predicament at the end of the book, is not so squeamish.) Several intimations of flatulence have appeared at intervals on the preceding pages:

Rrr. (11.1155)
Rrrrrrrsss. (11.1162)
. . . bloom felt wind wound round inside.
Gassy thing that cider: binding too. Wait. (11.1178)
. . . then all of a soft sudden wee little wee little pipy wind.
Pwee! A wee little wind piped eeee. In Bloom's little wee. (11.1201)
Rrrrrr.
I feel I want. . . . (11.1216)
Wish I could. Wait. (11.1224)
I must really. Fff. Now if I did that at a banquet. (11.1247)
Must be the cider or perhaps the burgund. (11.1268)

The final release is therefore the culmination of a little private drama, a kind of interior dialogue, and we are left in no doubt as to the sound represented by the letters on the page before us. (Though some readers of refined sensibilities may have taken the problem to be the less embarrassing one of an urge to belch: the text seems to offer this possibility in its references to the gassiness of the cider and to the Persian custom of burping at banquets, and in the apparent, if deceptive, hint in "Must be the bur." Such an uncertainty as to oral and anal alternatives would be entirely in keeping with the rest of the episode, as my argument in the next chapter will suggest.) The same letters can in fact perform very different onomatopoeic tasks: in *Ulysses* a sequence of *es* stands not only for a release of wind, as in "A wee little wind piped eeee," but for a stick trailing along a path ("Steeeeeeeeeeeephen!" [1.629]), a creaking door ("ee: cree" [7.50] and "ee" [11.965]), a turning doorhandle ["Theeee!" [15. 2694]), and a distant trainwhistle ("Frseeeeeeeefronnnng" [18.595], "Frseeeeeeeeeeeeeeeeeeeeefrong" [18.874], "sweeeee . . . eeeee" [18.908]). In the last example the context does not allow us to distinguish that trainwhistle from Molly's own anal release.

(6) For onomatopoeia to work at all, however, it is not enough to know from the context what sound is supposed to be represented; it is also necessary to have some prior familiarity with that sound. The capacity of any sign to refer, for a given individual, is subject to this condition, as C. S. Peirce clearly saw (at the same time acknowledging that this was not an immediately obvious truth to everyone):

> The Sign can only represent the Object and tell about it. It cannot furnish acquaintance with or recognition of that Object; for that is what is meant in this volume by the Object of a Sign; namely, that with which it presupposes an acquaintance in order to convey some further information concerning it. No doubt there will be readers who will say they cannot comprehend this. They think a Sign need not relate to anything otherwise known, and can make neither head nor tail of the statement that every sign must relate to such an Object. But if there be anything that conveys information and yet has absolutely no relation nor reference to anything with which the person to whom it conveys that information has, when he comprehends that information, the slightest acquaintance, direct or indirect—and a very strange sort of information that would be—the vehicle of that sort of information is not, in this volume, called a Sign. (*Philosophical Writings*, 100)[23]

[23]Socrates advances a related argument in Plato's *Cratylus:* if names are purely conventional, as Hermogenes argues, we must already know what it is they name, as words will not inform us (433e). E. H. Gombrich cites and discusses a pertinent comment from Philostratus' third-century life of Apollonius of Tyana: "No one can understand the painted horse or bull unless he knows what such creatures are like" (*Art and Illusion*, 181–82, 260–61). To the extent that language can be shown to be constitutive of experience rather than a reflection of it, of course, this argument loses its force.

The onomatopoeic representation, even when it breaks free from the restrictions imposed by the lexicon, does not escape this general semiotic rule. Bloom produces a sound with which we are all familiar, but we are less likely to know what a 1904 Dublin tram sounded like and so are less likely to be impressed by the imitative appropriateness of Joyce's phonetic formulae. To take a more extreme example, readers who do not know the sound of a badly adjusted gaslight (among whom I number myself) will not be able to find out what it is from the letters given to represent the noise in the "Circe" episode: "Pooah! Pfuiiiiiii!" (15.2280). (We might suspect, from the much more helpful lexical description *the gasjet wails whistling,* that there is a Circean extravagance about this utterance as about so many utterances in that chapter, but even if the representation were as accurate as letters could make it, we would still be little the wiser.) Onomatopoeia is not a means of gaining knowledge about the world; after all, we can praise a literary text for the precision of its descriptions only if we are already fully acquainted with what the text purports to be describing.

(7) Even when these two conditions, an unambiguous situating context and prior familiarity with the sound, are met, the imitative effects of onomatopoeia—even of this very direct type—remain extremely imprecise. What, for instance, are we to make of "Oo"? Is this a voiced (or thought) exclamation of Bloom's? An accompanying burp? A noisy passage in the anal performance? (As every actor knows, the letter "O" can represent a wide variety of speech sounds.) Are the "rrr" sequences here and earlier to be taken as stomach rumbles, or as premonitory activity in the bowels? And what aspects of the tram's sound are represented? The other noises made by trams in the novel provide no help: earlier they are to be heard "honking" (5.131) and "clanging ringing" (7.10), and in "Circe" a sandstrewer bears down on Bloom, "its trolley *hissing* on the wire," while the motorman "*bangs* his footgong" and the brake "*cracks* violently" (15.186, 187, 190). One reader, at least, does not even hear a tram at the end of "Sirens," but something more euphonious: David Hayman, in a plot summary of *Ulysses,* refers to Bloom's "carefully releasing a final fizzle of fart to the sound of band-music."[24] Most readers would no doubt regard this

---

[24]Hayman, *Ulysses: The Mechanics of Meaning,* 142. Compare 112–14, where Hayman takes Bloom's thoughts about a drummer in a military band as evidence that there is a real band on the Liffey quay.

as a highly idiosyncratic interpretation, but it does testify to the lack of a wholly obvious sonic referent.

Only a few nonvocal sounds, in fact, can be imitated with any degree of closeness by the speech organs, and the significance (and pleasure) to be drawn from Bloom's fart lies partly in its exceptional character: it is unusually amenable to vocal imitation in being a sound produced by an orifice of the human body. This fact enables the sequence "fff" to be appropriate in both the ways open to onomatopoeic imitation, in its articulatory processes and in its acoustic properties—it is both produced like and sounds like a fart. (Even then, we take little pleasure in accuracy of imitation for its own sake: a more precise rendition of a fart than "Pprrpffrrppffff" would be "Ffffffffffffff.")[25] Few of the sounds that we hear, and that writers attempt to convey, are as well qualified as this one is for imitative representation. We might even say that the only fully successful onomatopoeia occurs when the human voice is imitated, which is what written language, in a sense, does all the time—except, that is, when it is attempting nonlexical onomatopoeia.

(8) A further complication is most obvious in the case of nonlexical onomatopoeia, though it remains a possibility in all onomatopoeic devices. The reader who responds to these strings of letters as attempts at direct representation of familiar sounds is likely to go beyond the normal phonological rules of English in essaying an imitation (in the imagination if not in actual utterance) more accurate than language normally permits. Doing so amounts to treating the sequences as instructions to the reader: [*sound of fart*], [*sound of passing tram*]. If we look at it in this way, mimetic precision in the string of

[25]Occasionally, it is true, there is pleasure to be had from an author's ingenuity in exploiting the limited resources of the English phonological system to represent a sound very different from the human voice, as when, in the "Sirens" episode, the changing configuration of the oral cavity in producing a sequence of vowels mimics the alteration in the sound-producing properties of a gradually filling chamber pot: "Diddleiddle addleaddle ooddleooddle" (11.984). But even here the effect depends on the context, on conventional onomatopoeic devices, on lexical associations (e.g., "widdle," "piddle," "puddle," "little," "diddy"), and on visual patterns, and we enjoy the sequence more for its unlikeliness than for its accuracy. (The technique of heightening the reader's awareness of vowels as sounds by varying them in a sequence in which the consonants remain unchanged had already been used in *A Portrait*: "From here and from there came the sounds of the cricketbats through the soft grey air. They said: pick, pack, pock, puck: like drops of water in a fountain slowly falling in the brimming bowl" [41].)

letters is completely unnecessary, and the reader is in fact likely to do a better job of imitating or imagining the sound required if he or she is unhindered by the writer's attempt to make it compatible with the normal phonological properties of the English language. Difficulty in pronunciation according to the normal rules of English may also encourage the reader's inventiveness: strictly speaking, for example, it is impossible to give a plosive any degree of duration, but the doubling of *p* in the final onomatopoeic effusion of "Sirens" may suggest a continuant very close to the sound represented. And most readers probably take the unpronounceability of "Mrkrgnao!" as an invitation to imitate a cat's cry in a way less stylized than the conventional "Miaow!" In "Circe" Joyce plays with the curious relationship between stage directions describing utterances and the utterances themselves, as in the gasjet's wailing whistle, and we might ask whether in "Lestrygonians" Davy Byrne's yawn "Iiiiiichaaaaaaach!" (8.970), which Hugh Kenner praises for its "deftness of rhythmic imitation" (*Ulysses*, 85), would even be recognized without a prior announcement of what is coming. (When Byrne is assigned a similar string of letters in "Circe"—"Iiiiiiiiiaaaaaaach!" (15.1697)—interpretation is again aided by the stage direction [*"yawning"*].) At the same time, the extraordinary sequence of letters clearly gives the reader more scope for a bravura performance and in so doing provides greater pleasure than would a mere "Davy Byrne yawned loudly."

It can be demonstrated, then, that any sense of appropriateness which an example of nonlexical onomatopoeia may produce is not primarily the result of an unusually close resemblance between the sounds of language and the sounds of the external world. This being the case, it is easier to understand how the experience can be accompanied by a heightened consciousness of the sounds of language themselves. Indeed, the inevitable incongruity of such devices frequently intrigues and amuses the reader, even while the letters successfully perform their referential duties. Jakobson's double emphasis seems justified, therefore, at least as far as nonlexical onomatopoeia is concerned: the series of linguistic sounds *and* their referents receive simultaneous, if separate, enhancement. But this pleasurable double foregrounding is achieved by something other than the art of imitation.[26]

[26]"Concrete poetry" that eschews recognizable lexical items has to rely on the conventions and signifying procedures discussed here, and the more it dispenses with these

"Liquor for His Lips": Lexical Onomatopoeia

"Sirens" is rich in lexical onomatopoeia, and several varieties, not sharply distinguishable, can be enumerated. Nearest to the examples we have been discussing are words that, by convention, represent the occurrence of sounds themselves, puncturing the narrative in the same way as do the sounds suggested by nonlexical onomatopoeia: "Jingle" (11.212), "Tink" (11.286), "Smack" (11.413), "Twang" (11.811), "Tap" (11.933–1274 passim). Or, less directly, the sound is referred to by a verb, adjective, or noun that seems to function onomatopoeically as well as semantically, often drawing neighboring words into the imitative network as well: "its buzzing prongs" (11.316), "Clock clacked" (11.383), "Jingle a tinkle jaunted" (11.456), "One rapped on a door, one tapped with a knock" (11.986). The individual words may have no semantic connection with sounds and still have this effect, as in these contrasting evocations of some of the chapter's music: "Brightly the keys, all twinkling, linked, all harpsichording" (11.324); "the voice of dark age, of unlove, earth's fatigue made grave approach and painful" (11.1007). Or the symbolism may involve some aspect of the scene in addition to, or other than, its sounds: "Sauntering sadly, gold no more, she twisted twined a hair" (11.82); "Shebronze, dealing from her oblique jar thick syrupy liquor for his lips, looked as it flowed" (11.365); "His gouty paws plumped chords. Plumped, stopped abrupt" (11.452). There are also instances that fall between the lexical and nonlexical categories, where the word is deformed for onomatopoeic purposes: "end-lessnessnessness" (11.750), "hissss" (11.985), "lugugugubrious" (11.1005). (Again, as these examples indicate, the visual properties of language play an important part, though in the discussion that follows I confine myself to questions of sound.)

In all these examples the reader is likely to sense a peculiar involvement in the physical features referred to by the words, more potent than anything achieved by nonlexical onomatopoeia. Clearly, a large part of the experience is derived from factors we have already discussed: lexical onomatopoeia is dependent for its effectiveness on the reader's internalization of the rules of English graphology, pho-

---

as well the more empty of signification (and, to many readers or hearers, interest) it becomes. Joyce's method in *Finnegans Wake* is the reverse: to *maximize* lexical associations.

nology, and morphology, as well as on a knowledge of the onomatopoeic conventions of a specific literary culture. Thus we can trace the operation of phonesthetic constellations (behind "twinkling, linked," for instance, hover such words as "tinkle," "clink," "ting," etc.) and of conventional onomatopoeic associations, such as those of the back vowels in "The voice of dark age, of unlove." As with nonlexical onomatopoeia, any feeling of precision must depend both on the fictional context and the reader's familiarity with the sensory phenomenon in question, and on the degree to which the reader treats the onomatopoeia as an invitation to perform mimetically. In addition, there is the sheer power of certain *semantic* features in conveying sensory impressions (the neologism "unlove," for instance, or the verb "plumped"). But all these factors seem inadequate to account for the specific and distinctive quality of many of Joyce's examples, in which the physical world does seem to come closer than is usually possible in language. With cases of lexical onomatopoeia we cannot test the words' imitative power by removing them from their semantic context, as we could with Bloom's fart and the passing tram. That context is present in the words themselves, and it is virtually impossible to hear a sound *as* a sound when it simultaneously informs us what sound it is supposed to represent.[27] W. K. Wimsatt has observed that "it seems probable that any name of a sound we can think of in our own language will strike us with a degree of onomatopoeic force," and he cites, among others, "fizz," "bang," "boom," "tinkle," "jingle," "jangle," "click," "clank," "clang." "Try to think," he challenges the reader, "of the name of a sound that does *not* have a degree of such suggestiveness" ("In Search of Verbal Mimesis," 65).[28] Here our in-

[27]Sometimes, however, the context that gives the clue to the "mimetic" effect is separated from the onomatopoeia itself, as in William Carlos Williams's "I can hear an engine / breathing—somewhere / in the night: / —soft coal, soft coal, / soft coal!" ("The Injury"). Although the last line uses normal words for its "imitation," it is closer to nonlexical onomatopoeia than to the lexical items under discussion.

[28]In *A Portrait* Joyce dwells on the power of this kind of suggestiveness in early life. Thus the young Stephen mediates on a word that he has heard at school: "Suck was a queer word. . . . The sound was ugly. Once he had washed his hands in the lavatory of the Wicklow Hotel and his father pulled the stopper up by the chain after and the dirty water went down through the hole in the basin. And when it had all gone down slowly the hole in the basin had made a sound like that: suck" (11). Stephen is obviously responding to the connotations of the word (and, perhaps, to a phonic association with another word with special power of which he is dimly aware). Later, the word "kiss" is made to seem equally onomatopoeic: "His mother put her lips on his cheek; her lips were soft and they wetted his cheek; and they made a tiny little noise: kiss" (15).

vestigation—which is to say, Joyce's investigation—of nonlexical onomatopoeia has a special usefulness: if a great part of our sense of the phonetic appropriateness of "Rrrpr" or "kran kran kran" has to do with our knowledge of the English language, of the rhetorical traditions of English literature, of the scene already laid before us in the novel, and not with the imitative accuracy of their sounds as such, we can be reasonably sure that objective similarity is of little importance in these lexical examples.

If, then, readers experience a sense of "rightness" about the sounds of these passages—and the praise that has been lavished on "Sirens" to this effect suggests that it is a common response—it is clearly not to be explained in terms of realistic imitation. On the other hand, the notion of a "set toward the message" does not help very much either, because we no longer have the immediate self-advertisement of non-lexical onomatopoeia. Jakobson argues that the distinctive "poetic" response is produced by "parallelism" in poetic language,[29] but as a sufficiently refined analysis could be used to demonstrate the presence of complex sound patterns in virtually any specimen of language, it remains to be explained why in a particular piece those patterns function onomatopoeically. The reader's experience is, after all, not consciousness of speech sounds as pure sounds. To the degree that *non*lexical onomatopoeia functions directly as mimesis, it may be perceived in this way: there would be some truth, at least, in saying that the letters in Joyce's "fff" encode sounds, not signifiers (which is why such devices can only be occasional features, fissures in the semantic web of the text which remind us that language is *not* generally mimetic). But the experience we are trying to account for in lexical onomatopoeia—the experience that nonlexical onomatopoeia does not offer—is one of *heightened meaning,* and an approach that emphasizes "sheer sound," although it provides a useful corrective to the notion of onomatopoeia as a form of realism, fails to explain this experience and the special pleasure associated with it.

[29]For example: "Notwithstanding the varied proofs of speakers' and listeners' thorough attention to speech sounds, the pattern of ordinary language is nowhere near the autonomous, in fact guiding role sounds and their distinctive features play in poetry, which promotes the deliberate accumulation of similar sounds and sound groups to the constitutive device of the sequence" (Jakobson and Waugh, *Sound Shape,* 230). In "Linguistics and Poetics" Jakobson had more scrupulously insisted that the notions of "parallelism" and "equivalence" were not identical with patterning and similarity (see Attridge, "Closing Statement"), but in the case of onomatopoeia it is clear that patterning of physically similar sounds is crucial.

I would argue instead that what is important—and pleasurable—in a successful example of lexical onomatopoeia (an example that has more effect than the mere deployment of onomatopoeic conventions would have) is the momentary and surprising reciprocal relationship established between phonetic and semantic properties, a mutual reinforcement that intensifies *both* aspects of language. Not only do the phonetic properties point to the semantic content, but the semantic content points back to the sounds. We have seen that this cannot be a simple relationship of imitation or resemblance. It seems to depend upon a semantic content that is relatable to some aspect of the physical characteristics of speech, whether that aspect is objectively present, like the expulsion of air or a quality of rhythm, or produced by the conventions of onomatopoeia, like "hard" and "soft" consonants. (For an example of a physical property that cannot be given special vividness in this way, we might think of color, which can be enhanced onomatopoeically only through a metaphorical translation into properties that do occur in our conventional notions of speech, like "gentleness" or "harshness.") The strongest effects of this kind occur when both levels are marked, when a more than usually powerful semantic evocation of a suitable physical property is achieved in words that constitute a more than usually patterned phonetic sequence (*whether or not* that patterning involves anything that could be deemed specifically appropriate to the properties in question).[30]

One of these properties of language might be able to operate on its own: if the semantic content has a sufficient intensity (through the use of uncommon lexical items, verbal accumulations, unusual metaphors, sharp sensory detail, etc.) and is concerned with a striking physical property of the right sort, it may light up an otherwise unnoticeable pattern at the level of sound. A possible example is "His gouty paws plumped chords." On the other hand, a strongly marked sound pattern ("One rapped on a door, one tapped with a knock") or a transgression of the linguistic rules ("lugugugubrious") may induce a more acute appreciation of a relatively unemphasized semantic con-

---

[30]"More than usually" conceals, of course, all the problems of linguistic deviation that are at issue in this book. My claim is not that there is a measurable degree of deviance from some norm at which these effects begin to operate; it is simply that the *perception* of unusual semantic salience or patterning may function in this way. Whether this perception occurs in any given instance of reading is dependent on a host of factors determining the specific interpretative situation in question and the cultural context in which it occurs.

tent, as long as it has some suitable physical association. We cannot, in any case, tell for certain if one or the other level has priority, because the experience is always one of interdependence and indivisibility between semantic and phonetic properties (and in this respect lexical onomatopoeia is very different from nonlexical onomatopoeia, in which the two properties are liable to diverge). The result is neither direct apprehension of the physical world nor a focus on the sounds of speech as sounds; rather, it might be called a heightened experience of language *as language*. By that I do not mean language as a mere sequence of sounds, or a series of physical articulations, or even as sounds given identity by a system of differences, but language in the act of *producing meaning* and thereby momentarily fusing the abstractness of *langue* and the concreteness of *parole*, the ahistoricity of the system and the historicity of this moment in time, the shared social convention upon which language depends and the individuality of my vocal activities as I speak these words.

An example may make the argument clearer. When we read (aloud or with a mental image of the sound) the description of Boylan's sloe gin as "thick syrupy liquor for his lips," we respond on the one hand to an image powerfully physical by virtue of the tautologically double adjective, the slight unexpectedness of "liquor" instead of "liquid," and the focus on a part of the mouth with connotations of sexual rather than alimentary pleasure. We respond on the other hand to the pattern of sounds, which connects "thick" to "syrupy" by way of "liquor" and "lips," creating what we might call a "nonce-constellation."[31] But it is their *conjunction* which has the further effect that characterizes strong lexical onomatopoeia, the effect of heightening those features of the spoken English language (or indeed all speech) which might be deemed appropriate to the referent of the passage— here, its richness of texture, its fluidity, the way it is molded and savored by the lips and other organs of the mouth. The mind, in responding to the semantic content of the verbal sequence, is sensitized to certain physical properties of speech; simultaneously, in

[31]Bella Millett has pointed out to me that "liquor" and "lips" are also connected by an implied pun on the absent word "lick"; the adjective "oblique," recently restored in the corrected text ("Shebronze, dealing from her oblique jar thick syrupy liquor for his lips, looked as it flowed"), strengthens this phonic implication and shares echoes with "dealing" and "looked" as well. The operation of nonce-constellations is probably more significant than genuine phonesthemes in onomatopoeic effects; see, for instance, John Hollander's exemplary account in *Vision and Resonance,* 157, of Tennyson's regularly cited murmuring bees.

responding to the foregrounding of the physical properties of speech achieved by the unusual patterning of˙ phonemes, it is sensitized to certain features of the semantic content. Any feeling of *precision* the reader experiences is the product of this mutual reinforcement, not of some perfect match between the sounds of language and the properties of sloe gin. (Indeed, a feeling of precision may stem from an avoidance of detailed description in favor of a device that achieves intensity and immediacy by virtue of its phonetic properties. Thus the "bluehued" flowers on the table [11.458], though only vaguely described, are vividly "present" because of the aptness of those sounds in the aural texture of a chapter studded with plays on Bloom's surname.)

The achievement of referential intensity in this phrase, therefore, is not a matter of the specific "mimeticism" of the phones [i] or [l] or [p] in relation to sloe gin or the drinking thereof, as traditional accounts of onomatopoeia or sound-symbolism would argue; such imitativeness is, as we have seen, a very small part even of nonlexical onomatopoeia and could probably be "discovered" in any sounds by sufficiently ingenious and persuasive critics.[32] All speech involves muscular movements in the oral cavity, rhythmic contractions of the diaphragm, the tensing and relaxing of the larynx, sensations of changing pitch and volume, the passage of air over the surfaces of the speech organs, and so on; and the particular aspects of this complex physical process which function in a given example of onomatopoeia depend less on the specific configurations of the phonetic sequence in question than on the meaning of the passage.[33] The result is a diversion of attention away from the referent in itself to the *activity* of referring carried out by language—a diversion achieved in this example both by the semantic content, with its emphasis on physical tex-

[32]See my discussion of etymological associations in chapter 4 above, p. 108. An example of the critical traps that can be laid by onomatopoeia occurs in Joyce's description of a "dusty seascape" in the Ormond hotel: "A lovely girl, her veil awave upon the wind upon the headland, wind around her" (11.591). The patterning of iambic rhythm, assonance, consonance, and repetition draws attention to the visual interrelations of the picture, and vice versa; but many readers deduce from the sound-qualities of the phrase that it describes a song being sung in the bar-room (including Zack Bowen in the standard reference-book *Musical Allusions in the Works of James Joyce*, 172–73).

[33]An exception might be when the passage refers to speech-sounds and the activity of the speech-organs in producing them, as occurs on the opening page of Humbert Humbert's story in Nabokov's *Lolita:* "the tip of the tongue taking a trip of three steps down the palate to tap, at three, on the teeth. Lo. Lee. Ta" (see Attridge, *The Rhythms of English Poetry*, 292).

tures and oral experience, and by the phonetic content, with its artful patterning. And it is that focus of attention on the materiality of language *as it does its work of bringing meaning into being* that has so often been interpreted as mimetic or iconic representation, because the experience is unquestionably one of increased vividness or intensity of signification.[34] The texture of the words Joyce has chosen to describe sloe gin does nothing to specify the substance's qualities further than the words' meaning already does (in cooperation with the reader's familiarity with syrupy liquids and appreciation of the fictional context, which includes an awareness of Boylan's sensualism), but it creates what Valéry calls the "illusion" (and in literature illusions are what matter) of a more direct involvement in those qualities than language normally attains.[35] And it is only an apparent paradox that this illusion is created—as Jakobson realized—by means of a heightening of our apprehension of the medium that stands *between* us and direct experience itself. Understood in this way, onomatopoeia might be seen as a model for all literary language.[36]

The Art of Onomatopoeia

What emerges from Joyce's verbal antics is that the notion of onomatopoeia as objective similarity between the linguistic sign and

[34]This account of "poetic" language as involving a heightened awareness of the production of meaning by language is, I would argue, more amenable to a materialist philosophical (and political) position than an emphasis on the material signifier alone, which is often invoked in such contexts. As Jameson trenchantly puts it, "the Lacanian notion of a 'material signifier' . . . and a few feeble allusions to the sonorous vibration of language in air and space are appealed to as a grounding for some genuinely materialistic view. Marxism is, however, not a mechanical but a historical materialism: it does not assert the primacy of matter so much as it insists on an ultimate determination by the mode of production" (*The Political Unconscious*, 45).

[35]It is perhaps significant that Jakobson, in quoting Pope's line "The sound must seem an echo to the sense," replaces "seem" with "be" ("Quest for the Essence of Language," 357). Jakobson's positivistic stance has little room for illusions.

[36]De Man touches on the significance of onomatopoeic effects in some suggestive paragraphs in "The Resistance to Theory" (9–11). He detects a tension within the writing of Jakobson and Barthes between a desire to endorse the Cratylist position and a recognition that "the convergence of sound and meaning [is] a mere *effect* which language can perfectly well achieve, but which bears no substantial relation, by analogy or by ontologically grounded imitation, to anything beyond that particular effect. [It] operates on the level of the signifier and contains no responsible pronouncement on the nature of the world—despite its powerful potential to create the opposite illusion" (10). De Man expands this point to a consideration of imitation more generally, insisting, on the same grounds, that literariness is not primarily a *mimetic* quality.

its referent, or between signifier and signified, trivializes a fruitful, complex, and characteristic feature of literary language and reduces reading to a mechanical, rule-governed routine. (We might extend this moral to wider domains of mimetic theory and ideology.) It is not at all difficult to write a sentence with open, back vowels which evokes vast palls of darkness or large, hollow, resounding vaults, or a sentence with close, front vowels which depicts shrill insects or little, pinched, squeezed niches (word processors, I have read, can now be programmed to produce sentences with such patterns). But it is extraordinarily difficult to write a sentence that offers endlessly repeatable (and variable) pleasures in its very turns of sound. Another of Valéry's comments on the subject emphasizes the unamenability of such achievements to any precise explanation or prediction: "The power of verse stems from an *indefinable* harmony between what it *says* and *is*. 'Indefinable' enters into the definition. This harmony must not be definable. When it is, it becomes imitative, and that is not good. The impossibility of defining this relationship, together with the impossibility of denying it, constitutes the essence of verse."[37] No doubt the effects I have pointed to are only part of the explanation for the peculiar density and inexhaustibility that language, as material medium, is capable of in its literary manifestations; but I hope it is clear that the complexities of the reading experience involve both the Hermogenist illusion of the self-reflexive word and the Cratylist illusion of unmediated signification. Jakobson's desire to retain in his definition of poetic language *both* a heightened attention to the sounds of language and their organization into structures *and* an intensified experience of their semantic import is justified, although his attempt to crush several kinds of verbal effect into a single phenomenon and to promote it to the defining feature of literature may not be. Onomatopoeia as I have described it is a feature of a particular literary tradition and a particular mode of reading. It may highlight, as I have suggested, some more general aspects of the operation of literary texts within that tradition, but it cannot be used as a litmus test of what is and is not literature.

Against my argument it might be said that Joyce gives us merely a *parody* of onomatopoeia, always on the verge of incapacitating itself by its own indiscreetness, and that the real thing involves a process of imitation far more subtle than anything in "Sirens"—taking effect, it

[37]*Tel Quel, Oeuvres* 2:637; quoted by Genette in "Valéry and the Poetics of Language," 366–67.

might be felt, at a completely unconscious level and operating in intimate conjunction with all other aspects of language. But if this is parody, it is achieved only by heightening and isolating what must be present in any device that we claim to be onomatopoeic. If onomatopoeia is to be judged in terms of the accuracy with which it enables the sounds of language to reproduce the sounds and other physical characteristics of the nonlinguistic world, then the more successful it is (and, as we have seen, it is only within severe limits that it can ever be successful), the more it is bound to come into conflict with the necessarily abstract nature of the language system, foregrounding the physical properties of speech (and writing) and drawing attention to itself as a rhetorical device instead of melting away in a presentation of unmediated reality.[38] The more it succeeds, that is, the more it fails, and the critic who points out a subtle onomatopoeic effect only adds to the failure by making readers more conscious of the onomatopoeia—unless we relinquish the idea of onomatopoeia as a mode of realism, and see it as a literary device that can generate a variety of pleasures, all of them focused on language itself and on its capacity to elude and exceed any rules we might construct for it.[39]

This discussion raises, of course, the whole question of art as imitation. We need remark only what has often been remarked before, that if art were to imitate its subject perfectly it would cease to be art. It is therefore precisely in its distance from the world of nonart, its "artificiality," that its raison d'être, and the sources of the pleasure it

[38]In *The Rhythms of English Poetry* I made a distinction between iconic devices that function *mimetically*, as part of the reading process, and those that function *emblematically*, by the application of a conscious interpretative strategy (288). But to the extent that onomatopoeia is appreciated for what it is, it becomes emblematic; on the other hand, so long as its working remains subliminal or unconscious, we have no direct evidence of its existence. As a literary device we can point to, that is to say, onomatopoeia does not achieve "transparency," in Ullmann's sense: it is, as the Group μ put it, "opaque to the extent that it shows itself before it shows the world" (*A General Rhetoric*, 12).

[39]Onomatopoeia, as I have described it, provides a reassuring and pleasurable sense of the smooth and powerful operation of language; but as soon as it becomes exorbitant, or involves the breakdown of lexical integrity (as occurs occasionally in *Ulysses* and continually in *Finnegans Wake*), it endangers the norms and procedures of language as they are generally understood to a greater degree even than purely nonlexical onomatopoeia, which can be accommodated as a momentary suspension of the rules. It also provides a comic challenge to the myth of fixed, authentic, and knowable meaning directly embodied in language. Most literary texts therefore avoid it in anything other than moderate and sparing manifestations.

offers, may be seen to lie.[40] Joyce, in his onomatopoeic acrobatics, is playing with the impossibility of language's ever escaping the condition of being language, the absurdity of the desire (which does not cancel the desire) to make language sound like nonlanguage, the inappropriateness (and at the same time the inevitability) of so much praise being lavished on fiction for its approximation to reality. Onomatopoeia therefore can be seen as a paradigm not just for all literary language, as I suggested earlier, but for all languages, indeed, for all representation; its effectiveness lies in the fact that it necessarily displaces that to which it refers.[41] In fiction there is a further paradox, that what language refers to is something that it created in the first place. Bloom's unforgettable fart is presented to us by the same linguistic event that asserts the impossibility of presenting it; its only existence is in those marks on the page which fail, so delightfully, to bring it into existence.

[40]This insight has a history as long as the identification of art with imitation, from Plato's observation that a name which fully reproduced the thing it referred to would not be a name but an instance of the thing (*Cratylus* 432d) to Derrida's discussion of Plato's "mimesis" in "The Double Session" (*Dissemination*, 185–93). For a discussion of eighteenth-century versions, see Todorov, *Theories of the Symbol*, chap. 4.

[41]Implicated in the question of imitation, therefore, is the question of the supplement, and the relation of art to nature, discussed in chapters 2 and 3 above. Derrida discusses this network of terms as they occur in Rousseau's *Essay on the Origin of Languages*, in *Grammatology*, 203–16; the following passage (215–16) and its quotation of part of Rousseau's discussion of musical imitation (the italics are Derrida's) indicate in outline the connections among these terms, as well as giving a sense of the degree to which Rousseau's writing anticipates the arguments of this chapter.

What does Rousseau say without saying, see without seeing? That substitution has always already begun; that imitation, principle of art, has always already interrupted natural plenitude; that, having to be a *discourse*, it has always already broached presence in differance; that in Nature it is always that which supplies Nature's lack, a voice that is substituted for the voice of Nature. But he says it without drawing any conclusions:

". . . Thunder, murmuring waters, winds, tempests, are but poorly rendered by simple chords. Whatever one does, noise alone does not speak to the spirit at all. The objects must speak in order to be understood. *In all imitation, some form of discourse must substitute for the voice of nature.* The musician who would represent noise by noise deceives himself. *He knows nothing of either the weakness or the strength of his art,* concerning which his judgment is tasteless and unenlightened. Let him realize that he will have to render noise in song; that to produce the croaking of frogs, he will have to have them sing. *For it is not enough to imitate them;* he must do so touchingly and pleasantly" (*On the Origin of Languages,* trans. John H. Moran and Alexander Gode [New York, 1966], 58).

Chapter 6

Literature as Deviation: Syntax, Style, and the Body in *Ulysses*

Norms and Deviations

*U*lysses is a text that fails to meet both of the contradictory demands the cultural tradition makes upon the language of literature, that such language be both clearly distinguishable from and closely related to the language of the quotidian world. The fact that, like *Dubliners*, it incorporates items of ordinary Dublin speech—including taboo words and precise personal and topographical references—was a cause of annoyance and resistance when the book appeared, and Joyce was held to have failed in the artist's task of filtering and shaping his linguistic source material. *Ulysses* went much further than *Dubliners* in this respect, of course, and added to the offending words and proper names long stretches of apparently nonliterary prose and the extensive use of clichés of a sort that good writers were supposed to avoid. At the same time, like *Finnegans Wake*, it has been held to betray the cause of fiction by distancing itself too far from the language of ordinary communication, through the use of extravagant verbal deformations and disruptions.

The complaints of early reviewers often yoked both responses together. Thus S. P. B. Mais moves from the first to the second and back again: "Our first impression is that of sheer disgust, our second of irritability because we never know whether a character is speaking or merely thinking, our third of boredom at the continual harping on obscenities (nothing cloys a reader's appetite so quickly as dirt)" (*Daily*

Express, 25 March 1922).[1] The *Sporting Times* reviewer, after making the notorious comment that the book "appears to have been written by a perverted lunatic who has made a speciality of the literature of the latrine," continues: "In addition to this stupid glorification of mere filth, the book suffers from being written in the manner of a demented George Meredith. There are whole chapters of it without any punctuation or other guide to what the writer is really getting at" (1 April 1922) (1:192). Holbrook Jackson, writing *To-Day,* comments on the expanses of apparently nonliterary and unselective writing: "There are the deadliest of Dead Seas in this ocean of prose. You get becalmed in them—bored, drowsed, bewildered. And there are gulfs and bays which are muddy and noisome with the sewage of civilization" (June 1922) (1:199). The double objection is summed up in Shane Leslie's graphic phrase "rotten caviar" in the *Dublin Review* for September 1922 (1:203). Better-known writers voiced the same complaints. Arnold Bennett objects to the difficulty of the language—"To comprehend *Ulysses* is not among the recognized learned professions, and nobody should give his entire existence to the job"—and its directness—"James Joyce sticks at nothing, literally. He forbids himself no word. He says everything—everything" (*Outlook,* 29 April 1922) (1:220–21). Rebecca West is more alert to the paradox that taboo words in literature represent but finds Joyce's use of them inartistic: "I would hesitate to say that some artist may not at some time find it necessary to use these Angle-Saxon monosyllables, which are in a sense so little used and in a sense so much, for the completion of some artistic pattern. But . . . Mr. Joyce is not that artist" ("The Strange Case of James Joyce," *Bookman,* September 1928) (2:431). Among the questions that this chapter considers is whether one of the ways in which *Ulysses* works as a powerfully revelatory (and extremely funny) literary text is by exploiting this contradiction in our expectations—by demonstrating, in a comic modality, that both of our demands take their strength from mythical or ideological imperatives, that our sense of what counts as "close to" or "distant from" the norm is largely given by our participation in a particular literary tradition not by our experience of ordinary language (whatever that might be).

If we look carefully at the language of the nameless narrator's passages in the "Cyclops" episode or Molly Bloom's monologue in the

---

[1]Quoted in Robert H. Deming, *James Joyce: The Critical Heritage* 1:191. Further page references in this paragraph are to this work.

"Penelope" episode—parts of the book that have been found "convincing" in their faithfulness to real uses of language, in one case speech and in the other thought—we find that although these styles of utterance deviate from the norms of one kind of literary language, they do so only to exploit another: the familiar tradition of colorful, unrestrained "character" speech, the talk of Sam Weller and his father in *Pickwick Papers* or of Miss Bates in *Emma*, with its defiance of the norms of syntax and prose discourse dutifully observed by the narrator and the majority of the other characters. We also find overtly literary styles in *Ulysses*, styles that have never pretended to exist in the city streets, such as the cheap romance style of Gerty McDowell's section of "Nausicaa" or the succession of pastiches in "Oxen of the Sun," though in these cases too Joyce is comically exploiting, not simply employing, the styles in question. Among the chapters that are more difficult to place in this way are "Sirens" and "Eumaeus," chapters that could be said to challenge the norms of both "literary" and "nonliterary" language. "Sirens" plays havoc with the rules of lexical formation, syntax, and discourse on which any continued use of language depends; "Eumaeus" seems to follow all too faithfully the norms of an overblown, self-conscious rhetoric, a crass journalistic or speech-day conception of "high style" from the late nineteenth century. I use a few morsels from these chapters to consider some of the ways in which linguistic deviation can work in literary language and to explore the effects of Joyce's peculiar language on our grasp on the world, and its grasp on us.

Lipspeech

The English language allows very little independence to the organs of the body: most verbs of conscious behavior require a grammatical subject implying an undivided, masterful, efficient self of which the organ is mere slave or satellite. In the sentences *James wears a ring* or *He turns the page* it is only from the verb and its object that we deduce the role of finger or hand, as they make no appearance in the sentence. If it becomes necessary to stipulate the organs involved, we do so by suggesting that they are places where, or accessories by means of which, the controlling individual performs the activities in question: *James wears a ring through his nose* or *He turns the page with his toes*. We seldom stop to question the easy transition from subject to verb, to consider what a totalizing and naturalizing gesture it is to constitute in language a complete, homogeneous, individual subject ("James," "he"), a single, coherent, separable activity ("wears," "turns"), and a relation between them of pure transitivity. If, however, the verb is given a subject that is only a part of the whole individual, the sentence immediately registers as anomalous: *James's finger wears a ring* or *His hand turns the page*. Nor is it just the feeling of tautology that produces the oddness here; we are even more unsettled by statements in which the subject is *not* implied by the rest of the sentence: *James's nose wears a ring* or *Joyce's toes turn the page*. What is perturbing is that the grammatical subject is no longer a human subject: syntax and our sense of the world have ceased to coincide.[2] Even when the activity is fully localized in the conscious mind, we prefer to specify the individual as a mental and physical unity: *She thought hard* not *Her mind thought hard*. The totalizing pronoun "she" satisfies us by providing a fully constituted human subject, answerable to the rules and norms of the society that confers identity upon all subjects; "her mind," on the other hand, disturbs us as an isolated and ungovernable potency. (We do, however, say "my head hurts" where French, for example, has "j'ai mal à la tête," an even more stringent insistence on a dominating central subjectivity. In other languages the fusion of individual and action extends to a verbal system that does without personal pronouns; thus *cogito, sum*—I think, I am.)[3]

Ulysses, however, frequently fails to conform to these widespread syntactic expectations. Take, for example, the narrative statement "His hand accepted the moist tender gland and slid it into a side-pocket" (4.181). Such a sentence, in which the transaction between Leopold Bloom and the pork butcher Dlugacz becomes a transaction between two organs, hand and kidney, challenges momentarily our untroubled belief in the human subject as unitary, unconstrained, and capable of originating action from a single center of consciousness. Here the sharp focus that is the goal of traditional realistic narrative has been narrowed to a point at which it threatens the subjective unity it usually serves to sustain. Only when the unity of

[2]A useful discussion of the "lack of fit" between syntax and the perceived world, as exploited in *Ulysses*, is Roger Moss, "Difficult Language."

[3]The linguistic representation of persons, whether through a system of pronouns or through inflections of the verb itself, sustains a sense of the individual self which is not necessarily given outside language; see Emile Benveniste, "Subjectivity in Language," chap. 21 of *Problems in General Linguistics*, and John Lyons, *Semantics*, 2:636–46.

mind and body is actually broken does it seem legitimate—though still troubling—for the organ to command its own intentional verb, as in young Patsy Dignam's memory of his father's death: "I couldn't hear the other things he said but I saw his tongue and his teeth trying to say it better" (10.1171). Even the body acting as a whole must be behaving abnormally if it is to be permitted the privilege of functioning as the subject of a verb of this kind: "Once, sleeping, his body had risen, crouched and crawled in the direction of a heatless fire and, having attained its destination, there, curled, unheated, in night attire had lain, sleeping" (17.854). (Roy K. Gottfried, in *The Art of Joyce's Syntax*, comments briefly on the occurrence of such sentences, finding in them a "drift into apparently mere patterning and mechanics" which leaves Bloom "almost a passive object" [70]; he views them, that is, as having a traditional expressive function, aimed at representing human behavior as mechanical.) The verbs we are accustomed to finding with organs of the body as subject usually involve involuntary and localized muscular behavior (or behavior that is so perceived by a particular character or point of view). Thus in "Aeolus" we find "His mouth continued to twitch unspeaking in nervous curls of disdain" (7.709)—and even here "disdain" seems to reintroduce the intentionality expelled by the automatic "twitch."

Not surprisingly, among the organs whose independent initiative is stringently circumscribed by these linguistic norms are those which produce language: we guard the right of the "speaking subject" to be master of the speech apparatus, to speak through it, not to let *it* speak. However ten lines into "Sirens," whose title indicates its special concern with voices, we come across this:

—In the second carriage, miss Douce's wet lips said, laughing in the sun. (11.72)

This sentence refuses the usual automatic move from vocal activity to a free, originating subject; we stop at the lips, which have somehow managed to displace Miss Douce as author of the statement. Is this, as Gottfried would no doubt have it, an indication of the barmaid's mindlessness as she produces mechanical chatter—or, to be more accurate, as she passively lets her speech organs produce it for her? Perhaps; but the device occurs rather too often in the "Sirens" chapter, and in relation to rather too many characters, to be seen as only the reflex of a particular state of mind. Lips act again and again beyond the reach of a mastering self:

> Her wet lips tittered:
> —He's killed looking back.   (11.76)
> Lenehan's lips over the counter lisped a low whistle of decoy.   (11.328)
> Lenehan still drank and grinned at his tilted ale and at miss Douce's lips that all but hummed, not shut, the oceansong her lips had trilled. (11.377)
> Down she sat. All ousted looked. Lips laughing.   (11.727)
> Sour pipe removed he held a shield of hand beside his lips that cooed a moonlight nightcall, clear from anear, a call from afar, replying.   (11.854)
> See. Play on her. Lip blow.   (11.1088)
> Miss Mina Kennedy brought near her lips to ear of tankard one.
> —Mr Dollard, they murmured low.   (11.1167)
> Yes, her lips said more loudly, Mr Dollard.   (11.1175)

Here are six different pairs of lips, all engaged in activities we normally regard as the proper province of the whole individual acting under the command of a central will: they say, titter, lisp, hum, trill, laugh, coo, blow, and murmur. To this list of independently acting speech organs in the episode we might add the "bootssnout" that sniffs a rude reply to Miss Douce (11.100), Bob Cowley's Adam's apple that "hoarsed softly" (11.589), and Richie Goulding's breath and teeth that "fluted with plaintive woe" (11.632), as well as the strange reversal of agency in the statement "Speech paused on Richie's lips" (11.625). There is clearly too much vocal and emotional energy of different kinds being expended here to allow "mechanical behavior" to stand as a satisfactory explanation.

It is in the "Sirens" episode that examples of independently acting speech organs cluster most thickly. The words "lip" and "lips," for example, occur twenty times in the episode, and on more than half of these occurrences they function in this deviant manner; the next most frequent appearance is in "Circe," which has only half the number, all of them functioning normally.[4] Nevertheless, interesting examples

---

[4] I derive these figures from the extremely useful *Handlist to James Joyce's "Ulysses"* prepared by Wolfhard Steppe with Hans Walter Gabler from the critical reading text; this handlist replaces the venerable *Word Index,* by Miles L. Hanley.

appear elsewhere in the text, and it is evident from the less deviant instances that Joyce is, as so often in *Ulysses,* pushing a traditional novelistic device beyond its normal limits. Take, for instance, the use of the noun "voice" in the first episode of the novel, which operates on the borders between orthodox Victorian or Edwardian narrative style and self-conscious parody of that style. In common narrative practice a "voice" can be said to utter a speech if the voice comes from outside the scene being depicted and its owner has not yet been identified by the narrator or the commanding consciousness. Thus "A voice within the tower called loudly" (1.227) is a perfectly normal reference to Haines before he appears or is named. (Equally, "Circe" is not at all deviant with respect to dramatic textual conventions in frequently identifying offstage speakers as "A VOICE.") The effect becomes excessive when it is continued after Haines has been referred to by name:

—We'll be choked, Buck Mulligan said. Haines, open that door, will you?
Stephen laid the shavingbowl on the locker. A tall figure rose from the hammock where it had been sitting, went to the doorway and pulled open the inner doors.
—Have you the key? a voice asked. (1.318)

It is as though the narrator, in spite of Mulligan's address, remains in ignorance of Haines's identity (and even gender: the "figure" is scrupulously referred to as "it"). This exaggeration of the convention points up the faint absurdity of an apparently omniscient narrator having to feign ignorance of the names of characters merely because they have not yet been introduced to the reader.

The technical device shades into something more clearly a signal of "fine writing," an example of elegant variation or periphrasis: thus "Buck Mulligan's gay voice went on" (1.40); "The drone of his descending voice boomed out of the stairhead" (1.237); "A voice, sweettoned and sustained, called to him from the sea" (1.741). It becomes less securely serious in its tone in other examples, which one might analyze in terms of "free indirect discourse" or "empathetic narrative"—that is, Stephen's critical view of his fellow tenants colors the narrator's language. For example, "He saw the sea hailed as a great sweet mother by the wellfed voice beside him" (1.106), or "—Of course I'm a Britisher, Haines's voice said" (1.666). And the criticism becomes insistent when the milkwoman's deference to Mulligan and Haines is described as though directed toward their voices alone: "Stephen listened alone in scornful silence. She bows her old head to a voice that speaks to her loudly, her bonesetter, her medicineman: me she slights. To the voice that will shrive and oil for the grave all there is of her. . . . And to the loud voice that now bids her be silent with wondering unsteady eyes" (1.418). Significantly, Stephen's own utterances are never described in this way; one is much less likely to reduce one's own subjectivity to a vocal production. The same is true for Bloom, whose interlocutors are sometimes given this trait and thus diminished. One interesting exception, however, suggests perhaps a moment of sudden self-consciousness and self-distancing on Bloom's part—or an exuberant parody of this novelistic mannerism:

> He said softly in the bare hall:
> —I'm going round the corner. Be back in a minute.
> And when he had heard his voice say it he added:
> —You don't want anything for breakfast? (4.52)

To move from "voice" to "lips" is unquestionably to start to put the novelistic style under pressure. A sentence from the first episode might pass for orthodox if it stopped halfway through: "His curling shaven lips laughed and the edges of his white glittering teeth" (1.131). The mildly erotic fictional style by means of which Gerty McDowell is presented in "Nausicaa" allows the trick occasionally— "The pretty lips pouted awhile" (13.125), "Gerty's lips parted swiftly to frame the word" (13.581)—but the antinovelistic style used for the representation of Molly Bloom's thoughts in "Penelope" does not permit it at all. In the latter case, although the word "lips" occurs several times, only once does it act as a subject, and then to describe what is presumably an involuntary action: "didnt I cry yes I believe I did or near it my lips were taittering when I said goodbye" (18.673).[5] Only in "Sirens" are the normal limits unmistakably suspended, and lips do not merely laugh, pout, part, and taitter but speak.

[5] I have not been able to find "taitter" in any dictionary. What is interesting is how the context—the specific sentence, and beyond it the conventions already established by Molly's monologue—leads the reader to guess at an action that is out of Molly's control. The same sentence in a third-person narration in another part of the novel would not impose these limits upon interpretation. (In *Notes for Joyce*, Don Gifford and Robert J. Seidman assert that the word is "English dialect" and means "tilting, seesawing," which, though they could be involuntary actions, do not seem appropriate to lips.)

One way of attempting to account for the independence of the speech organs in "Sirens" is to appeal to the figure of synecdoche. We find a familiar textbook example of this trope, somewhat fragmented, among Bloom's meditations in this chapter: "Her hand that rocks the cradle rules the. Ben Howth. That rules the world" (11.183). And in "Circe" Stephen recites the customary description of the trope in connection with another example: "Doctor Swift says one man in armour will beat ten men in their shirts. Shirt is synechdoche. Part for the whole" (15.4402).[6] This definition in terms of a straightforward substitution implies a reassuringly reversible movement that allows the momentarily challenged unity to be retrieved, so we are not shaken in our assurance that mothers, not hands, rock cradles (and rule the world). We can also, however, regard the naming of the whole individual when only a part of the body is active as itself a figure of speech, albeit one that we use all the time and therefore take for granted; in fact the classical definition of synecdoche also allows the substitution of whole for part. This synecdochic tendency in colloquial speech is most striking when the entire individual is substituted for the genital organs in euphemistic references to sexual activity. "You can apply your eye to the keyhole and play with yourself while I just go through her a few times," says Boylan to Bloom in "Circe" (15.3788), and it is no feat of interpretative subtlety to translate "yourself," "I," and "her" into the appropriate sexual organs. Joyce also uses puns to convey the easy convertibility of organ to subject and vice versa: thus the barmaids can refer to the "old fogey in Boyd's" in terms of his facial features—"O greasy eyes!" "Married to the greasy nose!"—and the narrator can quickly transform these phrases into "greasy I knows" (15.124–77).[7] One way of regarding the variously busy lips of "Sirens," therefore, is as a more *literal* rendering of human vocal activity than is normally

[6]The uncommon spelling "synechdoche" is retained by Gabler in the corrected text, as a variant vouched for by the *OED*.

[7]To refer to "the narrator" is, of course, to reintroduce the notion of a single continuous voice under the control of an individual consciousness, which is to misrepresent the way the chapter operates. It is only readers' strong expectations of such a consistent subjectivity as the origin of the third-person passages which produce in "Sirens" the ghost of a narrator (or an "arranger," as this masterful figure has sometimes been called). The voices that speak in these passages could be more accurately seen as detached from an overriding will, as are so many of the other voices in the chapter. I refer to the narrator, therefore, merely as a shorthand way of indicating the third-person passages that interweave with the representations of thought, speech, and song—not that the distinction between these categories is always clear.

166

promulgated by the linguistic convention of representing all conscious human behavior as if it were the product of a single, coherent subjectivity and by the ideology that this convention serves and promotes. Joyce's transgressions of the selectional restrictions of English syntax can be regarded as strategems that liberate the body from a dictatorial and englobing will and allow its organs their own energies and proclivities.

A further effect of this organic liberation is erotic arousal: sexuality thrives on the separation of the body into independent parts, whereas a sexually repressive morality insists on the wholeness and singleness of body and mind or soul. The business that engages all the lips I have quoted in "Sirens" is in one way or another sexual: Lenehan's flirting with the barmaid, Bloom's recollection of Molly's first appearance, Simon Dedalus's memory of moonlight barcaroles, Bloom's fantasies of oral sex, and of course the titillating ministrations of the Sirens themselves. Miss Douce and Miss Kennedy know the power of a sexuality radiated from a single organ, as did their Homeric counterparts (the Sirens heard by Odysseus sang both *of* and *in* a "honey-sweet voice that issues from our lips" as they lured men to death by sexual enchantment [12.187–8]), and the Ormond Hotel barmaids offer not only erotically independent lips and voices but a rising and falling bosom, a smackable thigh, and a masturbatory finger and thumb. The "Sirens" chapter teems, in fact, with the names of parts of the body (as so often, Joyce's well-known schema for the novel, which singles out the ear as the special organ of this chapter, favors only one of many contenders).[8] We find the following organs in the first hundred and fifty lines of the chapter proper: head (four times), lips (twice), hair (four times), ear (five times), eyes (nine times), hand (four times), neck (twice), skin (twice), face, fingers, nose, nosewings, nostrils, throat, mouth, beard, breast, thumbnails, and arm. Why should a chapter whose main thematic concern is music be so taken up with parts of the body? One answer is that during this chapter the most important physical event of the narrative takes place, the sexual union of Molly and Boylan, but another answer—quite in keeping with the book's mode of verbal operation—is in terms of the polysemy of the word "organ." Toward the end of the chapter Bloom recalls the music of the "organ in Gardiner street," then the organist himself in the

[8]In "Miroirs aux Sirènes," Daniel Ferrer has shown how well the "Sirens" episode responds to interpretative schemata that "officially" belong to other episodes.

significantly named "cockloft" (11.1197); a few sentences later Bloom is surprised by his own organic wind-music, an event I discussed in connection with onomatopoeia in the previous chapter. (It might be relevant, too, that the book's first sentence referring to Bloom informs us of his relish for organs and that, having had kidney for breakfast, he is now devouring a piece of liver.)

Once the parts of the body are separated, the possibility arises of replacing one with another. When lips are said to hum, coo, and murmur, they are doing duty for other parts of the vocal apparatus. In this chapter a bust hums (11.387), eyes ask (11.886), lips and eyes listen (11.266). Bloom even tries, in a fantasy of remote-controlled seduction across the barroom, to commandeer another organ to serve in place of both voice and lips: "Ventriloquise. My lips closed. Think in my stom" (11.1095). (His most notable utterance in "Sirens" does indeed proceed from the lower rather than the higher organs; having begun with uncontrollable laughter, the chapter ends with another human noise notorious for its independence of the individual's volition.) We hardly need Freud to persuade us that on this substitutability of organs depend the development of the individual's libidinal potential and the varied richness of his or her sexual life. Lips may be a synecdochic substitute for the whole individual of which they form a part, but they may also be a metaphoric substitute for another organ that they resemble. (Ivan Fónagy has noted that in several languages the word for "lips," in addition to its literal reference to the mouth, metaphorically designates both the vocal cords and the lips of the vulva.)[9] Miss Douce's lips are twice given the adjective "wet," and she complains after a laughing spree induced by a series of double entendres, with ambiguous reference, "I feel all wet" (11.182)—to which the well-bred Miss Kennedy responds "You horrid thing!" (Compare Molly's exclamation that, in the same chapter, Bloom recalls her screaming while collapsing with laughter in the wake of Dollard's departure in trousers so tight as to reveal his genitals: "Oh saints above, I'm drenched!" [11.558].)

This traffic between vocal and sexual organs occurs throughout the chapter, the word "organ"—as we might expect—providing one of the bridges:

—Sure, you'd burst the tympanum of her ear, man, Mr Dedalus said through smoke aroma, with an organ like yours.

[9] Ivan Fónagy, *La vive voix*, 85. Fónagy surveys a number of studies concerned with the equivalence between the mouth and the vagina.

In bearded abundant laughter Dollard shook upon the keyboard. He would.
—Not to mention another membrane, Father Cowley added. (11.536)

The substitution here is not only of one powerfully penetrative male organ for another, penis for voice, but of vagina for female ear, and in the background is the similar displacement in one traditional account of the Virgin's conceiving in Christian mythology. The latter reference becomes more explicit in "Circe" when Virag produces an anti-Christian version: "Panther, the Roman centurion, polluted her with his genitories . . . Messiah! He burst her tympanum" (15.2599). The possibility therefore arises of a double reading of Miss Kennedy's coy refusal to hear about the old fogey's sexual advances: she "plugged both two ears with little fingers" (11.129). (This is also, of course, a reference to Odysseus' stratagem for sailing past the Sirens without harm by plugging his men's ears with wax, itself a kind of prophylactic against sexual assault.) The idea of sexual penetration through the ear returns, and is related to oral sex in another movement of displacement, when Bloom muses over Miss Douce's hairstyle later in the chapter: "Hair braided over: shell with seaweed. Why do they hide their ears with seaweed hair? And Turks the mouth, why? Her eyes over the sheet. Yashmak. Find the way in. A cave. No admittance except on business" (11.941).

The slippage from voice to genitals occurs frequently, at times by means of words that suit both organs, whether male—"Tenderness it welled: slow, swelling, full it throbbed" (11.701)—or female—"Gap in their voices too. Fill me, I'm warm, dark, open" (11.974). In Bloom's musings on Ben Dollard, voice and testicles are associated through the obvious physiological connection: "With all his belongings on show. . . . Well, of course that's what gives him the base barreltone. For instance eunuchs" (11.557–60). And later: "Good voice he has still. No eunuch yet with all his belongings" (11.1026). In Tom Kernan's highly condensed anecdote of a promising vocal career cut short, the context of adulterous sex encourages a double reading of the word *throat:* "Authentic fact. How Walter Bapty lost his voice. Well, sir, the husband took him by the throat. *Scoundrel,* said he, *you'll sing no more lovesongs*" (11.927). This fusion of throat and testicles, voice and sexual potency, becomes more explicit in "Circe" when the nymph exclaims to Bloom: "Satan, you'll sing no more lovesongs. . . . (*she draws a poniard and, clad in the sheathmail of an elected knight of nine, strikes at his loins*)" (15.3459). The phrase used first to refer to Dol-

169

lard's genitals also proves applicable to Molly's sexual endowments, in another sliding of organic allusion: "She looked fine. Her crocus dress she wore lowcut, belongings on show" (11.1056). In Molly's case too there is an association between these sexual attributes and the voice, made possible by the double applicability of the word "full"; "Full voice of perfume of what perfume does your lilactrees. Bosom I saw, both full, throat warbling" (11.730).

The vocal and the vaginal also become indistinguishable at times; Simon Dedalus, agreeing that Molly has a fine voice, adds, "The lower register, for choice" (11.1222). (Once again, "Circe" is outrageously explicit, for in that chapter Bella's "sowcunt barks" [15.3489].) And returning to the wetness noted earlier, we can trace a pattern whereby the flow of the singing voice flows into the flow of genital arousal. This language of flow, like the language of flowers, is the language of Henry Flower's synecdochic love for Martha Clifford, whose stimulating letter (and flower) he is busy replying to in the Ormond Hotel: "Flower to console me and a pin cuts lo. Means something, language of flow. Was it a daisy? Innocence that is" (11.297). And ten pages later:

> Tenors get women by the score. Increase their flow. Throw flower at his feet. When will we meet? (11.686)

> Flood of warm jamjam lickitup secretness flowed to flow in music out, in desire, dark to lick flow invading. Tipping her tepping her tapping her topping her. Tup. Pores to dilate dilating. Tup. The joy the feel the warm the. Tup. To pour o'er sluices pouring gushes. Flood, gush, flow, joygush, tupthrob. Now! Language of love.[10] (11.705)

One can almost conceive of the chapter as a version of Diderot's *Les bijoux indiscrets:* a conclave of talkative (not to say musical) genitalia.

Many organs other than the vocal apparatus prove sexually substitutable: ears, hair, skin, hands, fingers, nose, and eyes all function as genital surrogates in the course of the chapter. The barmaids work each other up into an almost orgasmic ecstasy of erotic allusion with the

---

[10]For further discussion of the language of flow in "Sirens" see Robert Young's contribution to the panel entitled "Sirens without Music" in *James Joyce: The Centennial Symposium,* ed. Morris Beja et al., 57–92. Complementary perspectives on the episode are provided by Maud Ellmann, Daniel Ferrer, André Topia, and Jean-Michel Rabaté in their papers at this panel.

aid of such displacements, taking off from a well-established catch-phrase, "your other eye,"[11] and moving to "his bit of beard" and "the greasy nose." At the same time the text works its own displacement from the "old fogey" to Leopold Bloom, walking, unthought of by the barmaids, along the Liffey quay (11.148–80). The association is purely verbal, from Miss Douce's "your other eye" to the narrator's "Bloo-whose dark eye," and from her "married to the greasy nose" to the narrator's "Married to Bloom, to greaseabloom," but the implication is perhaps that sexual desire may track across the same organs on differ-ent bodies as well as focus on the whole person. The link is perpetuated when Bloom is engaged in providing a cover for his erotic pen-manship: "Down the edge of his *Freeman* baton ranged Bloom's, your other eye" (11.856). And the metaphor is reversed in the final chapter of the book as Molly recalls her first sight of an erect penis: "it had a kind of eye in it" (15.816). When the barmaids reappear in "Circe" as erotically aroused witnesses of Boylan's and Molly's copulation, the stage directions once more bring out the sexual expressiveness of their facial organs—("*her eyes upturned,*" "*her mouth opening*")—and Miss Kennedy is given a statement that neatly encapsulates the reliance of eroticism upon the fragmentation of the body: "O, he simply idolises every bit of her" (15.3800).

The description of Miss Douce's hand on the beerpull transforms even that object into a phallic substitute: "Fro, to: to, fro: over the polished knob (she knows his eyes, my eyes, her eyes) her thumb and finger passed in pity: passed, reposed and, gently touching, then slid so smoothly, slowly down, a cool firm white enamel baton protruding through their sliding ring" (11.1113). This action triggers for Bloom the memory of Molly's erotic touch during their early lovemaking on Ben Howth, in a passage I have already partly quoted: "Beerpull. Her hand that rocks the cradle rules the. Ben Howth. That rules the world" (11.1183). It is not, after all, maternal but sexual instincts that rule the world, and they exercise their power through specific and erotically separable organs. (We might recall the professional excuse

[11]The use of "eye" to suggest other organs has been current at least since the time of Chaucer, who refers to Alison's anus as her "nether ye" (lower eye) in the *Miller's Tale*. It would have been a particularly familiar usage in 1904 owing to its frequent occur-rence in music-hall songs of the period, especially those of Marie Lloyd, who made an early hit with "Then you wink the other eye" and reused the phrase in further songs; see Erlene Stetson, "Literary Talk," 180–81. The phrase is further discussed by Wilhelm Füger in "Bloom's Other Eye."

that has brought Molly and Boylan together for their adulterous act while the events of this chapter are unfolding: the performance of an operatic duet in which genital union is emphasized as a union of hands, Da Ponte and Mozart's "La ci darem la mano.")

What we have seen in this discussion is how one aspect of the linguistic deviation of "Sirens" works to explore and test assumptions about the relationship between parts of the body and the individual subject, assumptions coded in the language we habitually employ. There are, of course, many other kinds of verbal deformation in the chapter, as well as manipulations of more strictly literary conventions, all of which multiply and complicate the chapter's powers of comic dismantling and destabilizing. The result of this process, however, is not to reinforce the stability and certainty of the norm, and the sharp distinction between literary and nonliterary language that depends upon it, but to put in question the norm itself. This is at least a possible way of reading the chapter, a reading that does not merely offer an "explanation" of its linguistic adventures but participates in them, enjoying and learning from them at the same time.

With Apologies to Lindley Murray

It is commonplace of Joyce criticism that in the language of the "Sirens" episode *Ulysses* comes closest to the verbal extravagance of *Finnegans Wake*. The reasons for this view are obvious. Most, if not all, of the linguistic deviations that characterize Joyce's last book are present in embryo in "Sirens," including puns, portmanteau words, syntactic deformations, insistent onomatopoeic and rhythmic patterns, various forms of reduplication, and repeated verbal motifs, and our examination of a small sample of the episode's use of language could easily be extended to the later text. The "Eumaeus" episode, on the other hand, seems to be at the opposite end of the linguistic spectrum: instead of newly coined lexical forms we have all-too-familiar clichés, instead of an intense concentration of meaning in a confined linguistic space we have sense spread thinly across a seemingly endless flow of words, instead of syntax that flaunts its disregard of the rules we have pedantic adherence to conventional forms, and instead of rhythmic and sonic patterning that approaches the aural salience of verse we have flaccid and sprawling prose. Where "Sirens" kaleidoscopically detaches sentences from speakers (or thinkers) and organs from bodies, "Eumaeus" proceeds as if from a single all-embracing consciousness that gives voice to a continuous unfolding of thoughts and perceptions. If the earlier chapter subverts ways of conceiving identity and sexuality which are central to what might be labeled (with all the crudity of such labels) the bourgeois tradition, the later one appears an apotheosis of bourgeois values and habits of mind.

To investigate the validity of this opposition, we need to examine a piece of continuous prose from "Eumaeus"—one indication of the difference between the chapters being that it is not possible, as it was with "Sirens," to get a sense of the text's procedures and peculiarities from scattered fragments.

> The spirit moving him he would much have liked to follow Jack Tar's good example and leave the likeness there for a very few minutes to speak for itself on the plea he so that the other could drink in the beauty for himself, her stage presence being, frankly, a treat in itself which the camera could not at all do justice to. But it was scarcely professional etiquette so. Though it was a warm pleasant sort of a night now yet wonderfully cool for the season considering, for sunshine after storm. And he did feel a kind of need there and then to follow suit like a kind of inward voice and satisfy a possible need by moving a motion. Nevertheless he sat tight just viewing the slightly soiled photo creased by opulent curves, none the worse for wear however, and looked away thoughtfully with the intention of not further increasing the other's possible embarrassment while gauging her symmetry of heaving *embonpoint*. In fact the slight soiling was only an added charm like the case of linen slightly soiled, good as new, much better in fact with the starch out. Suppose she was gone when he? I looked for the lamp which she told me came in to his mind but merely as a passing fancy of his because he then recollected the morning littered bed etcetera and the book about Ruby with met him pike hoses (*sic*) in it which must have fell down sufficiently appropriately beside the domestic chamberpot with apologies to Lindley Murray. (16.1456)

One way of responding to this prose style is to treat it as "expressive form," to ask what kind of character or state of mind we are expected to deduce, according to the norms of the literary tradition, from this language. We then have the option of applying this description to the narrator of the chapter or, in accordance with what Hugh Kenner calls "the Uncle Charles principle" (which allows us to transfer an apparent peculiarity of the narrator to the character appearing in the narrative), to the main character in the episode, Leopold Bloom (*Joyce's Voices,* chap. 2). Hence we have the frequent suggestion that the style reflects Bloom's tiredness at this hour of the night or, as argued by Kenner (who finds the style anything but exhausted) that it reflects the kind of chapter Bloom himself, with his stale notions of high-class written style, would write (130–31). If Bloom is not asked to shoulder responsibility for the style—which has always seemed to me to attribute both too little and too much to him (he would be capable neither of the dreadful pomposity on the surface nor of the brilliant parody and verbal play that underlies it)—an alternative is to think in terms of an individualized narrator or even of Joyce himself at a moment of exhaustion in his artistic labors. But there is nothing obligatory about this interpretative leap; it is, after all, only the product of a certain strategy of reading which demands some kind of linkage between a particular style—especially if it is an unusual style—and an imaginary human being, whether narrator or character. By this point in the book the reader might be wary of this strategy. As we have already noted, there is a difficulty in identifying a single narrative presence in "Sirens," and to whom do we ascribe the headlines in "Aeolus," the interpolations in "Cyclops," or the stage directions in "Circe"?

I shall concentrate instead on the language itself without trying to identify it with somebody's voice. Although the style is quite unlike that of "Sirens" in that it is not strongly marked by deviations from the rules of morphology or syntax, the "Eumaeus" episode does not simply replicate a self-important, "leader-writerly" prose. While taking such a style as its major norm it constantly twists, overextends, exaggerates, fractures, and undermines it in ways that comically exhibit not only the absurdity of the rhetorical mode in question but the inexhaustible potential that exists at this level of language (the level of style, rhetoric, or discourse) for shifts and slippages not very far removed in their effects from those produced at the more strictly linguistic level in "Sirens." Its deviations tend to be deviations from the norms of what traditionally constitutes "good" style, norms that one finds spelled out in such handbooks as Hodgson's *Errors in the Use of English* and Fowler's *Modern English Usage* or, unprescriptively, in studies of "text linguistics" and suprasentential rules;[12] it is very con-

---

[12] In "Reflections on Eumaeus" Alistair Stead has discussed Joyce's use in this chapter of William Ballantyne Hodgson's 1881 *Errors in the Use of English* (a copy of which Joyce

scious of the possibility of stylistic solecism, however, and its hypercorrectness can be as ludicrous as its unintentional lapses. This inefficient, self-referring, self-propagating language requires the reader to process it with extreme alertness in order to avoid misinterpretation or confusion—which appears to justify the handbooks' rules, except that the formulation of and insistence upon such rules is itself part of the problem, producing a style that is continually scrutinizing itself to assess its own tastefulness and impressiveness and looking over its shoulder to check its models and rules of decorum.

It is possible to isolate, somewhat arbitrarily, different kinds of deviation from (or excessive adherence to) "good style" in this extract. What follows is a list of ten varieties, with some comments on the effects they are likely to have on readers.

(1) Cross-referencing is a normal part of any discourse, but in this episode it occurs across abnormally large distances; thus "Jack Tar's good example" refers back to an incident witnessed by Bloom—a sailor relieving himself—which had been described over five hundred lines earlier. In terms of *fictional* time the reference is not particularly far back, but the prolixity of the style makes it an inordinately long span for a reader's memory to cross. At the level of sentences, similarly, pronouns refer back over unusually long gaps to the nouns they are standing in for; thus the "her" of "her symmetry" comes as something of a surprise, because Molly has not been mentioned for several sentences.

(2) A repetition of words and lexical roots confuses the reader by at first seeming to carry some significance (according to Jakobson's principle of equivalence in literary language); for instance, "he would much have *liked* . . . to leave the *like*ness"; the photo is "*creased*" and Bloom fears "in*creasing*" Stephen's embarrassment. A whole chain of repetitions appears in the sequence "a *kind* of *need*" "a *kind* of inward voice" "a *possible need*" and "*possible* embarrassment." This technique amounts at times to tautology; Bloom feels a *need* to satisfy a *need* to *move* a *motion* (having already been *moved* by the spirit). After attempting to extract some significance from these repetitions, the reader has to conclude that they are accidental and semantically vacuous. There

___
had in his Trieste library). Fowler's *Modern English Usage* was not published until 1926, but Kenner is right to note that it is, nevertheless, "a useful guide to the rhetoric of this episode" (*Ulysses*, 131).

is also a graceless repetition of suffixes: "sufficiently appropriately" (a long-winded way of saying "appropriately enough"?).

(3) On the other hand, we encounter the self-conscious use of "elegant variation" in accordance with one of the conventional imperatives of polished style. The sailor therefore becomes "Jack Tar," again a formulation liable to mislead the reader not on the wavelength of the jocular rhetoric. Stephen, we notice, is "the other."

(4) There are several incomplete sentences in this passage; once more the reader has to do some uncustomary work in filling in the ellipses (even more after the mid-1980s than formerly, because the newly established critical text removes the graphic indications of ellipses which were apparently added by a well-intentioned typist and retained in all texts between 1922 and 1984).[13] The first one, for instance, occurs after "on the plea he" and could be continued as "on the plea he needed to urinate," but numerous other possibilities are not excluded by the text. Others are: "But it was scarcely professional etiquette so," "for sunshine after storm," "Suppose she was gone when he?"

(5) There is a wholly unorthodox mixture of registers. Much of the phrasing is that of an artful, not to say arch, *written* style ("The spirit moving him," "her symmetry of heaving *embonpoint*," "(*sic*)"), but it is constantly interrupted by speech locutions: "frankly," "a warm pleasant sort of a night," "good as new, much better in fact." (Fritz Senn has written valuably about the "Eumaeus" style's constant self-corrections, a feature that does not, of course, occur in normal written prose; see "Dynamics of Corrective Unrest," in his *Joyce's Dislocutions*, 67–68.) The seesawing indecisiveness—Bloom wants to leave, *but* it's scarcely professional etiquette, *though* it's a warm evening, *yet* it's cool, and he *does* feel a need, *nevertheless* he sits tight—is excessive even for the spoken language and requires strenuous attention if the reader is to keep abreast of it.

(6) The sequencing of items frequently gives the reader pause, demanding either a rereading or a reading-on to make sense. Thus "a

---

[13]In addition to the ellipses, the new edition removes several hundred commas, dashes, and quotation marks from the hitherto established text of "Eumaeus."

kind of need there," which seems to refer to the *place* where Bloom feels the need (his bladder, perhaps), has to be reinterpreted as the idiomatic phrase "there and then." Similarly, "to follow suit like" appears to introduce a comparison relating to the act of following suit but has to be reread as referring back to "need" when it continues "like a kind of inward voice." It is not, presumably, the "opulent curves" that are "none the worse for wear" but the photo; nor was it the apologies to Lindley Murray—the author of a standard school grammar-book—which fell down beside the chamberpot. A nonsequitur in the first sentence is typical of the style's lack of attention to the implications of the syntagmatic chain: "He would much have liked to follow Jack Tar's good example and leave the likeness there." The example set by the sailor in fact has nothing to do with leaving a photograph, and the reader has to deduce from the earlier event what Bloom would like to do. Mid-sentence referential shifts produce strange effects, as when the photo is said to be "creased by opulent curves" and the surface of the paper gives way without warning to the image upon it, or when the adjective "heaving" suddenly turns the photograph into a moving picture. And there are contradictions from one part of the sentence to the next: the single movement of "Nevertheless he sat tight just viewing the slightly soiled photo . . . and looked away thoughtfully" manages to make it sound as though Bloom is performing these two incompatible actions simultaneously.

(7) The printed text—especially in the critical edition—at times lacks the punctuation necessary to disambiguate verbal sequences, forcing a reinterpretation when the mistake becomes obvious. Thus the absence of quotation marks (and of any introductory comment) leads the reader hopelessly astray when a sentence begins "I looked for the lamp" and appears to go on "which she told me came into his mind." Only familiarity with the words of Tom Moore's "Song of O'Ruark" could, on a first reading, supply the missing quotation marks around "I looked for the lamp which she told me" and allow it to register as an unfinished quotation ("I look'd for the lamp which, she told me, / Should shine when her Pilgrim return'd"). Knowledge of the song's story of a returning husband who finds his wife has left home would then help elucidate the meaning and unexpressed continuation of the previous question, "Suppose she was gone when he?", which appears to come from nowhere. (This example also raises the question of the knowledge presupposed by the Eumaean style—a

distorted echo of the assumption of shared cultural reference points which marks one kind of public utterance and depends on elitist educational practices while pretending to draw on universal commonplaces.)

(8) The abstract is allowed to become momentarily concrete through badly chosen collocations of words, as when, for instance, "the case of linen" turns out to be not a box but an example. Similarly, metaphorical usages always run the risk, in this style, of sliding into other metaphors or of becoming literal: "moving a motion" may be a term from committee procedure but in this context may also mean "defecation," and the final word of "he sat tight" tends to turn from a relatively empty phrase indicating immobility to a description of Bloom's straining sphincter muscles.

(9) There are, of course, the famous clichés, not just well-worn phrases but phrases that are slightly inappropriate or falsely jocular and that often add nothing but length (and sometimes confusion) to the narrative. Instances in this passage include "The spirit moving him," "good example" (why good?), "drink in the beauty," "stage presence" (what stage?), "a treat in itself," "the camera could not at all do justice to," "professional etiquette" (which profession?), a string of (contradictory) weather clichés, "follow suit," "inward voice," "sat tight," "an added charm," "good as new," "a passing fancy," "the domestic chamberpot" (what other kind could it have been?), "with apologies to."[14] At one point two clichés are nicely combined into what we might call a portmanteau-cliché: "none the worse for that" and "worse for wear" fuse into "none the worse for wear." Another pair of clichés, "the likeness" and "to speak for itself," are the *disjecta membra* of a cliché from a previous paragraph: "a speaking likeness" (16.1444).

(10) Finally, we may note, with all these lapses at the level of discourse, only two *syntactic* deviations in the strict sense: the bit of apparent gibberish "met him pike hoses" and the solecism "must have *fell* down." Significantly, both are self-consciously acknowledged in the text itself, the first by the editorial insertion "(*sic*)," the second by the apology to the grammarian Lindley Murray.

[14]A valuable study of the role of clichés in Joyce's writing is Jennifer Levine's "Originality and Repetition."

All these points—and they by no means exhaust the deviations from accepted style which occur in the chapter—involve the reader in a tangle of verbiage, requiring sharp wits and a readiness to reread and reinterpret in order to negotiate it. Further complexity is added by the fact that the chapter plays not only with the norms of various styles and registers outside the text but also with the conventions established by the earlier parts of the text itself. Any extended literary text is involved in a double process: it constantly evokes norms that preexist it in the cultural community, but it also constantly establishes its own norms, which it then challenges or confirms as it goes on. This particular passage entails the conversion of the Bloomian interior monologue style, which has its own set of (by now naturalized) linguistic conventions, into another style with the different set of conventions that govern reported speech.[15] Thus what in the "initial style" would have been the interior question "Suppose she is gone when I?" here becomes "Suppose she was gone when he?", the conventions of indirect speech replacing those of direct speech to alter tense and person. Yet the sentence retains a trait typical of Bloomian interior monologue, breaking off before its end so as to avoid the explicit presentation to consciousness of embarrassing or painful thoughts. Similarly, the isolated "her" mentioned in the first point above continues Bloom's characteristic reference to Molly by pronoun rather than by name. What we reach when we get through the refracting glass of the Eumaean style is another refracting glass.

We may notice too that the recollections of earlier episodes are frequently based on *language* rather than events or objects. "Opulent curves" and "heaving *embonpoint*" are not merely descriptive phrases in a comically inappropriate register. They are tags from the erotic novel *The Sweets of Sin* which have regularly recurred in Bloom's interior monologue since he first read a few sentences from it in "Wandering Rocks" ("opulent curves of the" has in fact just appeared in the previous paragraph [16.1448]). The odd phrase "embarrassment while gauging her symmetry" points back to its earlier appearance in the "Aeolus" episode, when Bloom recalls Martin Cunningham's spelling conundrum: "It is amusing to view the unparalleled embar-

---

[15]There is also liberal use of "free indirect discourse," in which the narrator's report is colored by the diction and syntax of the original utterance (or verbalized thought), though it is frequently impossible to decide whether a given locution is Bloom's or the reporting narrator's. "The spirit moving him" is presumably the narrator's phrase, while "wonderfully cool for the season" is presumably Bloom's. But what about "none the worse for wear, however," or "with apologies to Lindley Murray"?

rassment of a harassed pedlar while gauging the symmetry of a peeled pear under a cemetery wall" (7.166). (The word "view" is another link between the two sentences.) The conundrum is associated, as it was then, with Bloom's still lingering embarrassment over the incident with John Henry Menton, to whom he wished he had said, apropos of his dinged hat, "Looks as good as new now" (7.173), another phrase that the passage under discussion picks up. (That the allusion serves to equate Molly's heaving *embonpoint* with a peeled pear adds another pun and another humorous association—one that has already been exploited in the "Circe" episode, where the conundrum allows the prostitute Zoe's breasts to be referred to as "peeled pears" [15.1993].) As Schutte's *Index of Recurrent Elements* informs us, "move a motion"—which is easily treated as an example of the "Eumaeus" style's particular brand of tautology—has been used before, in "Oxen of the Sun" (14.1527). And the syntactic mistakes, so unusual in a chapter that prides itself on its grammar while getting everything else wrong, are, of course, unmistakably identifiable as Molly's. "Met him pike hoses" is Molly's pronunciation of "metempsychosis" (as recalled by Bloom), and it is Molly whose earlier "It must have fell down" (4.326) threatens to embarrass the shade of Lindley Murray (though, curiously, neither Bloom nor the narrator made any remark on it at the time).[16]

Although the episode is sometimes referred to as if it were a compendium of bad examples, a treatise on how not to do things with words, the fluidity and instability of language demonstrated so hilariously in this chapter is effective in ways that go beyond comedy. The domain in which most of the verbal uncertainties and slidings occur is, as in "Sirens," that of the sexual and excretory functions of the body (two sets of functions between which there is, in Joyce as in Freud, an easy passage), and this fact is worth exploring. We have seen, for instance, how "moving a motion" and "sat tight" hover on the edge of anal signification. The spirit that moves Bloom to go outside, leaving Stephen with Molly's photograph, may be a simple physical need, or it may be a more indirect and unconfessed desire to engineer a sexual liaison between Stephen and Molly; it is the euphemism, at first sight just a sample of Eumaean roundaboutness, that allows both desires to be present at once. The ellipsis after "plea he"

---

[16]On some of the points on which the text remains oddly silent, see Hugh Kenner, "The Rhetoric of Silence."

also leaves open the possibility that a more devious strategy in Bloom's mind is interfering with the proclaimed, or almost proclaimed, urinary need. As Bloom urges himself to go ahead with his plan, however we read it, the hackneyed words dally with alternative meanings: "though it was a warm pleasant sort of a" leads only to "night" when it might have led elsewhere. The potential misreading of "he did feel a kind of need there" already mentioned gives his desire a physical location, whether it be excretory or sexual.

The possibility that one feature of Bloom's sexual universe at this moment is an interest in arousing Stephen's desire for Molly—as a physical object—emerges in part through words that are trying to remain on the level of the aesthetic; the trouble is that the clichés of aesthetic conversation, like "drink in" and "treat," have physical shadows that appear when the context permits them. The descriptions of the photograph and of Molly's image keep shifting toward expressions of sexual invitation—even the apparently innocent "frankly" takes on an added hint of bodily exposure, especially in the light of the previous paragraphs, which have referred to the image of "a large sized lady with her fleshy charms on evidence in an open fashion," in a dress cut "to give a liberal display of bosom with more than vision of breasts" (16.1428–30) (although her figure, we learn as we shift to Bloom's viewpoint, "did not come out to the best advantage in that getup" [16.1445]—another nice example of the abstract cliché becoming comically, and erotically, concrete). I have already referred to the way the photograph's creases unexpectedly turn into those of Molly's body, but we might note too that the portmanteau-cliché "none the worse for wear," though on semantic grounds it refers to the photograph, is so positioned as to appear to refer to the "opulent curves." A world of sexual fantasy is also evoked by the references to *Sweets of Sin*, with Molly cast as the desirable temptress. And once we have, thanks to the multiple imprecisions of this style, associated the soiled and creased photograph with Molly's anything-but-virginal (and all the more available) body, the insistently (or is it clumsily?) repeated references to "slight soiling" taken on further resonances. To move from the "symmetry of heaving *embonpoint*" (a pompously general description of a fairly specific portion of Molly's anatomy, tinged, we remember, with memories of a peeled pear, or, if we recall that the point of the sentence was a spelling test, perhaps a pair of pears) to an assertion that "the slight soiling was only an added charm" is indubitably to attribute to Molly's ample breasts a history of sexual experience, especially as the word "charms" is just the term this style would use as a euphemism for "breasts." The slightly soiled linen, therefore, cannot but suggest copulatory and excretory stains, and Bloom's expressed preference for linen "with the starch out" must also be, at some level, a preference for a maturely flexible bust.[17]

Any doubts about this further range of meaning in what is presented merely as a description of a crumpled photograph are settled by the next sentence ("Suppose she was gone when he?"), which does not quite come from nowhere, as I suggested earlier: thoughts about the availability of Molly's body lead inevitably to fears about her present whereabouts after the assignation with Boylan. The statement of this scarcely voiceable fear dies in the utterance but is displaced, characteristically, onto a popular song that realizes it in fiction. There is then a moment of reassurance when the comforting memory of Bloom's last encounter with Molly is recalled, with all its verbal peculiarities. The sexual/excretory images are still there, however: the bed, the cheap eroticism of *Ruby, the Pride of the Ring,* the phallic images and suggestions of adultery in the monosyllables of "met him pike hoses," the chamber pot, perhaps even the "etcetera" (on one level the epitome of Eumaean vagueness but on another, as the *OED* has it, a "substitute for a suppressed substantive, generally a coarse or indelicate one"). What the style of "Eumaeus" achieves, for all its attempts at propriety, is a vivid demonstration of the impossibility of fixed boundaries and significations when the structures of language are permeated by the dissolving energies of erotic desire. At the same time it confirms language's power to engage with and embody the unconscious or surreptitious movements between the proper and the improper which will undermine any fixed ideal of "correctness" in speech and thought.

In its constant play with the conventions of normal discourse and with the language of the earlier parts of the book, and in its opening out of multiple and uncertain meanings even as it tries to clamp down on language's semantic evasiveness, this passage is representative of the chapter as a whole. "Eumaeus" does not take its bearings from some notional "ordinary" language but from some of the dialects of turn-of-century public utterance in English, spoken and written (jour-

[17]In "Calypso" Bloom lifts an armful of Molly's "soiled linen" on to the bed (4.265), and in "Lotus-Eaters" his fantasies about the conquest of "reserved" women include the thought "Possess her once take the starch out of her" (5.106).

nalism, essays, speeches, pedagogic oratory), just as "Telemachus" engages with the Victorian novel and parts of "Ithaca" with popular scientific writing. Its achievement is not primarily the representation of a fictional character's mental world (the interior monologue style would be more justly described in these terms) or of a particular cultural moment; its peculiar language cannot be recuperated within some notion of "state of mind" or "state of civilization." Though it is true enough to say that Bloom's motivation with regard to Stephen is complicated and ambiguous, the ways in which the language of this episode permits slippage and uncertainty, deception and detour— features that also function as themes throughout the episode—go beyond a particular character's mental condition and spring from the propensities and liabilities of language itself, even when language scrupulously avoids the kinds of verbal deformation that mark the style of "Sirens."[18]

With these qualities in mind we might feel that the episode has a claim equal to that of "Sirens" as an anticipation of the textual operations of *Finnegans Wake*. Kenner has observed that "it is in 'Eumaeus' that we find the principles of *Finnegans Wake* on display, congesting foreground and middle distance with verbal phantoms. And if we open *Finnegans Wake* at random, it is 'Eumaeus'-like syntax that we are apt to find" (*Joyce's Voices*, 37). Senn comments on an extract from "Eumaeus" that "the passage quoted might easily be touched up to become an item of the convoluted defence of H. C. Earwicker," and he remarks of the Eumaean penchant for self-correction, "we are of course uncannily close to *Finnegans Wake*, the microcosmic verbal integration of doubt" ("Dogmad or Dubliboused?" in *Joyce's Dislocutions*, 110–11). The *Wake* has also been subject to a reading that attempts to locate all its exfoliating semantic suggestiveness and its frequently incompatible multiple meanings within a single mind, but this reading is testimony to the strength of interpretative conventions and readerly desires rather than to the qualities of Joyce's writing, which takes to its limit the demonstration of language's capacity to exceed the confines

---

[18]Now it can clearly be seen how Joyce's omission of much of the normal punctuation—an omission that cannot be explained in terms of the models he is parodying or of the consciousness he is representing—multiplies the uncertainties of the language. There is one striking passage in which lexical deviation is thematized: the newspaper report of Dignam's funeral (including the memorable transformation of Bloom's name to "L. Boom" [16.1248]). As with the two instances in the passage under discussion, the deformations are foregrounded and fully motivated.

of mental representation, character, or intention. The initial impression that "Eumaeus" represents, in contrast to "Sirens," the unfolding of a single consciousness's experiences and formulations, cannot survive close attention to Joyce's text. "Eumaeus" is far from repeating the effects of "Sirens," but it complements them by demonstrating in a quite different mode the same capacity on the part of the closely cooperating forces of the linguistic and the erotic to elude a mastering subjectivity.

Language, Ideology, and the Body

In both "Eumaeus" and "Sirens" these processes of displacement, decentering, sliding, and exchange can be seen as one aspect of the interpenetration of the categories of "form" and "content" which characterizes *Ulysses,* going well beyond (and indeed undermining) any simple notion of mimesis or iconicity. We saw in the previous chapter that the sounds of language constitute not a given resource that the writer freely bends to his or her own purposes but a complex set of conventions that can be exploited in a number of ways, including a heightening of the reader's awareness of their conventionality (which need not take away their expressive or aesthetic power). In a similar way the use of language that is recognizably deviant, lexically, syntactically, or stylistically, does not simply register a degree of distance from a norm for artistic effect but raises questions about the stability of any possible norm.[19] These conventions are socially con-

---

[19]Gottfried's study of Joyce's syntax in *Ulysses* is typical of the traditional methods of stylistics in dealing with deviation. It is built on the assumption that the deviations which characterize much literary language can be limited at a certain point, before they do any real damage to the status quo. Among the "characteristics of the Joycean sentence," Gottfried claims, are "a freedom within bounds, an extension of certain expected patterns of syntax to the limit of their rules, but not beyond" (9). It is the familiar double demand that literary language be deviant but not too deviant (compare J. P. Thorne's influential theory of poetic grammar, which is governed by the following constraint: "Although it contains rules which are not rules of Standard English, they must relate to rules of Standard English" ["Generative Grammar and Stylistic Analysis," 195]). The connection between this view and a wider political outlook is made explicitly by Gottfried: "The language of *Ulysses* is a freedom within bounds, a freedom which takes its definition, *as all freedoms do,* from the order it makes free with" (11–12, my emphasis). This freedom, whether understood linguistically or politically, is never allowed to be the kind that exposes the restrictions of freedom upon which it relies.

stituted, and they therefore encode aspects of a society's or a language community's ideology; the process of exposing them and turning them into comedy is therefore, potentially at least, a politically significant one. Essential to Joyce's method in *Ulysses* is the way his writing moves in and out of the established conventions (problematizing the borderline it transgresses), thus resisting the processes of naturalization which are an inevitable product of close familiarity with a language and which lead us to assume that the distinctions and continuities given in our own language or languages are "normal" or "real." Joyce's work has, of course, been subject to a massive exercise of systematization and abstraction, but it has also played its part in raising these very questions, whose careful discussion has in turn made it possible to return to Joyce with different expectations and tools of analysis.

As this discussion has shown, one area in which language encodes assumptions that are also challengeable through language is the ideology of the body.[20] The liberation of the bodily part from the whole, and the possibility of condensation and substitution, can occur only because the meaning of an organ is not exhausted by its place and function in the economy of the unified individual as determined by the cultural and ideological context. Each organ has its own physical properties and patterns of behavior which displace and subvert the central, commanding, conscious will and open up the possibility of continual reinterpretation. As wide variations from culture to culture indicate, the parts of the body acquire their meanings through a specific set of signifying systems, which is possible only if the relation between these meanings and the actual physical properties of the organs in question is, in part at least, arbitrary—although signifying systems, of which language is the most poweful, work ceaselessly to

---

[20]Though my prime concern—and Joyce's—is the English language, the tendencies discussed here are apparent in a wide variety of other languages. When these tendencies serve, in a particular society at a particular time, the interests of a dominant class— when, for instance, the unquestioned notion of the subject as a freely acting, fully conscious, internally hierarchical unity of mind and body is part of a prevailing liberal-humanist ethos that inhibits the kind of collective consciousness and collective activity which might challenge an exploitative socioeconomic system—we can justifiably regard them as having an ideological function. This is quite different from saying that it is "language" as some transcendent and suprahistorical entity that constitutes ideological systems. The interplay between the language or languages of a given social group and its relations of domination or resistance is inevitably complex and subject to historical change.

dissolve any awareness of that arbitrariness. One organ may thus be substituted for another at a given point in the system, or the resistant materiality of the organ may refuse the abstracting power of the network of differences. In just the same way every item of speech or writing has its own sound and shape independent of its authorized function in the language system, and this material specificity and independence prohibit complete transparency, fixity, and singleness of meaning; words, even letters, have lives of their own in *Ulysses* (and even more so, of course, in *Finnegans Wake*).[21] Because the syntactic system is purely differential, one item in the chain may be paradigmatically replaced by another in defiance of semantic restrictions ("her lips" for "she"), and because the relation between a materially specific signifier and that which it signifies is arbitrary, a single word or part of a word may point in several directions at once ("swelling," "nose," "frankly," "etcetera"). (In the "Sirens" episode Bloom himself reflects on this potential in language—and achieves another vocal/genital transfer—in bringing to mind the sounds of Molly's urination: "Chamber music. Could make a kind of pun on that" [11.979].) Nor is this semantic instability just a matter of highly charged language studded with puns and syntactic deviations: "Eumaeus" demonstrates that uncertainties of meaning also spring from a certain emptying out of sense, which allows the signifiers—words, phrases, whole sentences—to work in several ways at once.

Ouside the literary domain these properties of language tend to be treated as accidental features whose effects have to be kept to a minimum if language is to function properly. Both the system of differential patterning which allows for an infinite series of replacements and the arbitrary relation between the resistant materiality of the signifiers and the senses they bear threaten the efficient transmission of meaning from one whole consciousness to another, a transmission that relies on the illusion of words which perfectly serve their meanings, without slippage and without residue. Yet these properties make the functioning of language possible. Without them there would be only some clumsy, ostensive method of communication like that which Gulliver encounters in the Academy of Lagado. Time and again in *Ulysses* these properties are foregrounded and exploited, and

---

[21]On the evasive and unfixable properties of the letter (and what is built on the letter, name and identity) as it functions in Joyce's writing, see Maud Ellmann, "Disremembering Dedalus" and "Polytropic Man."

they become the structural principle of the language of *Finnegans Wake*.

In "Sirens" these two processes come together: bodily displacements and substitutions are enacted in the displacements and substitutions of language, and the apparent naturalness of both systems of meaning is challenged by the specificity and unpredictableness of its elements. The episode explores the way in which the body is conventionally conceived of as unitary and simple, without recognition of its potential for multiple, shifting, and ambiguous significations, its separability into independent parts whose meanings are not given in advance, and its limitless openness to new interpretations and new sources of pleasure. As with language, this potential exists because of, not in spite of, its material being, and language has to conceal its own materiality in order to promote the ideology of an indivisible and biddable body. Throughout *Ulysses* there is a questioning of the straightforward blending of a mind and a body in a unity that can be called by a single proper name or pronoun; most obviously, "Circe" and "Ithaca" use deviant language to disturb and dissolve that unity, and the uncertain reference of many of Molly's pronouns in "Penelope" is another well-known instance. "Eumaeus," too, dethrones the controlling subject, whose language is seen to be a tissue of slightly soiled phrases, all too available to the first-comer. These episodes, by means of their play with organs and with words, and the desires that pass between them, insist that neither language nor the body can be seen as merely secondary and subservient to a nonmaterial, transcendent, systematic, controlling principle, whether we call that principle "meaning" or "the self." More important, they demonstrate some of the pleasures, sexual and textual, that we owe to this fact.

Chapter 7

Unpacking the Portmanteau; or,
Who's Afraid of *Finnegans Wake*?

O NE aspect of Shakespeare's writing Samuel Johnson, for all his admiration of the dramatist, could not stomach: its use of puns. This blind spot of Johnson's is well known, but it is worth paying attention to the apparently extravagent terms he employs in the famous passage from the Preface to Shakespeare:

> A quibble is to Shakespeare, what luminous vapours are to the traveller; he follows it at all adventures, it is sure to lead him out of his way, and sure to engulf him in the mire. It has some malignant power over his mind, and its fascinations are irresistible. Whatever be the dignity or profundity of his disquisition, whether he be enlarging knowledge or exalting affection, whether he be amusing attention with incidents or enchaining it in suspense, let but a quibble spring up before him, and he leaves his work unfinished. A quibble is the golden apple for which he will always turn aside from his career, or stoop from his elevation. A quibble, poor and barren as it is, gave him such delight, that he was content to purchase it, by the sacrifice of reason, propriety and truth. A quibble was to him the fatal Cleopatra for which he lost the world, and was content to lose it. (74)

Though Johnson's grandiose metaphors may seem exaggerated, the attitude they reflect is not one that the intervening centuries have

188

entirely expunged.[1] The pun remains an embarrassment to be excluded from "serious" discourse, a linguistic anomaly to be controlled
by relegation to the realms of the infantile, the jocular, the literary. It
survives, tenaciously, as freak or accident, hindering what is taken to
be the primary function of language: the clean transmission of a pre-
existing, self-sufficient, unequivocal meaning. It is a characteristic
mode of the dream, the witticism, the slip of the tongue: those irrup-
tions of the disorderly world of childhood pleasures and unconscious
desires into the clear, linear processes of practical and rational
thought, those challenges to what Johnson precisely articulates as the
domain of "reason, propriety and truth." The pun represents a trick
of art, imposing duplicity and self-consciousness upon the singleness
and simplicity of nature.

The pun has this power because it undermines the basis on which
our assumptions about the communicative efficacy of language rest:
in Saussure's terms, that for each signifier there is an inseparable
signified, the two mutually interdependent like two sides of a sheet of
paper.[2] To the extent that a language, natural or artificial, fails to
match single signifiers to single signifieds, it is held to fail as language.
The possibility of the pun is a mark of our fallen condition—our
language, it seems, like every other aspect of our existence, is touched
with imperfection. But the possibility of the pun is not, of course, the
pun itself, merely the presence of ambiguity in language. And linguistic theory has learned to handle ambiguity—indeed, ambiguity

[1]In the opening pages of *Shakespeare's Wordplay*, M. M. Mahood discusses the antag-
onism toward the pun which originated in the seventeenth-century demand for communicative efficiency, noting that Johnson, for all his hostility, had a sharper ear for
Shakespeare's puns than his nineteenth-century successors. Sylvan Barnet, in "Coleridge on Puns," observes that despite Coleridge's disagreement with Johnson over
Shakespeare's word-play, and his own penchant for punning, his approval of the practice is strictly circumscribed. Thus Coleridge several times claims there are no puns in
Macbeth (making it necessary to argue that the porter's equivocations are by another
hand), and in the *Philosophical Lectures* he endorses the view that the minds of young
pupils should be guarded against the deceptive force of puns. For some valuable
comments on the threat so often perceived in the pun, see Richard Rand, "Geraldine,"
298–99 and n.16.

[2]Many possible taxonomies are applicable to the range of effects we call "the pun"; I
am concerned only with the general phenomenon of homonymy in language and its
exploitation in literature. See the suggestions by James Brown in "Eight Types of Puns"
and L. G. Heller in "Toward a General Typology of the Pun." Both these writers
regard the pun as representing a fundamental property of literary language.

plays a crucial part in the argument for a distinction between deep and surface structures which is central to transformational-generative syntactic theory. The same surface structure may have two distinct meanings—"The shooting of the hunters was terrible," "Visiting relatives can be tedious"—and it follows that each meaning must be derived from a different "kernel sentence" or correspond to a different "deep structure." Notice, however, that the same valorizing assumptions haunt the linguist's various metaphors: the single, unambiguous meaning is awarded the complimentary adjectives "kernel" or "deep," whereas ambiguity is associated with the husk, the superficial outside—duplicitous appearance and not monosemous reality.

In spite of its untoward tendency to polysemy, language works well enough, we are told, because it always operates in a disambiguating context. We are able to choose one of several potential meanings for a word or sentence because we are guided by the immediate verbal surroundings, the nature of the speech act in which the words are uttered and perceived, the social and historical setting, and so on. As speakers we construct our sentences in such a way as to eradicate possible ambiguities, and as hearers we assume single meanings in the sentences we interpret. The pun, however, is not just an ambiguity that has crept into an utterance unawares, to embarrass or amuse before being dismissed; it is ambiguity unashamed of itself, and this characteristic is what makes it more than just an inconvenience. The context of a pun, instead of being designed to suppress latent ambiguity, is deliberately constructed to *enforce* ambiguity, to render impossible the choice between meanings, to leave the reader or hearer endlessly oscillating in semantic space.

Pope's reference to Cambridge University in the Fourth Book of the *Dunciad* furnishes a well-known example for discussion:

> Where Bentley late tempestuous wont to sport
> In troubled waters, but now sleeps in Port.   (lines 201–2)

In most of our encounters with the word *port* the context in which it occurs (verbal and pragmatic) suppresses large areas of its potential signification. Pope's achievement in this couplet is to leave unsuppressed two apparently incompatible fields of meaning—*port* as in "harbor" and *port* as in "wine"—by inventing a context in which both are simultaneously acceptable. The noble conception of the tempest-tossed bark at last lying peacefully in harbor is radically undercut by the unseemly image of the great scholar reduced to drunken slumber by nightly overindulgence, and the movement between these two is as inescapable as it is perpetual. Bentley's slumber is thus rendered risible by the use of a trope associated with heroic endeavor. At the same time, however, something of that heroism rubs off on Bentley's adventures with the bottle.

Pope's lines do not release all the meanings associated with the word *port*, of course; there is little likelihood of a reader bringing into play the idea of "external deportment, carriage, or bearing" or "the left-hand side of a ship." The semantic movement initiated by Pope's couplet, though never-ending, is strictly controlled: the angel of reason dancing on a pun. If we should encounter the word *port* in a severely impoverished context—it appears on a scrap pushed under the door, for instance, or is uttered in an otherwise silent dream—the range of meaning widens, and the pleasure we take in the word's ambiguity disappears. No longer is language's potential for semantic expansion hinted at but simultaneously kept at bay; it has become threatening and confusing. Remove even more of the context, and the expansion accelerates rapidly—imagine the word being encountered by someone who knows no English, or no Indo-European language, or no human language. Eventually its meaning becomes infinite and, at exactly the same moment, disappears.

It is not surprising, therefore, that the pun is marginalized in our most common uses of language. Outside the licensed domains of literature and jokes, and the uncontrollable manifestations of parapraxes and dreams, the possibilities of meaning in any given use of a word are stringently limited by context. The more that context bears down upon the word, the less the word will quiver with signification, until we reach a fully determining context under whose pressure the word will lie inert, pinned down, proffering its single meaning. But at this point something else will have happened: the word will have become completely redundant. The context will now allow only one meaning to be perceived in the gap that it occupies, and anything—or nothing at all—can be interpreted as providing that meaning. In the terms of information theory, the more predictable is a given item in a message, the less information it carries, and so the totally predictable word conveys, in itself, absolutely nothing. What we have, then, is a continuum from the totally powerless item, devoid of meaning because already completely specified by its surroundings, to the infinitely powerful item, devoid of meaning because completely *un*specified.

Meaning resides between the two. What we call the pun is one stage along the way, what we call "single meaning" is another.[3] Exclude the pun, and you exclude the process on which all language rests, the process whereby context constrains but does not wholly constrain the possibilities of meaning.

We can approach the pun from another direction, from which we can again see it as a phenomenon that is part and parcel of the normal procedures of language. The semantic fields of *port* in the sense of wine and of *port* in the sense of harbor have no evident synchronic connection. One's understanding of each normally remains un-colored by one's understanding of the other, because of the constrain-ing effect of context already discussed. The two words usually func-tion quite differently, and it is an arbitrary quirk of the specific language system of English which associates them at all. Yet what Pope has done is to invent a context in which that arbitrary link comes to seem motivated: taking the language as he finds it, he has suc-ceeded in shifting the world into a pattern in which harbors and wine are superimposed. The material envelope of the sign—its phonemes and graphemes—has been allowed to take the initiative and has brought about a coalescence of otherwise distinct fields of reference. This dominance of the signifier, of course, goes against all the rules. Phonemes and graphemes should be servants, not masters, and the mere coincidence of outward similarity should have no bearing on the meanings within. If this were not the case, language would never get off the ground—we would expect all words beginning with the same letter to be semantically related, for instance, or assume that historical or dialectal changes in pronunciation must entail changes in meaning.

The insubordination revealed by the pun is, of course, a feature of all poetic language. The independence of meaning from its material representation required by the linguistic system is challenged by *every* use in poetry of sound or appearance to make connections or to establish contrasts—every effect of rhyme, rhythm, visual patterning,

---

[3]The attempt to use polysemy as a defining characteristic of literature—it is one of the criteria suggested by Ronald Carter and Walter Nash in their interesting essay "Language and Literariness," for instance—needs careful qualification. Certain cultur-al traditions undoubtedly valorize certain kinds of polysemy in the texts they deem literary, which may or may not include both the polysemy produced by an extremely rich context (Shakespeare, Dickens) or by a relatively impoverished one (William Carlos Williams, John Ashbery), but the extremes (*Finnegans Wake*, Dada) tend to be viewed with understandable suspicion.

alliteration, or assonance—and the pun is only a particularly extreme case of such articulation at the level of the signifier, relying as it does on *complete* coincidence of sound between two words. Once we generalize the pun in this way, we realize that its mode of operation is not, in the end, peculiar to poetry. For if other manifestations of language completely excluded this mode of establishing relationships of meaning, the only linguistic connections and contrasts with any significance would be those already given (but how?) by extralinguistic reality. Meanings would have to relate to meanings by their own nature, and signifiers would be left to form innocent patterns, mere diagrams of froth on the surface of a profound and unplumbable sea. Such a theory not only disqualifies the characteristic mode of poetry, of popular wisdom and humor, of any discourse that uses the verbal schemes of rhetoric (and what discourse does not?); it also ignores the perfectly normal syntactic and morphemic function of patterning at the level of the signifier. It is not mere chance that there is a similarity of sound between "book*s*" and "cat*s*" or between "look*ed*" and "hop*ed*," and the oppositions single/plural and present/past are not experiential givens that preexist the linguistic patterns which produce them. More generally, to the extent that language is held to affect or determine the subject's perception and categorization of the world, patterning in the signifier must have semantic force, because language has no medium in which to operate other than the patterns of sonic and visual substance. Clearly, there *is* meaning in the coincidences of the signifier, and an absolute separation between the functions of signifier and signified is impossible.[4] Once again the pun turns out to be not an aberration of language but a direct reflection of its "normal" working.

I have suggested two approaches to the pun, both of which reveal it as a product of language's necessary mode of operation: as one signifier with two possible signifieds, which in a particular context are simultaneously activated, and as two identical signifiers, which in a particular context are made to coalesce. Each approach associates the

[4]The operation of "folk etymology," which is a significant factor in the diachronic changes in any language, depends on the assumption in the minds of speakers that coincidences of sound are not accidental—an assumption not unreasonably derived from the patterning of morphology and the process of analogical change (see chapter 4 above). Mitsou Ronat usefully relates the portmanteau word to folk etymology in "L'hypotexticale."

pun with a feature especially characteristic of literary language. The first is polysemy, the second the semantic use of purely formal similarities, and the pun combines these features in a way that heightens the power of both. But it does so at some cost. The effect has to be created by a carefully constructed linguistic envelope (Pope needs fourteen words to prepare us for a bisemous reading of *port*), and it is limited to exact correspondence of sound. Other kinds of polysemy (a word with one primary meaning and several secondary associations, for example) and other kinds of assonance (rhyme, alliteration, etc.) are much more readily available in the language and need no such elaborate scaffolding in order to work. By the same token, however, they are much weaker: the reader can more easily ignore or subdue them, dismissing secondary associations as "irrelevant" or allowing rhyme words to lie side by side without mutual interference, as if chastely separated by a chivalric sword.

Banished from utilitarian discourse, then, the pun finds a home in the literary tradition as long as it is well-behaved, limiting its field of operation in terms of genres (preferably nonserious writing), frequency (punning too often is a sign of immaturity), and the range of its multiple meanings (preferably only two, both clearly defined by the context). But what if there were a way of combining the power of the pun with the ready availability of those weaker effects of polysemy and patterning, of bringing into the foreground those otherwise dismissable associations, and of coupling together in a simultaneous experience those meanings which lie separate in such verbal echoes as rhyme and assonance? And what if the operation of this device could be signaled independently of context and in a completely inescapable way? If this fusion were to be achieved, the processes of exclusion which operate already on the pun would be put into action with redoubled energy, because the new device would expose even more thoroughly the myths of a monosemous language and a preexisting structure of meaning, and it would put even more strongly in question the belief in language's transparency, stability, and rationality. The spirit of Dr. Johnson would prove to be still very much alive, and the new device, together with the text and author employing it, would meet with the same hostility that in the eighteenth century greeted Shakespeare's use of puns. Johnson's denunciation needs very little rewriting to bring it up to date: "A portmanteau word, poor and barren as it is, gave Joyce such delight that he was content to purchase it by the sacrifice of reason, propriety and truth. A portmanteau word was to him the fatal Issy for which he lost the world, and was content to lose it."

The Power of the Portmanteau

Published responses to *Finnegans Wake* afford examples of this hostility in profusion. That the last major work of one of the language's most admired and influential writers—the product of some sixteen painful years' labor—has remained on the margins of the literary tradition is an extraordinary but well-established fact. That the phenomenon is so evident does not mean that it requires no explanation; on the contrary, if we could properly account for it, we might throw light on the processes of reading and evaluation which determine the shape of the literary canon. Those who find little appeal in Joyce's earlier writing are unlikely to have a good word to say for the *Wake*, but what is more remarkable is that many of those who have written admirably about Joyce's other works testify to difficulties with his last book. Sometimes, as a result, an introductory text that one might expect to offer encouragement to the new reader in tackling Joyce's most ambitious work can have the opposite effect. Thus John Gross asks, in his volume on Joyce in the widely selling Modern Masters series, "What was Joyce's object in devising so outlandish a style?— always assuming, that is, that the entire book isn't best regarded as a hoax?" And he sums up his position as follows: "In the end the *Wake* seems to me a dazzling failure, the aberration of a great man. Viewed as a whole, I don't believe it is nearly worth the effort which it demands" (*Joyce*, 79, 89). S. L. Goldberg says of *Finnegans Wake* in another introductory book on Joyce's entire output: "The work itself seems to me an artistic failure; and despite the enthusiastic assertions of its admirers, the questions it prompts the ordinary reader to ask remain, I believe, still the most important—questions concerned less with its verbal "meaning" or its machinery than with its value: why Joyce ever undertook it, why it seems so laborious and, more particularly, so unrewarding to read through" (*Joyce*, 103).[5] And A. Walton Litz, in his study *The Art of James Joyce*, comments that "at one and the same time the *Wake* is too abstract and too concrete. Paradoxically, it

[5]Goldberg's phrase "read *through*" suggests one reason for the problems he has with the *Wake*.

displays a detailed point-by-point fidelity to Joyce's early experiences without reflecting—as do *Portrait* and *Ulysses*—a full sense of the reality of those experiences. The result is an infinitely rich texture combined with a tedium of basic thought. That sense of 'felt life' which Henry James considered the essence of literary form infuses Joyce's artifice by fits and starts" (124). Litz goes on to use the same word as the other two critics, referring to "this failure I find in the *Wake*." Yet it is clear from his valuable discussion of Joyce's writing of the *Wake* that Litz's reservations do not arise from any lack of sympathy, sensitivity, or effort; he seems almost unwilling to reach the conclusion he feels he has to. In his later introductory book on Joyce one hears the same tone:

> I have spoken earlier of the triumphs and limitations of *Finnegans Wake*, which force me to conclude that it is a partial failure. Any set of standards that will account for the essential greatness of *Ulysses* must, I feel, find a certain sterility in *Finnegans Wake*. Even the comic spirit which, much more than the elaborate structural patterns, gives the *Wake* its unity, seems to me ultimately self-defeating. In *Ulysses*, parody and satire have direction because they serve a moral vision; but in *Finnegans Wake* they turn upon themselves and destroy their own foundations. (*James Joyce*, 118)

The many readers who find the *Wake* a source of great pleasure, the many teachers and students who find it a delight to discuss in a small class (once initial prejudices are overcome), will regret that comments like these, sincere though they are, put obstacles in the way of others who might find in the work pleasures similar to their own. But our present task is to ask what about Joyce's last book is so resistant to the efforts of many well-disposed and well-qualified readers to find enjoyment in it. There can be no doubt that a major reason for this negative reaction is the work's intensive use of the portmanteau word, which is what makes the style "outlandish," demands "effort" from the reader, renders the work "laborious" and "unrewarding," inhibits the communication of "felt life." The portmanteau word is a monster, a word that is not a word, that is not authorized by any dictionary, that holds out the worrying prospect of books which, instead of comfortingly recycling the words we know, possess the freedom endlessly to invent new ones. We have learned to accept novels without firm plots or consistent characters, novels that blend historical periods or submerge the authorial presence, even novels that pun and rhyme; but sixty years after it first started appearing, the novel—if it can still be called a novel—that makes the portmanteau word a cornerstone of its method remains a troublesome presence in the institution of literature.[6]

My argument so far suggests an explanation that goes beyond discomfort with the unusual and dislike of the difficult, understandable though these reactions are. The portmanteau word challenges two myths on which most assumptions about the efficacy of language rest. Like the pun, it denies that single words must have, on any given occasion, single meanings; and like the various devices of assonance and rhyme, it denies that the manifold patterns of similarity which occur at the level of the signifier are innocent of meaning. It does so with the pun's simultaneity of operation but more flagrantly and with less warning. There is no escape from its insistence that meaning is an *effect* of language, not a presence within or behind it, and that the effect is unstable and uncontrollable. Notice, too, that whereas the pun can easily be contained by being treated as the index of an imperfect language, allowing ambiguity where it should insist on univocity, the conclusion is harder to escape that the portmanteau can be nothing other than a defining feature of language itself, because the portmanteau derives from the fact that the same segments (letters, phonemes, syllables) can be combined in different ways to encode different meanings. A language in which portmanteau formations were impossible would be a language in which every signified was matched with a unique and unanalyzable signifier—that is, not a language at all.[7]

---

[6]In *Adultery in the Novel,* Tony Tanner comments that "puns and ambiguities are to common language what adultery and perversion are to 'chaste' (i.e., socially orthodox) sexual relations. They both bring together entities (meanings/people) that have 'conventionally' been differentiated and kept apart; and they bring them together in deviant ways, bypassing the orthodox rules governing communications and relationships. (A pun is like an adulterous bed in which two meanings that should be separate are coupled together.) It is hardly an accident that *Finnegans Wake,* which arguably demonstrates the dissolution of bourgeois society, is almost one continuous pun (the connection with sexual perversion being quite clear to Joyce)" (53). As I have tried to show, the pun can constitute a thoroughly respectable coupling, which is why the *Wake* is not, *pace* Tanner, essentially a punning text. Tanner's remark is more appropriate to the promiscuous liaisons of words and meanings in the portmanteau.

[7]The portmanteau exploits to the full the language's potential for what in chapter 5 I called "nonce-constellations": groups of words with similar sounds which create the

Not surprisingly, therefore, the portmanteau word has had a history of exclusion much more severe than that of the pun. Outside the language of dreams, parapraxes, and jokes, it has existed chiefly in the form of malapropism and nonsense verse—the language of the uneducated, the child, the idiot. (The very term "portmanteau word" comes from a children's story, *Alice Through the Looking-Glass*, and not a work of theory or criticism.)[8] And the literary establishment has often relegated *Finnegans Wake* to the same border area. How else can it avoid the claim made by the text that the portmanteau word, far from being a sport, an eccentricity, a mistake, is a revelation of the processes upon which all language relies? How else can it exclude the possibility that the same relation obtains between *Finnegans Wake* and the tradition of the novel, that what appears to be a limiting case or a parody, a parasite on the healthy body of literature, is at the same time central and implicated in the way the most "normal" text operates? It is the familiar logic of the Derridean supplement or *pharmakon* I have already discussed in relation to Puttenham's writing: the "artifice" to be excluded from the category of "natural" literature (with its "felt life" and "full sense of reality") which nevertheless reveals the artificial character of literature itself.[9] In the *Wake*'s deconstruction of the oppositional structures of the literary tradition, the portmanteau word proves to be a powerful tool, but its very power has rendered it ineffective. (This is not, of course, to argue that those who find the *Wake* hard going are party to a conspiracy dedicated to the preservation of a metaphysical conception of language; we can never be fully conscious of the reasons for our preferences, and to attempt to explain the acceptance or rejection of a literary text is not to award praise or lay blame.)

To demonstrate the operation of the portmanteau and to explore the reasons why, for all their superficial similarity, the portmanteau and the pun are very different kinds of linguistic deviation, a specific

---

impression of a particular appropriateness between those sounds and the dominant semantic content of the group. In the portmanteau the words in question are presented not as a sequence but as a combined unit. Dwight Bolinger's discussions of sound and sense in *Forms of English*, referred to in that chapter, are highly relevant to the language of *Finnegans Wake*.

[8]A text such as Francis Huxley's *The Raven and the Writing Desk*, which treats Carroll's portmanteaux with the comic brilliance they deserve, is equally likely to be overlooked by the literary establishment.

[9]See ". . . That Dangerous Supplement . . . ," in *Of Grammatology*, 141–64, and "Plato's Pharmacy," in *Dissemination*, 61–171.

example is needed. The following passage was chosen at random, and the points I make about it could be made about any page of *Finnegans Wake*.

> And stand up tall! Straight. I want to see you looking fine for me. With your brandnew big green belt and all. Blooming in the very lotust and second to nill, Budd! When you're in the buckly shuit Rosensharonals near did for you. Fiftyseven and three, cosh, with the bulge. Proudpurse Alby with his pooraroon Eireen, they'll. Pride, comfytousness, enevy! You make me think of a wonderdecker I once. Or somebalt that sailder, the man megallant, with the bangled ears. Or an earl was he, at Lucan? Or, no, it's the Iren duke's I mean. Or somebrey erse from the Dark Countries. Come and let us! We always said we'd. And go abroad. (620.1)[10]

At the risk of seeming to posit the very things I have said the text undermines—themes, plot, characters—let me tender a bald and provisional statement of some of the threads that can be traced through the passage, in order to establish an initial orientation. The predominant "voice" in this part of the text—its closing pages—is what Joyce designated by **△**, the shifting cluster of attributes and energies often associated with the initials ALP and the role of wife and mother. The addressee is primarily the group of characteristics indicated by **Ⅲ**, the male counterpart frequently manifested as the letters HCE. Two of the prominent narrative strands involving this couple in the closing pages are a walk around Dublin in the early morning and a sexual act, and both are fused with the movement of the river Liffey flowing through Dublin into the sea. Contradictory tones and modes of address are blended, in particular the eager admiration of a young girl for her energetic lover and the disappointment of the aging wife with her now impotent husband. Here ALP is asking HCE to don his new, expensive clothes and go out with her on a jaunt, but she is also inviting him to demonstrate his naked sexual potency. (At first, the words are also those of a mother to her young son; they echo, too, a letter of Joyce's to Nora on 7 September 1909: "I want

---

[10]References to *Finnegans Wake* are to the standard Faber/Viking edition of 1939 and indicate page number and line number on that page. Where a quotation is of more than one line, only the first line number is given. In commenting on this passage I have made use of several of the standard reference books on *Finnegans Wake*, and I gratefully acknowledge the labors of their authors.

you to look your best for me when I come. Have you any nice clothes now?" [*Letters*, 2:251].) At the same time what we hear is the river addressing the city of Dublin (reversed in "nill, Budd"), with its green belt and modern comforts. The relationship is also reminiscent of that between Molly and Leopold Bloom in *Ulysses*. "Blooming in the very lotust" points to the earlier novel, especially the "Lotus-Eaters" chapter; Sinbad the Sailor ("somebalt that sailder") is also associated with Bloom as he goes to bed in "Ithaca"; and Molly's own closing chapter has something in common with ALP's final monologue. It includes, too, the exploitative relationship of England and Ireland ("Proud-purse Alby with his pooraroon Eireen": perfidious Albion and poor Eire or Erin). The passage enunciates a series of ALP's sexual memories, all of which turn out to be memories of HCE in one or other of his guises: as sailor (Sinbad, Magellan, and Vanderdecken, the captain of the *Flying Dutchman*); as military figure (the man with the bandolier, the duke of Wellington, and the earl of Lucan—whether the hero of the Williamite wars or the Lord Lucan who fought at Balaclava); and as the stranger (the man with earrings, the man from the Dark Countries) who is also an Irishman (not only Wellington but Lucan as a village on the Liffey, "Iren" as Ireland, and "erse" as Irish). That the exploits of these figures are partly sexual (or excretory, for the two are not kept distinct in the *Wake*) emerges from the "gallant" of "megallant," "erse" understood as "arse," and another echo of *Ulysses*, this time of Bloom's pamphlet advertising the "Wonderworker," "the world's greatest remedy for rectal complaints" (17.1820).[11] Once phallic suggestions begin to surface, they can be discovered at every turn: a few examples would be "stand up," "straight," "I want to see you" (an instance of the familiar synecdoche discussed in the previous chapter), *bod* (pronounced *bud*) as Gaelic for "penis," "cosh" (a thick stick), "bulge," the "wonderdecker" again (*decken* in German is to copulate), the stiffness of iron, and the Wellington monument. And the evident ellipses (reminiscent of those in the "Eumaeus" episode of *Ulysses*) can easily be read as sexual modesty: "a wonderdecker I once . . . ," "the Iren Duke's . . . ," "Come and let us . . . ," "We always said we'd. . . ." I have provided only an initial indication of some of the meanings at work here, and one could follow other motifs through the passage: flowers, sins (several of the

---

[11] See *Ulysses* 11.1224, 15.3274, and 18.716 for further references to this invention, which "claims to afford a noiseless inoffensive vent."

seven deadly ones are here), tailoring and sailing (the two often go together in the *Wake*), and battles. All of these are associated in one way or another with sex.[12]

Let us focus now on one word from the passage, "shuit." To call it a word is of course misleading—it is precisely because it is *not* a word recognized as belonging to the English language that it functions as it does, preventing the immediate move from material signifier to conceptual signified. Unlike the pun, which exists only if the context brings it into being, the portmanteau refuses, *by itself,* any single meaning, and in reading we therefore have to nudge it toward other signifiers whose meanings might prove appropriate. Let us, first of all, ignore the larger context of the whole book and concentrate—as we would for a pun—on the guidance provided by the immediate context. We seem to be invited to take "shuit" as an item of clothing, one that can have the adjective "buckly"—with buckles—applied to it. Three lexical items offer themselves as appropriate: *suit, shirt, shoes.* The first two would account for the portmanteau without any unexplained residue, but "buckly" seems to point in particular to *shoes,* partly by way of the nursery rhyme "One, two, buckle my shoe." A writer employing orthodox devices of patterning at the level of the signifier might construct a sentence in which the separate words *suit, shirt,* and *shoes* all occur in such a way as to make the reader conscious of the sound-connections between them, thus creating what I called earlier a nonce-constellation, but it would be a rather feeble, easily ignored, device. "Shuit" works more powerfully because it insists on a productive act of reading, because its effects are simultaneous, and because the result is an expansion of meaning much more extensive than that effected by the pun. The pun, as we saw in the example by Pope, carries a powerful charge of satisfaction: the specter of a potentially unruly and ultimately infinite language is raised only to be exorcised, the writer and reader are still firmly in control, and the language has been made to seem even *more* orderly and appropriate than we had realized, because an apparently arbitrary coincidence in its system has been shown to be capable of semantic justification. But "shuit" and its kind are more disturbing. The portmanteau has the effect of a *failed* pun—the patterns of language have been shown to

---

[12]Needless to say, the relation between shifts and indeterminacy in the language and intimations of sexual desire is not fortuitous. See the discussion of the "Sirens" and "Eumaeus" episodes of *Ulysses* in chapter 6 above.

be partially appropriate but with a residue of difference where the pun found only happy similarity. And though the context makes it clear that the passage is about clothing and thereby seems to set limits to the word's possible meanings, one cannot escape the feeling that the process, once started, may be unstoppable. In the case of Pope's couplet the dictionary (or our internal lexicon) tells us the accredited meanings of "port," and we can acknowledge at once that the context excludes all those meanings besides "harbor" and "wine." But no reference book or mental register exists to tell us all the possible signifiers that are or could be associated in sound with "shuit," and we have learned no method of interpretation to tell us how to go about finding those signifiers or deciding at what point the connection becomes too slight to be relevant. Certainly other signifiers sound like "shuit," and if similarities of sound can have semantic implications, how do we know where to draw the boundary?

The answer to this question may seem straightforward: like the pun, the portmanteau will contain as much as the verbal context permits it to contain and no more. But the answer brings us to a fundamental point about the *Wake,* because the context *itself* is made up of puns and portmanteaux. So far I have spoken as if the context were a given, firm structure of meaning which has one neatly defined hole in it, but this notion is of course pure interpretative fiction. The text is a web of shifting meanings, and every new interpretation of one item recreates afresh the context for all the other items. Having found *suit* in "shuit," for example, one can reinterpret the previous word to yield the phrase *birthday suit,* as a colloquial expression for "nakedness," nicely epitomizing the fusion of the states of being clothed and unclothed which the passage implies—one more example of the denial of the logic of opposites which starts to characterize this text with its very title. Thus a "contextual circle" is created whereby plurality of meaning in one item increases the available meanings of other items, which in turn increase the possibilities of meaning in the original item. The longer and denser the text, the more often the circle will revolve, and the greater will be the proliferation of meanings. It is important to note, however, that the network of signification remains *systematic:* the familiar accusation that "there is no way of denying the relevance . . . of any meaning any commentator cares to find," to quote Goldberg again (*Joyce,* 111), is without substance. In a text as long and as densely worked as *Finnegans Wake,* however, the systematic networks of meaning could probably provide contexts for most of the associations that individual words might evoke—though an individual reader could not be expected to grasp them all. This sense of a spiraling increase in potential meaning is one of the grounds on which the *Wake* is left unread, but is this not an indication of the way *all* texts operate? Every item in a text functions simultaneously as a sign whose meaning is limited (but not wholly limited) by its context and as a context limiting (but not wholly limiting) the meaning of other signs. There is no escape from this circle, no privileged item that yields its meaning apart from the system in which it is perceived and which can act as a contextless context or transcendental fixing-point to anchor the whole text. The enormous difference between *Finnegans Wake* and other literary works is, perhaps, a difference in degree, not in kind.

The next word, "Rosensharonals," provides another example of the operation of contexts in the *Wake*. As an individual item it immediately suggests "Rose of Sharon," a flower (identified with crocus, narcissus, and others) to go with bloom, lotus, and bud and to enhance further the springlike vitality of the male or his sexual organ. It gives us a reference to the Song of Solomon (itself a sexual invitation), reinforcing the text's insistence that apparently "natural" human emotions are cultural products: love and sexual desire in this passage are caught up not only with the Hebraic tradition but also with Buddhism (both in the lotus and in "Budd"), with *Billy Budd* (a story whose concerns are highly relevant), with *Sinbad the Sailor* (as a tale from the *Arabian Nights* or as a pantomime), and with popular songs (*Eileen Aroon*—"Eileen my darling"—and phrases from "I will give you the keys to heaven"). (I suspect there may also be a song called "The Man with the Bandolier," though I have not been able to trace it; in fact the text problematizes that very urge to "verify" what offers itself as an "allusion.")[13] The sense of new beginnings is also heightened by a suggestion of Rosh Hashanah, the Jewish New Year. In the context of clothing, however, the name sounds more like that of the Jewish tailor who made the garment in question: "the buckly shuit Rosensharonals near did for you," bringing to mind the story of Kersse the tailor and

---

[13]Charles Peake has suggested to me a possible reference to the once-popular song "The Bandolero" (private communication). The word "bandolier" is also associated with Leopold Bloom: he is recalled as a school pupil in "Oxen of the Sun," "his booksatchel on him bandolierwise" (14.1047); and in "Circe" he appears with "*fieldglasses in bandolier*" (15.538). The French word "bander," to have an erection, is perhaps in the background.

the Norwegian captain from earlier in the book (311–32), a story that involves a suit with a bulge in it, apparently made necessary by a hunchback. But once we move to the context of the whole work, another story, from the same earlier chapter (337–55), comes into prominence: the tale of Buckley and the Russian general, which appears in the text at many points and in many guises. Buckley is a common Irish soldier in the Crimean War who comes upon a Russian general with his pants down, in the act of defecating, and either does or does not shoot at him. The story interweaves with other stories of encounters involving exposure and/or voyeurism, such as the much-discussed event in Phoenix Park involving HCE, two girls, and three soldiers. It has to do with the attack by the younger generation on the older, and the older generation's fall from power before the younger, the drunkenness of Noah and the drugging of Finn MacCool by his young bride being other versions. (It is typical of the *Wake*'s method that an indecent anecdote which Joyce heard from his father is accorded the same status as religious myth and epic narrative.) So in the middle of a passage of praise for the virility of HCE comes a reminder of his loss of control, and "near did for you" becomes a reference not to tailoring but to an attempt at, or a resisted temptation to, murder. And our portmanteau *shuit* unpacks itself further, yielding both *shoot* and *shit*.[14]

Pariah and Paradigm

My aim is not to demonstrate the plurality of meaning in Joyce's portmanteaux; that is easily done. It is to focus on the workings of a typical portmanteau to show both how crucial they are to the method of *Finnegans Wake* and how they help make the book conceivable as a central, rather than a peripheral, literary text. The portmanteau shatters any illusion that the systems of difference in language are fixed and sharply drawn, reminding us that signifiers are perpetually dissolving into one another: in the never-ending diachronic development of language; in the blurred edges between languages, dialects, registers, idiolects; in the interchange between speech and writing; in

[14]Horne Tooke would have found these multiple associations unsurprising. For him they would have revealed the historical processes of the language—see my summary of his etymological account of the word *shit* in chapter 4, p. 102 above.

errors and misunderstandings, unfortunate or fruitful; in riddles, jokes, games, and dreams. *Finnegans Wake* insists that the strict boundaries and discrete elements in a linguist's "grammar of competence" are a neoplatonic illusion.

But the portmanteau problematizes even the most stable signifier by showing how its relations to other signifiers can be productive; we find that we can quite easily relate *suit* to *shirt* just as we do in fact relate *suit* to *suits* or *suited*. Instead of saying that in learning a language we learn to ascribe meaning to a few of the many patterns of sound we perceive, it may be as true to say that we learn *not* to ascribe meaning to most of those connections (Freud takes this view in his book on jokes)[15]—until we are allowed to do so again to a certain degree in rhetoric and poetry, and with almost complete abandon in *Finnegans Wake*. The result, of course, is that as we read the *Wake* we test for their possible associations not only the obvious portmanteaux but every apparently normal word as well. The phrase "bangled ears" does not present itself as a portmanteau, and in most texts it would be read as a somewhat odd, but semantically specific, conjunction of adjective and noun. But the context of the *Wake*'s portmanteau style encourages us, as I have suggested, to hear it also as "bandolier," to combine the attributes of the savage or stranger with those of the soldier. Even the most normal and innocent word will invite such treatment. As Jean-Paul Martin has said of *Finnegans Wake*, "the portmanteau word, but also every word, every fragment of a word or of an utterance, marks the interlacing of sinuous and diverse chains of associations which cross codes and languages" ("La condensation," 189). Another theoretical distinction becomes blurred, that between synchronic and diachronic dimensions, because a pertinent meaning may be retrievable from the history of a word. "Erse," for instance, offers both a Middle English word for "arse" and an early Scottish word for "Irish." Here, too, the *Wake* heightens a process that operates in all language, in spite of the Saussurean enterprise of methodically separating synchrony and diachrony (see chapter 4 above).

---

[15]Freud refers to a group of jokes ("play upon words") that make "the (acoustic) word-presentation itself take the place of its significance as given by its relations to thing-presentations" and observes, "It may really be suspected that in doing so we are bringing about a great relief in psychical work and that when we make serious use of words we are obliged to hold ourselves back with a certain effort from this comfortable procedure" (*Jokes*, 167–68). See also my comments on linguistic motivation in chapter 5 above, p. 141.

The implications of the portmanteau word, or rather the portmanteau text, go further, however. The portmanteau undermines the notion of authorial intention, for instance, in a way quite foreign to the traditional pun. The pun in fact strengthens the illusion of intention as a presence within the text: part of the satisfaction to be found in Pope's pun on *port* is the feeling of certainty, once the pun is grasped, that it was intended by its witty and resourceful author. The careful construction of context to allow both meanings equal force and to exclude all other meanings is not something that happens by accident, we feel, and this feeling makes the pun acceptable in certain literary environments because there is no danger that the coincidence thus exposed will enable language to wrest control from its users. But the portmanteau word, though its initial effect is often similar, has a habit of refusing to rest with that comforting sensation of "I see what the author meant." To find *shirt* and *suit* in *shuit,* and nothing else, might yield a satisfying response of that kind: "clearly what Joyce is doing is fusing those words into one," we say to ourselves. But when we note the claims for *shoes, shoot,* and *shit* as well, we begin to lose hold on our sense of an embodied intention. If those five are to be found, why not more? The polyglot character of the text, for instance, opens up further prospects. If French ears hear *chute,* one can hardly deny the relevance of the notion of a fall (or of the Fall) to the story of Buckley and the Russian general or to the temptation of HCE in the park.[16] And why should any particular number of associations, in any particular number of languages, correspond to the author's intention? Joyce has set in motion a process over which he has no final control—a source of disquiet for many readers. Litz, for example, complains that "in reading it one does not feel that sense of 'inevitability' or 'rightness' which is the sign of a controlled narrative structure" (*The Art of James Joyce,* 62). Others are more willing to accept the vast scale of what the multilingual portmanteau opens up. In "Finnegans, Wake!" Jean Paris observes that "once it is established, it must by its own movement extend itself to the totality of living and dead languages. And here indeed is the irony of the portmanteau style: the enthroning of a principle of chance which, prolonging the intentions of the author, in so far as they are perceptible, comes little by little to

---

[16]For a discussion of the effects of Joyce's coalescing of languages which focuses on a single (and apparently simple) portmanteau from the *Wake,* see Derrida, "Two Words for Joyce."

substitute for them, to function like a delirious mechanism, accumulating allusions, parodying analogies, and finally atomizing the Book" (60–61).[17] But *every* text, not just this one, is ultimately beyond the control of its author, *every* text reveals the systems of meaning of which Derrida speaks in his consideration of the word *pharmakon* in Plato's *Phaedrus:* "But the system here is not, simply, that of the intentions of an author who goes by the name of Plato. The system is not primarily that of what someone *meant-to-say* [*un vouloir-dire*]. Finely regulated communications are established, through the play of language, among diverse functions of the word and within it, among diverse strata or regions of culture" (*Dissemination,* 95).

Similarly, the portmanteau word leaves few of the conventional assumptions about narrative intact: *récit* cannot be separated from *histoire* when it surfaces in the texture of the words themselves. When, for instance, the story of Buckley and the Russian general is woven, by the portmanteau method, into a statement about new clothing, it is impossible to talk in terms of the narration of a supposedly prior event. Rather, there is a process of fusion which enforces the realization that *all* stories are textual effects. Characters, too, are never *behind* the text in *Finnegans Wake* but *in* it; ALP, HCE, Buckley, and the Russian general have their being in portmanteau words, in acrostics, in shapes on the page—though this, too, is only a reinforcement of the status of all fictional characters. Finally, consider the traditional analysis of metaphor and allegory as a relation between a "literal," "superficial" meaning and a "figurative," "deep," "true" meaning. The portmanteau word, and *Finnegans Wake* as a whole, refuses to establish such a hierarchical opposition, for anything that appears to be a metaphor is capable of reversal, the tenor becoming the vehicle, and vice versa. In the quoted passage we might be tempted to say that a literal invitation to go for a walk can be metaphorically interpreted as an invitation to sexual activity. At the level of the word one might say that "lotust" is read literally as *latest*, a reference to fashion, but that the deeper meaning is *lotus*, with its implication of sensual enjoyment. But the only reason for saying that the "deeper" meaning is the sexual one is our own preconception as to what counts as deep and what as superficial. All metaphor, we are made to realize by this text, is potentially unstable, kept in position by the hierarchies we bring to

[17]See also the discussion by Jean Paris of the portmanteau word in "L'agonie du signe."

bear upon it, not by its inner, inherent division into literal and figurative domains. I consider in the following chapter further consequences of the *Wake*'s destabilizing of conventional categories and hierarchies.

The fears provoked by *Finnegans Wake*'s portmanteau style are understandable and inevitable, because the consequences of accepting it extend to all our reading. Every word in every text is, after all, a portmanteau of sorts, a combination of sounds that echo through the entire language and through every other language and back through the history of speech. *Finnegans Wake* makes us aware that we, as readers, control this explosion, allowing only those connections to be effected which will give us the kinds of meaning we recognize—stories, voices, characters, metaphors, images, beginnings, developments, ends, morals, truths. We do not, of course, control it as a matter of choice. We are subject to the various grids that make literature and language possible at all—rules, habits, conventions, and all the boundaries that legitimate and exclude in order to produce meanings and values, themselves rooted in the ideology of our place and time. Hence our feeling of security in reading Pope's couplet, for we share both the language and the joke. Nevertheless, to obtain a glimpse of the infinite possibility of meaning kept at bay by those grids, to gain a sense that the boundaries upon which our use of language depends are set up under specific historical conditions, is to be made aware of a universe more open to reinterpretation and change than the one we are usually conscious of inhabiting. For many of its readers *Finnegans Wake* makes that glimpse an experience of exhilaration and opportunity, and as a result the book comes to occupy an important place in their reading; but for many others it can be only a discouraging glimpse of limitless instability.[18] So the book is treated as a freak, an unaccountable anomaly that merely travesties

[18]Someone who was able to go further than most in reading a wide range of literature against the grain of established codes, prefiguring the strategies required by *Finnegans Wake*, was Saussure; but he too took fright at the infinite possibilities he opened up, as Jean Starobinski documents in *Words upon Words*. Starobinski's comments have an obvious relevance to the anxieties and pleasures of reading *Finnegans Wake:* "If this approach [the theory of hypograms] had been further developed, it would soon have become a quagmire. Wave upon wave of possible names would have taken shape beneath his alert and disciplined eye. Is this the vertigo of error? It is also the discovery of the simple truth that language is an infinite resource, and that behind each phrase lies hidden the multiple clamor from which it has detached itself to appear before us in its isolated individuality" (122).

the cultural traditions we cherish, and its function as supplement and *pharmakon,* supererogatory but necessary, dangerous but remedial, is thereby prolonged.

When the *Wake* is welcomed, however, it is often by means of a gesture that simultaneously incapacitates it, either by placing it in a sealed-off category (the impenetrable and inexpressible world of the dream) or by subjecting it to the same interpretative mechanisms that are applied to all literary texts, as if it were no different: the elucidation of an "intention" (aided by draft material and biography), the analysis of "characters," the tracing of "plot," the elaboration of "themes," the tracking down of "allusions," the identification of "autobiographical references," in sum, the whole panoply of modern professional criticism. The outright repudiation of the Joycean portmanteau, though it may one day seem as quaint an attitude as Johnson's rejection of the Shakespearean quibble, is perhaps preferable to this industrious program of normalization and domestication. Johnson's passionate lament for his flawed idol involves a fuller understanding of the implications of the pun than many an untroubled celebration of textual indeterminacy, and to be afraid of *Finnegans Wake* is at least to acknowledge, even if unconsciously, the power and magnitude of the claims it makes.

Chapter 8

Deconstructing Digression:
The Backbone of *Finnegans Wake*
and the Margins of Culture

Theme (from a Filleted Wake)

I N order, no doubt, to minimize the risk of putting the most notoriously unreadable book ever published into a paperback edition, in 1975 Faber and Faber attempted to woo hesitant purchasers of *Finnegans Wake* with a reassuring statement on the back cover. The statement, by Anthony Burgess, asserts that in this book "the puzzle element is less important than the thrust of the narrative and the shadowy majesty of the characters." This piece of promoters' wishful thinking exemplifies the immense need felt by readers and publishers of literary texts (especially long ones) for the firm center that narrative and character provide; it is the tip of an iceberg of academic labor that has taken as its goal the production—which it usually sees as the "discovery"—of such a center in *Finnegans Wake*.

Anthony Burgess has also sought to aid the reading public by producing a *Shorter Finnegans Wake,* and it is instructive to watch him about his business, filleting out the backbone of the text (to use his own rather surprising metaphor)[1] and serving it up without the flesh. After a ritual protest—"*Finnegans Wake* is one of the few books of the

---

[1]"The backbone of *Finnegans Wake* is easily filleted out" (*SFW,* 9). What in fact follows this statement is an account of Vico's historical cycles, whose relationship to the narrative described by Burgess is not immediately clear.

world that totally resist cutting" (5)—he proceeds to sharpen his instruments by way of a brisk introduction entitled "What It's All About." And what it's all about, we quickly learn, is the dream of a Dublin publican called Mr. Porter after a hard Saturday night in the bar, interrupted by a spell of wakefulness that occurs toward the end of the book.[2] Unfortunately for the reader who may be sustained through several hundred dense pages by Burgess's promise of daylight at the end, it turns out, when Mr. Porter wakes up, that the author has *also* been asleep, and remains so to the book's final word.[3] This separation between the publican's dream and the author's dream of the publican's waking moments is, however, far from straightforward, for ("surprisingly," as Burgess concedes) in the middle of the publican's dream (II.3), we come upon him wide awake in his bar, dealing with customers on a busy evening—the source, we must assume, of Burgess's conviction (and that of many others) that the dream which is supposed to occupy most of the book is the dream of a publican after a busy night in the bar, a night of "rumbustious carousal," as Burgess calls it in another summary of what he sees as the book's central narrative (*Here Comes Everybody*, 193).[4] And, sure enough, we are told that when, within his own dream, the landlord is left alone in his bar (after a threat of lynching is revealed as "a dream within a dream" [*SFW*, 19], dreams being as tightly nested as Russian

[2]The inventor of this notion that the whole book is a representation of the dream of a Dublin publican—a notion that the text itself does little to suggest—seems to have been Edmund Wilson. In 1929 Wilson announced that Joyce's new book was going to "occupy itself with the single night's sleep of a single character" ("James Joyce," 91) and followed this up after the publication of *Finnegans Wake* with a highly influential two-part essay, the second part of which was entitled "The Dream of H. C. Earwicker"—supposedly the publican's dream name. A modified version of this interpretative framework, in which HCE falls asleep at the end of II.3 and dreams from then on, was popularized by Joseph Campbell and Henry Morton Robinson in their 1944 *Skeleton Key to "Finnegans Wake."* In both versions much of III.4, the penultimate chapter, is supposed to be concerned with the wakened dreamer, and the status of the last chapter is left somewhat uncertain.

[3]Burgess insists on this strange idea as though it clarified his argument instead of undermining it: "When HCE and his wife are awakened by the crying of one of the twins and when, after quietening the child, they attempt intercourse, Joyce does all the dreaming himself" (*SFW*, 9); "through the dreaming eyes of the author, we see the decadent times which Shaun's rule has brought about figured in the sterile rituals of marital sex" (*SFW*, 20); "the dream of our hero is thus temporarily dissolved, though the dream of the author continues" (*SFW*, 241–42).

[4]Burgess's conviction that the work has a "sleeping hero" called Mr. Porter is repeated in his more recent *This Man and Music*, 145.

dolls, apparently), he collapses in a drunken stupor and begins to
dream. The structure seems to be an instance of what Jacques Derrida
calls "invagination"[5]: enclosed by the book, the chapter also encloses
it. What follows, however, is not *Finnegans Wake* (how could it be?
We're on page 383 of *Finnegans Wake*). It is a version of the story of
Tristan and Isolde, colored by the familiar narrative perspective of
the four old men. Nevertheless, we are invited by Burgess to imagine
as we read this chapter that it is being dreamed by the publican asleep
on the floor of his bar, the publican's sleep being itself part of his
dream, and that the next three chapters are also dreams he dreams he
is dreaming, having dreamed that he has woken up and gone to bed
(*Here Comes Everybody*, 239).[6] When, after these dreams, he finds himself in bed again, we are assured—though it is not clear why he should
not once more be dreaming that he is in bed—that he is really awake.
Awake, that is, in James Joyce's dream.

The strain produced by this project of separating distinct dream
levels is evident enough in Burgess's account, as it is in all such attempts.[7] The argument is motivated, of course, by a desire to provide
the reader with a firm sense of *where* he or she is at any given point, an
explanation always ready to hand for the oddness of the writing, a
secure path through the threatening tangle of the text; but many
readers may find the task of imagining that what they are reading is
an account of a dream (or a dream of a dream, or a dream of a dream
of a dream) multiplies rather than reduces their difficulties. The
reader searching for a principle by which to distinguish what is central from what is digressive in Joyce's text is not given much assistance; after all, dreams are not generally characterized by a clear
separation between central core and digressive envelope (and that
very distinction must present itself as problematic to anyone who has
been impressed by *The Interpretation of Dreams* and recent readings of

[5]See Derrida, "Living On," 94–103, and "The Law of Genre," 216–19.

[6]Campbell and Robinson, from whom Burgess derives much of his version of the
Wake's "plot," create a bridge between II.4 and III.1 by deftly inserting a passage that in
fact occurs one hundred and fifty pages later. They thus allow us to imagine HCE/Por-
ter waking from his sleep on the barroom floor (the usual interpretation of the
"throne" into which, as King Roderick O'Connor, he "slumps" [382.26]) and creeping
to bed—where he dreams the first three chapters of Book III (*Skeleton Key*, 256).

[7]This includes Clive Hart's theory of "dream-layers" (*Structure and Motif in "Finnegans Wake,"* chap. 3) and Michael H. Begnal's view that the text is a web of distinguishable dreamers ("The Dreamers at the Wake").

it).[8] Burgess adopts a schoolmasterly tone to insist upon our duties as readers: "We are primarily in a bed above a bar in Chapelizod, Dublin, on a Saturday night, with a dry branch tapping or tipping at the window, and we must never let ourselves forget it" (*Here Comes Everybody*, 219)—as we are very likely to do without reminders of this kind from conscientious critics, as only a few pages of the text refer to this situation (or something like it: details like the day of the week or the dry branch appear to be commentators' inventions). It is not that such accounts can finally be proved "wrong" or that they serve no purpose; what is important is that they cannot be proved to be right, and many other interpretative tools are just as handy in providing a temporary hold on the book's Protean substance.

On what principle, then is the text reduced by more than half its length in *A Shorter Finnegans Wake*, to reveal what Burgess breezily terms "the gist of the book" (*SFW*, 6)? The gist seems to exclude a large number of passages that many readers regard as particularly delightful, or particularly accessible, or particularly significant (or all three). It might be thought surprising that Burgess leaves out the "museyroom" and "prankquean" episodes in the first chapter, HCE's encounter with the Cad in I.2, the trial of Festy King in I.4, the story of Burrus and Caseous in I.6, much of the rendering of Shem's (and Joyce's) life story in I.7, the washerwomen's speculation about ALP's first sexual experience in I.8, Glugg's guesses as to the color of Issy's underwear in II.1, the story of the tailor and the Norwegian Captain in II.3 (as well as the memorable moment when Buckley finds he hasn't the heart to shoot the defecating Russian general), the football match/lovemaking of Tristan and Isolde in II.4, Jaun's longings for a happier life and Issy's sentimental leavetaking in III.2, fifty pages of interrogation on the mound in III.3, the children in bed in III.4 (and the famous description of HCE's backside as Phoenix Park), St. Kevin and the bath in IV, and many more. My point is not that Burgess has or has not made a good job in his selection (against the list of omis-

---

[8]This is not to imply that the techniques of dream-work described by Freud do not offer an interesting model for the verbal distortions of the *Wake*, though this is by no means as simply an analogy as it is sometimes taken to be. (Some of the complexities are suggested by J.-F. Lyotard in "The Dream-Work Does Not Think" and Samuel Weber in *The Legend of Freud*, especially 8–83.) In any case, the complexities of the dream-work are not what attracts Burgess about the comparison of *Finnegans Wake* to a dream: they serve to emphasize, rather than eliminate, the overdeterminations of the text.

sions one could set a list of well-known and memorable passages he has included and some undeservedly neglected ones he has rescued) but that any selection is necessarily arbitrary, at least as far as the intrinsic structure of the text is concerned. The "narrative" and "characters" that Burgess produces for the *Wake* are created as much by his brief interpolated summaries as by the passages he reprints—perhaps more so. And the "backbone" he offers is a matter of moral as well as structural fiber, produced by the injection of evaluative attitudes into the connecting tissue whence they seep into the text; thus the passage describing the sexual union of HCE and ALP in III.4—whose final delightful sentence reads, "While the queenbee he staggerhorned blesses her bliss for to feel her funnyman's functions Tag" (590.27)—is deflatingly and moralistically encapsulated in Burgessese as "To bed it is then, for a quick and joyless tumble" (*SFW*, 247).[9]

The story thus constructed by Burgess out of the materials provided by the *Wake* (and by previous commentators on the *Wake*) is determined, as it must be, by his preconceptions as to what constitutes an acceptable narrative and his predilections as to moral commentary—which are by no means idiosyncratic but rather representative of a whole class of critics, who are in turn representative of a wider class of readers. (It is also clear that the practical demands of reprinting the text—maintaining wherever possible the same page format as the original printing while allowing room for Burgess's summaries—dictated many choices. The shortened text is thus the product of a more truly Wakean principle of selection, allowing the material contingencies of language as print to have their say.) To insist, as Burgess does, that *Finnegans Wake* must have a central core is to adopt a Shaun-like position: Shaun, it will be recalled, mistrusts Shem's writing on the grounds of its dispersal of meaning through ruses and plagiarism. Or as the text has it, echoing the deceived Isaac, "The gist is the gist of Shaum but the hand is the hand of Sameas" (483.03). All we can be given (and what in fact Burgess gives us) is a *sampling* of the text, because all we can ever do with a text like this is to sample it.[10]

---

[9]For another example of Burgess's reductive and moralistic view of marital sex in the *Wake*, see the second quotation in n.3 above. There is an equivalent tradition of moralizing commentary on *Ulysses*, which presents it as an attack on the lives and morals of its characters.

[10]One could generalize this point further, as Derrida does: "The utterances 'I am reading Joyce', 'read Joyce', 'have you read Joyce?' produce an irresistible effect of

One reason for this property of the text is that narrative in the *Wake*—of which there is a great deal—is not a linear extension from start to finish (as everyone knows, start and finish in this book are not so easily defined): it is woven through the text in a complex web, existing in varied and overlapping forms at every level from the whole book to sections to chapters to paragraphs to sentences and even to individual words.[11] The longer the span, however, the more rarefied the narrative, and the more limited are its satisfactions *as* narrative. Thus there is a perceptible movement from the fall of darkness at the end of Book I, through the evening activities in much of Book II and suggestions of night in Book III, to the intimations of dawn at the start of Book IV, but this movement is "plot" only of the most tenuous sort, and it is forgotten for much of the time in the richness and intricacy of the detail that fills it out. Who in enjoying the manifold delights of the "watches of Shaun" is actually conscious for any length of time of a nocturnal setting for these luxuriantly foliating speeches, dialogues, and cross-questionings? But if we take a subsidiary narrative unit such as the story of Buckley's shooting (or nonshooting) of the Russian general, or HCE's misdemeanor (or attributed misdemeanor) involving two girls and three soldiers in the park, we find it repeatedly recurring in constantly varied forms at every conceivable level of discourse (these two narratives are also, of course, versions of each other). The two-page account of the Battle of Waterloo in the "museyroom" passage (8–10) is a complex development of the same narrative nucleus that appears in the single phrase "nicies and priers" (196.21), the game "*Fickleyes and Futilears*" (176.13), and the "mamafesta" title "*Them Lads made a Trion of Battlewatschers and They Totties a Doeit of Deers*" (105.33). It occurs at slightly greater length in the nursery rhyme, "This liggy piggy wanted to go to the jampot. And this leggy peggy spelt pea. And theese lucky puckers played at pooping tooletom" (496.18). And it appears in the inculpatory exculpation offered by the long sentence in I.2, which is worth quoting for its characteristically indirect presentation of the story's outlines:

> Slander, let it lie its flattest, has never been able to convict our good and
> great and no ordinary Southron Earwicker, that homogenius man, as a

---

naivety, irresistibly comical. What exactly do you mean by 'read Joyce'? Who can pride himself on having 'read' Joyce?" ("Two Words for Joyce," 148).

[11]For a discussion of this use of multileveled narrative in *Finnegans Wake*, see Jean-Michel Rabaté, "Lapsus ex Machina," 83–86.

pious author called him, of any graver impropriety than that, advanced by some woodwards or regarders, who did not dare deny, the shomers, that they had, chin Ted, chin Tam, chinchin Taffyd, that day consumed their soul of the corn, of having behaved with ongentilmensky immodus opposite a pair of dainty maidservants in the swoolth of the rushy hollow whither, or so the two gown and pinners pleaded, dame nature in all innocency had spontaneously and about the same hour of the eventide sent them both but whose published combinations of silkinlaine testimonies are, where not dubiously pure, visibly divergent, as wapt from wept, on minor points touching the intimate nature of this, a first offence in vert or venison which was admittedly an incautious but, at its wildest, a partial exposure with such attenuating circumstances (garthen gaddeth green hwere sokeman brideth girling) as an abnormal Saint Swithin's summer and, (Jesses Rosasharon!) a ripe occasion to provoke it. (34.12)

Similarly, *How Buckley Shot the Russian General* appears frequently in versions of that summary title but is extended to seventeen densely packed pages in the dialogue of Butt and Taff (338–54), enfolding many other smaller-scale narratives within it.

This treatment of narrative shatters the illusion that sustains many readings of novels, and many sophisticated critical analyses and elaborate theoretical systems: that there is a sharp distinction between a set of pre-existing events and individuals and a secondary verbal representation of them. This distinction promotes to a central position those aspects of the text which disguise its textual and linguistic status and gives to the whole a teleological structure determined by the question "What happened next?" *Finnegans Wake* inverts and complicates this distinction: events, people, places, times are clearly constructed by the text (or, more accurately, by the reader in the encounter with the text), and attention is focused on the process of linguistic fabrication itself. The question we ask here is "What is happening in the text at this point?" and the *post hoc ergo propter hoc* logic (or antilogic) that powers narrative continuity is broken. At the same time *Finnegans Wake* could be said to glory in the *secondariness* of language, in its never-ending and ever-failing attempt to point to something beyond itself. The desire to interpret language, including fictional texts, as references to a "real world" cannot simply be annulled; on the contrary, the eliciting, teasing, thwarting, consoling, and occasional satisfying of that urge is the generative source of the *Wake*'s textual pleasures. Reading is not so simple an activity that one has to choose

216

between enjoying the evidently perpetual unknowability of the events in Phoenix Park and scrutinizing accounts of them for signs of "what *really* happened."

It is not only centralized narrative that disappears in *Finnegans Wake*. The mass of interlaced material makes it impossible to draw out *any* single thread as central—whether it be plot, time sequence, character, symbolic structure, mythic framework, voice, attitude, dogma, or any other of the threads that run through conventional novels.[12] There are far too many dissolves and montages, shifts and leaps, condensed phrases and multiple allusions, for a consistent center to emerge. Joyce's use of sigla and initials as labels to stick on to huge accumulations of verbal material (containing their own inner contradictions) has very little to do with traditional concepts of "character" and "narrative"—and, as Roland McHugh has demonstrated in *The Sigla of "Finnegans Wake,"* even these very broad categories merge ($\wedge$ and $\sqsubset$ becoming $\diagup\!\!\!\!C$), multiply ($\dashv$ becoming $\dashv\!\vdash$), or contain one another as ($\triangle$ contains $\wedge$, and $\sqcap$ contains $\sqsubset$). Place, time, tone, imagery, symbolic suggestiveness, moral judgment, all slide and propagate in this way, resisting, by means of the full exploitation of language's own alogicality, the erection of logically consistent patterns. This resistance, it should be noted, takes the form not of *refusing* these patterns but of proffering them in such abundance that none can stand as central or even consistent with the others. The title offers no passport to the book's inner chambers (though it tends, surprisingly, to be neglected by those seeking a "center"), and the text is shorn of all other traditional metatextual guideposts. *Finnegans Wake* is a book without a center; which is to say that it is a book without digressions, without anything that can be skipped, taken in at a glance, or read rapidly to get the gist. (Even what *looks* like supplementary material— such as marginal notes and footnotes or long lists of names—cannot be read as such.) Which is also to say that *everything* in it is capable of being skipped, because the book has no life-giving heart that might be injured. If, as Burgess says, *Finnegans Wake* totally resists cutting, it does so because it does not resist cutting at all.[13]

---

[12]The absence of a center in *Finnegans Wake* has been most clearly argued by Margot Norris, in *The Decentered Universe of "Finnegans Wake,"* though without following through all the consequences of this position. In chapter 7 above I discussed some of the ways in which the portmanteau style contributes to this decenteredness.

[13]As Fritz Senn puts it, in a characteristically acute remark, "*Finnegans Wake* is characterized by utter economy and extreme redundancy" (*Joyce's Dislocutions,* 115).

Deconstructing Digression

Is Joyce's last work best seen, for all these reasons, and in spite of the recuperative labors of Burgess and many others, as a digression from the central tradition of the novel?[14] Before answering this question, we need to examine the distinction between "center" and "digression" itself as it has been understood, and continues to be understood, in that tradition.

Digression

As we read a novel (and I use that term without any attempt at precision), we are continuously classifying the words we come upon according to the degree to which they appear progressive or digressive with regard to the movement of the narrative.[15] Although we do it unconsciously, this activity of classification influences the rhythm and tempo of our reading, the degree of our concentration at any given point, the selective operation of our short-term memory, and the formation of mental constructs relating to already held schemata of "character," "plot," "theme," and so on. Moreover, this constant monitoring of the internal relations of the text, crucial to our ability to make the text cohere, also produces formal pleasures analogous to those provided by a musical texture of digressions and returns in harmony, melody, rhythm, and timbre. What enables digression to operate in this way is that it carries with it the notion of subordination, unimportance, and ultimately dispensability: digressions in a novel are appendages, in some sense "unnatural" ones, which could be lopped off with only minor damage to the main body.

But any rigorous account of digression will quickly counter this view with an insistence that dispensability is only a (necessary) illusion. Classical and Renaissance definitions of *digressio* or *parecbasis* as a rhetorical device in oratory stress the contribution it makes to the main argument. Thomas Wilson, for example, states in his 1533 *Arte of Rhetorique* that by digression "we swerve sometimes from the mat-

[14]Though this essay may appear to privilege *Finnegans Wake*, its arguments could have been based on a number of other texts, most obviously *Ulysses*, which has experienced a similar history of filleting by critics in search of a center. But *Finnegans Wake* raises the questions that concern me in this chapter more forcefully than probably any other work.

[15]I take the opposition "progressive/digressive" from *Tristram Shandy* I.xxii; it is also used by Toby A. Olshin, "Genre and *Tristram Shandy*."

ter, upon just considerations, making the same to serve for our purpose, as well as if we had kept to the matter still."[16] In the *Arte of
English Poesie* Puttenham manages to emphasize both the apparent
randomness and the actual purposiveness of digression; he advises
the "perswader" to "talke farre from the principall matter, and as it
were to range aside, to th'intent by such extraordinary meane to
induce or inferre other matter, aswell or better serving the principal
purpose, and nevertheles in season to returne home where he first
strayed out. This maner of speech is termed the figure of digression
by the Latines, following the Greeke originall, we also call him the
straggler by allusion to the souldier that marches out of his array"
(233).

The Romantic conception of organic form (of which the Hegelian
dialectic may be considered a version) stresses both the importance of
internal digressive movements and the contribution they make to a
complex unity, as in Coleridge's description of the serpentlike motion
exhibited by the reader of an organically unified poem: "At every
step he pauses and half recedes, and from the retrogressive movement collects the force which again carries him onward" (*BL* 2:14). In
this century, structuralist attempts to formulate the codes whereby we
read narrative texts, the codes that have grown up with the novel and
constitute it as a readable object, emphasize that nothing in the literary text can evade the superefficient machinery of recuperation,
which operates on the simple principle that everything which is there
has meaning.[17] Roland Barthes gives a forceful statement of this principle in his survey of the structural analysis of narrative:

> A narrative is never made up of anything other than functions: in differ-
> ing degrees, everything in it signifies. This is not a matter of art (on the
> part of the narrator), but of structure; in the realm of discourse, what is
> noted is by definition noteworthy. Even were a detail to appear irre-
> trievably insignificant, resistant to all functionality, it would nonetheless
> end up with precisely the meaning of absurdity or uselessness: every-
> thing has a meaning, or nothing has. To put it another way, one could

[16]See Sister Miriam Joseph, *Shakespeare's Use of the Arts of Language*, 333. A similar
definition is given by Quintilian (*Institutionis Oratoriae* 4.3).

[17]Of course, "everything which is there" refers to everything that is *perceived* to be
there: every reading fails to register a great deal that is there for other kinds of reading.
Novels are not as different from films, or paintings from photographs, as is sometimes
maintained; it is merely that the presence of uncontrolled, contingent details is easier to
demonstrate in the latter.

say that art is without noise (as that term is employed in information theory): art is a system which is pure, no unit ever goes wasted, however long, however loose, however tenuous may be the thread connecting it to one of the levels of the story.[18]

According to this structuralist version of organicism, a digression that obstinately refuses to respond to all the recuperative strategies at the reader's command, a digression that cannot be read as supplementary information, symbolic parallel, illustrative exemplum, still offers itself as *digression,* as a model of the digressiveness of the mind or the world, as a demonstration of the impossibility or the undesirability of total and continuous relevance.

The functioning of digression as a structural principle clearly depends on its double nature—at once necessary and dispensable, part of the novel and excluded from it, inside and outside at the same time.[19] Its capacity to operate without threatening the unity of the text depends on its subordination as an irrelevancy, yet to subordinate it as irrelevant is to incapacitate it. What, then, are the forces that push digression in these two opposed directions, holding it within the text as an integral element and expelling it as an unnecessary addition? We can begin by looking at the former, the ways in which digression operates in the service of textual *cohesion,* and to do so it is useful to make a preliminary distinction between what might be called "flagrant" digression, which is openly announced as such, and passages of a more uncertain character, which we can term "equivocal" digression, where the reader postpones firm classification until further evidence is available. (These two kinds of digression are of course always merging into each other, and different readers and readings produce different categorizations of the same passage, but this consideration need not prevent us from discussing the strategies of interpretation and textual unification they each invite when they appear in relatively clear manifestations.)

[18]"Introduction to the Structural Analysis of Narratives," in *Image-Music-Text,* 89–90 (translation slightly modified). Barthes's later writing on narrative, of which *S/Z* is the most fully elaborated example, is less wedded to systematic interpretability.

[19]Digression shares this doubleness with such features as titles, headings, glosses, footnotes, prefaces, and appendixes, and more generally with every kind of "framing" device (see Derrida's discussion of the *parergon* in *La vérité en peinture,* 44–94). However, the fact that it is not *visually* signaled as such prior to reading renders its very undecidability undecidable.

Equivocal digression fails to announce openly its own relation to the rest of the text and, by keeping alive the possibility that it may be more progressive than at first it appears, encourages an alertness to potential links which acts as a powerful binding force in the reading and imbues the digression with all the interest of an enigma. What seems digressive at the time can, of course, be revealed in retrospect to have been progressive, like some of the apparently trivial incidents in *A la recherche du temps perdu* which blossom later into major constituents of the narrator's experience. Equally, what seems part of the central narrative at the time can turn out to have been a false trail, as often happens in detective fiction. The possibility that any digression may be redeemed, or revealed as a *felix culpa,* operates at all levels to keep the reader engaged, ensuring constant reinterpretation of earlier material and constant speculation about future directions. When an apparent digression is later retrieved, the resultant sense of an organic wholeness, and an all-embracing authorial Providence, is of a much higher order than could be produced without digressions. And the conclusion of a novel can function most conclusively when it finds in retrospect a place and a justification for all the wanderings that had seemed to defer and endanger it.[20]

Flagrant digression, by contrast, announces itself unmistakably as such, and the reader is left in no doubt as to its digressive status. It clearly departs from the main business at hand and may make use of a conventional introductory phrase as it does so ("Here we shall pause a little . . ."). Far from fracturing the text irredeemably, however, this kind of digression can have the effect of a strong guarantee of centeredness: to experience a passage as unmistakably digressive is to be reassured that what one took to be central *is* central, as it is so easy to know when one has strayed from it. It is also to be reassured in one's position as masterful and secure reader: in a digression that presents itself as digression, one knows exactly where one is (even though, or rather because, one is where one should not be). In its very resistance

---

[20]The way I have described the workings of digression may seem to apply only to a first reading, but one needs to ask if an absolute distinction is possible between a first and a later reading. The reader beginning a text, even if he or she has never come across references to the work or its author, must be familiar with the language, the genre, the textual and cultural context, etc.; while every later reading is to a greater or lesser extent a first reading, thanks to the limitations of human memory and the constant shifts in the mind's perspectives. For some suggestive comments on this question, see Barthes, *S/Z*, section IX, "How Many Readings?" (15–16), and passim.

to recuperation, flagrant digression enhances the recuperability of the progressive narrative: straining to make the digressive material "natural," we reinforce the easy and largely unconscious naturalization of the rest. To categorize an unassimilable section of the text as digression is to save the unity of the whole by means of a gesture of controlled separation; what we cannot file directly in the drawer marked "Center" we file in another drawer marked "Digression," and both drawers sit snugly in the same cabinet. The notion of "digression," therefore, implies and enforces a notion of "centrality." As long as the digression continues to be experienced as such, it is entirely at the service of the center that defines its digressiveness.

Some of the terms allied to "digression," such as "diversion" and "excursion" (or "excursus"), suggest, in their double signification of "detour" and "pleasant recreation," another function of this textual property. Digression's suspension of seriousness, its delight in its own irresponsibility, emphasizes the seriousness of what is left behind, operating like the licensed holiday that guarantees strict sobriety on all working days. (Occasionally the relationship is reversed, and the comic character of the whole is assured by the somberness of the digression, as in the Man of the Hill's story in *Tom Jones* or the supernatural tales in *Pickwick Papers*.) Again, by virtue of its subordinate status, digression serves the whole of which it is both part and not part.

Crucial to digression is its *temporary* nature. It always swerves back, and the return, the classical *reditus ad propositum,* is a moment of satisfaction and reassurance: we were right to retain confidence in the order and wholeness of the text, and in our own secure position as readers, and we taste the sweet pleasure of relevance in a way that would have been impossible without the digressive move. Barthes's description of "suspense" is equally applicable to the suspension achieved by digression: "a game with structure, designed to endanger and glorify it, constituting a veritable 'thrilling' of intelligibility" ("Structural Analysis of Narratives," 119). If a text that has swerved away does not in due course swerve back, the firm structure of center and digression collapses, and the reader is left groping, without secure bearings. Thus the second part of Blanchot's *L'arrêt de mort* (in its revised form) makes no overt reference back to the first part, and some of the nesting stories in Buñuel's film *Le fantôme de la liberté* never return to their enclosing narratives. One might even cite *The Taming of the Shrew,* in which the entertainment of the title starts as a diversion and ends as the play itself. In cases like these, our strategies of recuperation are stretched, our masterful position threatened; the narrative spins away out of our control. (We may devise tactics to regain control, of course, like those theater directors who resurrect a final scene from an inferior "Shrew" play to provide a secure closing frame for Shakespeare's text.)

Over a larger domain, digression is fundamental to all narrative design, in the wandering that constitutes the movement between the state at the beginning and the state at the end. Instead of taking the direct route from A to B, the narrative delays, dilates, and digresses (both in its events and in the discourse that produces them) before it reaches B—which often turns out to have more of A in it than one would have predicted from the errant paths traversed in between.[21] The end is experienced as a conclusion only because of the wanderings in the middle, the wanderings are acceptable only because they eventually lead to the conclusion.[22] Classical sonata form in music offers a parallel, the development section moving away from the material of the exposition in such a way as to promote both surprise and satisfaction at the return of this material, at once the same and different, in the recapitulation.

In these ways all digression, whether flagrant or equivocal, is retained securely within the text of the novel, contributing significantly to the novel's cohesion, its readability, its status as a model for an ordered, teleological, interpretable world, understood and controlled by self-knowing subjects. Yet it can function in this way only if it is kept firmly in a subordinate position. All its strength as a support for the text's unity—and for the assumptions about art, and about human experience and knowledge, that this unity serves—depends on this fact. But what guarantees its subordination? What advertises the di-

[21]Versions of this structure are discussed by M. H. Abrams in *Natural Supernaturalism* with particular emphasis on its Romantic manifestations. Romanticism is also associated with a revaluation of the "fragment," appreciated, like the digression, for its assurance of a wholeness against which it is defined (see Thomas McFarland, *Romanticism and the Forms of Ruin*, especially the Introduction). A Romantic text that succeeds in being both a fragment and, as its title suggests, a digression is Wordsworth's *Excursion*.

[22]The wanderings can become an end in their own right, holding out only tenuous hopes of homecoming (see Patricia A. Parker's discussion of this phenomenon in *Inescapable Romance*). The question of the relation of plot development to its conclusion also involves the problem of cause and effect within fictional narrative; see, for example, Cynthia Chase, "The Decomposition of the Elephants." Deviation and return are also valuably discussed, and related to Freud's *Beyond the Pleasure Principle*, by Peter Brooks in *Reading for the Plot*, especially chaps. 4 and 5.

gression *as* digression in the fullest sense, as diversion, interlude, excursion, supplement? (The mere presence of a conventional introductory phrase is obviously not sufficient.) What, in other words, pushes the digression toward the *edge* of the text and in so doing enables it to return toward the center?

The distinction between narrative center and digressive periphery in the "traditional" novel appears to be a simple one between that which "advances the plot" and that which does not. It may be described more precisely as a distinction between sections of the text which appear in the guise of mere reflection of a pre-existing series of events, carrying the writing along with them by the force of their causal logic and teleological motion, and sections that bring to the fore the writing itself, dallying and delaying, freezing the stream of events and revealing them to be secondary to the text that produces them. In the central narrative, language is experienced as a transparent medium through which the world is clearly observed, and the events recounted are enjoyed directly for their own intrinsic interest. In the digression the window grows opaque, and we focus on its texture and design. Jean Ricardou's account of *description* can be generalized to all forms of digression from the linear temporality of the plot: "This excessive disproportion between a segment devoid of action and a corresponding stretching of the text reveals in a pure space the *writing* itself. . . . With the break of the loose and confused parallelism reconciling the two axes, the *alibi* of the story is abandoned: the axis of narration being stabilized at the expense of that of the fiction, one realizes how the novel ceases to be the writing of a story to become the story of a writing." ("Time of the Narration," 11).[23] The episode of *Ulysses* perhaps most often treated by the reader as a digression is "Oxen of the Sun," where a great deal of language seems not greatly to advance the "plot" (the much more significant event at Westland Row Station which immediately follows this episode is, on the other hand, not narrated at all and has to be deduced from frag-

---

[23]Extended description is perfectly compatible with "readableness," however, as is indicated by its extensive employment in Ian Fleming's James Bond novels (Eco discusses their "relish for the inessential" in *The Role of the Reader*, 165–67); digression proper does not dwell on the describable content of the narrative but departs from it. Another opposition that, like "narrative"/"description," is related (but not in any simple way) to the opposition "narrative"/"digression" is the familiar "story" (*"fabula,"* *"histoire"*)/"discourse" (*"sjuzhet,"* *"discours,"* *"récit"*): a digression will usually, though not necessarily, bear more traces of "discourse," while the central narrative will seem to tell itself.

224

mentary retrospective references). Jennifer Levine, in "Reading *Ulysses*," comments on a passage from this episode that "there is such sheer exuberance in the writing: but to what effect? Instead of each additional phrase enhancing the expressive power of language (as each additional brushstroke on a canvas might increase our illusion of 'the real'), the accumulation of phrases is such that language itself is reified, and meaning (i.e. the thing 'out there' that language points to) recedes into the background" (271).

The commonest kind of digression interpolates a commentator or narrator, who is revealed as having the power to stop the flow of events or speed them up, to linger over this or that detail of character, to track backward and forward in time, to move entirely away from the plot, to introduce commentary, moralization, or subsidiary narrative—and in so doing to expose events, characters, time, and everything that is "interrupted" by the digression as already produced by the writing of the text (the same writing that produces the digressing commentator, of course, though this fact is usually disguised by the text). A narrating voice of this kind is not necessary for digressive effects to be felt, however. As soon as the stable ratio between the chronology of the events and the chronology of the discourse relating them—or, more generally, between words and matter—is broken, the construction of those events begins to obtrude, and writing, not the world, is felt to be in charge. The pastness of events is replaced by the presentness of narrating, a present that is already past when we read it and was never present to itself. The digression may, in spite of itself, attempt to substantiate the referential illusion by apologizing for its intrusion upon a real scene, or it may, on the contrary, revel in the breaking of that illusion, as in some of the initial chapters of *Tom Jones* or, more spectacularly, in the digressiveness of some of Samuel Beckett's highly unreliable narrators.[24] In digressions the language—

[24]This is what has been called *author's metalepsis*, in which the figure of the author reveals his or her power to determine the story (see Genette, *Narrative Discourse*, 234–35). It is interesting to note that Genette, citing Fontanier's 1818 *Commentaire raisonné sur "Les Tropes" de Dumarsais*, describes the device as "pretending that the poet 'himself brings about the effects he celebrates'" (234), and not—what would be more accurate—as a *dropping* of the pretense that he does *not;* this is, of course, true to the reader's experience of the trope. Genette extends the term *narrative metalepsis* to the narrator's pretense that the events are continuing to happen during the actual time of a digression (providing an example from Balzac's *Illusions Perdues:* "While the venerable churchman climbs the ramps of Angoulême, it is not useless to explain . . ."). This is in fact the reverse figure, implying that the author is helpless over the march of the events being related, but it pushes the "realist" claim so far as to have an equally subversive effect.

no longer yoked by the pretense that it is referring to a prelinguistic set of existents—can be given its head, deriving its energy from its own properties and proclivities. These include its capacity for intertextual allusion, polysemy, irony, recursiveness, patterning, all the byproducts of its existence as a system of differences realized in the materiality of print and sound (some of which I have discussed in chapters 5, 6, and 7). The central narrative, on the other hand, is at its purest, is least subject to being suspected of digressiveness, when these properties are repressed or masked, and language appears to obliterate itself in the act of referring and reporting.

What we are considering, then, is an opposition in which one member is defined as subordinate and is regarded as valuable in so far as it *is* subordinate, but the dominant member retains its dominance only by the systematic exclusion of those properties which characterize the subordinated opposite. This pattern brings to mind the similar pattern exhibited by many of the oppositions discussed in deconstructive readings by Derrida and others—literal and rhetorical, serious and nonserious, speech and writing, nature and culture, proper and improper, to name only a few—in which the subordinate member has been shown to be generalizable in such a way as to constitute a class of which the dominant member is a subspecies. So, for example, the properties of writing which result in its subordination to speech have been shown by Derrida to characterize all language (and all events that are capable of iteration)—indeed, to *constitute* language as language. The gesture of subordination and exclusion, which Derrida calls "the philosophical movement par excellence" ("Signature Event Context," *Margins,* 316), is designed to perpetuate, among other things, assumptions about the relation of language to its speaker, its referent, and its interpreter: assumptions of direct communication between subjects fully present to themselves of truths grounded firmly in a world independent of language and consciousness. And we find the opposition between central narrative and digression displaying this familiar logic. The properties that result in the subordination of digression are the very properties that constitute the entire text as a text, the properties of writing itself—its independence from origins, goals, referents, its ceaseless production of meaning, its material patterns and rhythms. The center is able to function as a center (and to uphold a conception of language as transparent communication) only by excluding those properties, by branding them as digressive and supplementary. To restore these properties to the entire text by a deconstructive reversal is to see the narrative as only one kind of writing among many, a form in which the material and diacritical character of language operates as forcefully and fruitfully as anywhere else. It is to see the world of plot and characters as vivid and shifting designs painted on the surface of the window.[25] It is also, of course, to view the secondariness of digression in a new light, not as the inherently subordinate status of a part of the text, guaranteeing the prime importance of the narrative and the organic unity of the whole, but as the product of only one of many ways of reading—among them (notwithstanding the long history of organic theories of form, including the structuralist variety) the possibility of letting some features or parts count for nothing, of treating the text as fragmentary, divided, or unstable. We may even come to feel that texts can only be read by privileging some aspects over others, and that an "organically unified" reading is achieved by just such a process of exclusion, a process repressed by reader and tradition, and visible only in its effects.

We are thus led to an account of reading which, in its allowance for heterogeneity as between readers and readings, and its acceptance of sampling and skipping, is probably a more accurate description of what actually happens in the encounter with a text than are idealized versions of total interpretation and hermeneutic rigor. But to displace narrative from its dominant position is to read against the pressure of current conventions and habits, and, given the primacy and power of narrative in our culture, such a mental set could probably be achieved only partially and fitfully. A few works, however, appear to cooperate more fully with a reading of this kind and in fact make the conven-

[25]It would be possible to show at length that the quality of "centrality" evinced by the narrative of a traditional novel rests on its conformity not with the reader's extranarrative experience but with the norms and conventions of narrative itself; these, however, operate over a much wider social and psychological terrain than that of literature and are determined by needs and power-relations well beyond the realm of the aesthetic. Mary Louise Pratt, drawing on the work of William Labov, has valuably discussed the relation between literary and nonliterary narrative in *Toward a Speech Act Theory;* see also Brooks's suggestions regarding an "erotics of narrative" in *Reading for the Plot.* *Within* the main narrative, certain tendencies are experienced as digressive, and the same pattern is evident here as in what is more usually called digression: these are moments at which the constructedness of the plot is revealed by its failure to conform to expected configurations. An extraordinary heightening of narrativity itself is achieved by the insertion of powerfully told stories within a sequence of events that flout the conventions of narrative (a sort of digression-in-reverse), as in Buñuel's *La voie lactée* and *Le charme discret de la bourgeoisie.*

tional gesture of exclusion impossible. These are works in which the "digressions" are so long or draw so much attention to themselves that they insist on a status equal, or even superior, to that of the central narrative. Examples come readily to mind. In Swift's *Tale of a Tub* the tale itself occupies about a quarter of the text; in *Tristram Shandy* Sterne weaves a web of digressions that prevent the ostensible autobiography from getting properly under way (we might note in passing here that Swift and Sterne are among the authors most frequently cited in *Finnegans Wake*); the digressions in Byron's *Don Juan* are as memorable as the story of its antihero; Melville's accounts of whaling in *Moby-Dick* vie for attention with the story of Ahab's quest for the White Whale. In such texts all the strategic systems for the recuperation of digression fail, because they all rely on digression's having a subordinate status; the hierarchical opposition between progressive and digressive, it might be argued, is deconstructed by the text itself. The result is that the reader is weaned from dependence on the illusion that novels are reports on the real world and is encouraged to enjoy the writing as writing, in all its uncertainty, prolixity, contradictoriness, and materiality.

In spite of their challenge to convention, however, the conservatively inclined reader of these texts need not relinquish a position of secure mastery. Once apprised of the reversal of priority between narrative center and digressive material, he or she can read for something *other* than the narrative while still enjoying the returns to the story, however exiguous, when they occur. The "reality effect" of the narrative sections may even be enhanced by the presence elsewhere of an obtrusive narrator, caught up in language's proliferations precisely—such a reader might say—because language is not being employed in its proper task of representing the world. What occurs is a split between two oppositions that are normally conflated, the progressive/digressive opposition and the dominant/subordinate opposition, and a reversal of the homology between them, so it becomes possible to read the digressive sections as dominant and the progressive ones as subordinate. The story of Peter, Martin, and Jack, the events of Tristram's early life, the adventures of Don Juan, the hunt for the White Whale, all remain structurally "central," but that centrality no longer guarantees pre-eminence. (The epigraph from Pliny to the seventh volume of *Tristram Shandy* reads "Non enim excursus hic ejus, sed opus ipsum est"—"For this is not a digression, but is the work itself.") One still knows *where one is* in reading the text, and one enjoys the comic or ironic effects of the reversal that has been achieved. The episodes that constitute the plot become episodes inserted into a continuous non-narrative sequence,[26] and it is possible to read the text for its digressive material, skipping the narrative entirely. (Thus *A Tale of a Tub* can be represented in the Nonesuch edition of Swift's works by its digressions alone.) What is lost in this kind of filleting, of course, is precisely the *digressive* quality of the digressions, their disruption of the generic conventions that arbitrate between dominant and subordinate in the text.[27]

Texts that make it impossible to read in terms of a structure of center and digression (with priority of one over the other) are very rare, perhaps nonexistent: we have seen that even *Finnegans Wake* has not escaped such readings. But what all these unconventional texts, and the history of their interpretation, show more clearly than orthodox novels is the degree to which such structures are *produced*, not given. Anthony Burgess's "backbone" belongs less to *Finnegans Wake* than to the ideology that provides Burgess with his moral out-

---

[26]The polysemy of *episode* illustrates neatly the reversibility of center and digression: as "that which comes in as an addition," it can refer to the entire action of Greek drama (which was added to the purely choral form), to a distinguishable *section* of the action (as in the modern "episodes" of a serial), and to a part of the plot which falls *outside* the main action—an "incidental narrative or digression," as the *OED* has it (one might compare, too, the term's musical sense). In Aristotle's *Poetics*, the word is used in all three ways—see Doran, *Endeavors of Art*, 273–77.

[27]Of the examples mentioned, *Tristram Shandy* is probably the most resistant to a strategy of reversal, and other techniques are often employed to diminish the potential disruptiveness of its digressive wanderings. Thus Wayne Booth proposes a second "story-thread," the story of Uncle Toby, running concurrently with the one announced in the title, so as drastically to reduce the novel's digressiveness ("Did Sterne Complete *Tristram Shandy?*"); and William Bowman Piper finds ways of justifying the digressive sections in terms of their function and their controlled structure (*Laurence Sterne*, 31–46). In both cases the critic tries to redeem the digressions (and deny the reader any pleasure in them *as* digressions). Booth notes, "In practically every case of Tristram's 'irresponsibility', as far as narrative devices are concerned, the reader in the long run finds himself fooled; the caprice was not caprice after all" (181 n.18), and Piper believes that Sterne has achieved "a web of life and opinion, of particular story and general statement which involves the trivial items of Shandy experience with general human truths in a fabric of great richness and density" (41). Equally typical is this statement from Olshin's "Genre and *Tristram Shandy*": "The digression which seemed irrelevant to Tristram's impatient reader has instead been shown to be needful: in the unity-in-diversity of subjective life, there are no irrelevancies" (368). Readers who experience an aleatory energy, and a potential endlessness, in the novel (both of which qualities the narrator draws attention to) are presumably being impatient or allowing themselves to be fooled.

look and his assumptions about reading. Even with conventional texts it is always possible for the reader—not as an absolutely free subject but as the focus of a set of forces operating at a specific time and place[28]—to privilege some feature other than narrative, to read Shakespeare for the patriotic sentiments, George Eliot for the moral wisdom, Joyce for the sexual explicitness. And editors have never been slow in publishing selections in accordance with contemporary preoccupations or their own preferences; *A Shorter Finnegans Wake* stands within a long and flourishing tradition.[29] If, however, structures of priority are produced and not intrinsic, they are necessarily unstable, dependent on readings and not on the text itself. Moreover, such oppositions (like the opposition between structure and event or cause and effect) have an *inherent* instability. To classify something as "digression" is to imply that the center from which it digresses is already firmly in place, yet to classify something as "center" is to imply that a digressive periphery is already in place. If either is experienced as "given," it is given not by the text itself, but by the conventions that govern its reading, conventions that themselves derive from a body of

[28]It is not possible to discuss here the degree to which the reader's "freedom" is circumscribed (or produced) by agencies beyond his or her conscious control; this issue has at least political, historical, psychoanalytic, biological, and philosophical dimensions. We have already noted that apparently individual literary judgments always occur within a framework provided by a cultural-political system, though the heterogeneity and uneven development of such systems necessarily leave spaces for some degree of choice. The classic structuralist position is stated by Barthes: "Subjectivity is a plenary image, with which I may be thought to encumber the text, but whose deceptive plenitude is merely the wake of all the codes which constitute me, so that my subjectivity has ultimately the generality of stereotypes" (*S/Z*, 10). For a lucid account of some aspects of the problem in relation to a digressive literary text, *Tristram Shandy*, see Samuel Weber, "The Critics' Choice."

[29]Shakespeare has been the favored victim of such ideological filleting, as the twenty-one columns under the heading "Selections and Extracts" in the Shakespeare entry in the 1964 British Museum Catalogue indicate. Included are such titles as *The Wisdom and Genius of Shakespeare, comprising moral philosophy, delineations of character, paintings of nature and the passions, and miscellaneous pieces*; *Shakespeare on Golf*; *Britons Strike Home; or, Shakespeare's Ghost to the British Armies* (extracts from the history plays); *Catholic Jewels from Shakespeare*; *Shakespear's Mental Photographs*; *Shakespeare on Temperance*; *The Sweet Silvery Sayings of Shakespeare on the Softer Sex* (Compiled by an Old Soldier); and innumerable editions of *The Beauties of Shakespeare*. The novel has not escaped this practice: one example is Alexander Main's highly popular *Wise, Witty, and Tender Sayings . . . Selected from the Works of George Eliot* (1872), and *Tristram Shandy* itself was known to many readers only through one of the numerous editions of *The Beauties of Sterne* published between 1782 and the early twentieth century.

texts that includes the one to which they are being applied.[30] The progressive and the digressive, in every literary text from the simplest tale to *Finnegans Wake,* depend on each other, invade each other, exchange with each other, in the never-ending production of reading and readings.

Return: The Wake *as Backbone*

I come now to the third and final part of this chapter, the part that should reveal whether the first part was a digressive prelude on *Finnegans Wake* in an essay on digression or the second part a digression on digressions in an essay on *Finnegans Wake.* Fortunately, the logic of my argument frees me of any obligation to settle the question, and I can leave it to the reader to produce—within the limits imposed by a particular position in time and space—her or his own structure of center and digression.

The question I left unanswered at the end of part 1—in true Shandean style—was whether *Finnegans Wake* should be seen as a digression (a flagrant digression, no doubt) from the central path of the novel as a tradition and a genre. Certainly this is how it *has* been treated, in obedience to the law I have already described, whereby the classification of something as "digression" helps reinforce the centrality and importance of what is not so classified. Certainly, too, the grounds on which this exclusion has been effected are the ones we have just been considering: *Finnegans Wake* is a digression because it fails to conform to the expectation that novels reflect a pre-existing reality, foregrounding instead the properties of language, its instability and shiftiness, its material patterns and coincidences, its intertextual slidings, its freedom from determining sources or goals, its independence from its referents, even its refusal to be bound by a single language system. The literary tradition (which now embraces most of Joyce's earlier writing) needs limit-texts against which to define itself: its sanctification of the novel tradition's "central" concern

---

[30]What is involved here, of course, is the whole question of "difference," originally raised by Saussure and much discussed in recent years. See, for example, Derrida's essay "Differance" in *Speech and Phenomena* and his second interview in *Positions,* "Semiology and Grammatology," 15–36.

with "the real world" or "humane values" or "common sense" is strengthened by the gesture with which it excludes *Finnegans Wake* for what it calls its "artificiality," its "shallowness," its "inaccessibility." (The familiar polarity between "nature" and "art" is once more detectable in this hierarchy.) Literary criticism rests on the givenness of the distinction between the serious and nonserious; it can accommodate the *comic* within the serious, but to protect its founding exclusion it has to banish *Finnegans Wake* to the realms of the nonserious, as a mere diversion or excursion.[31] And we can see clearly here how the distinction within the individual novel with which we have been concerned is also produced at the level of the canon by the ideologically determined needs of those who made it. (The attempt to situate *Finnegans Wake* within the tradition of the novel, and to give it the required seriousness, by producing a backbone for it—narrative or moral/thematic—serves, of course, the same ends. Indeed, a double gesture is frequently to be observed whereby the *Wake* is both excluded as a radical text and saved in the form of a grossly reduced and attenuated simulacrum.) What this process of marginalization fends off is the worrying possibility that *Finnegans Wake* may be not an aberration of the literary but an unusually thoroughgoing *exemplification* of the literary, of the very conditions of existence of *Middlemarch* or *Sons and Lovers* as literary texts—namely, the impossibility of ever being limited by originating intention, or external reference, or constraining context. To the extent that literary texts can be read as being so limited, that is to say, they perhaps fail to be literary or at least to be read as literary, offering themselves instead as if they were reports, arguments, confessions, sermons.

Does this argument hold? Could we—not as a matter of theory but in practice—reverse the priority in the opposition between the progressive mainstream and the digressive aberration as it operates in the canon by placing *Finnegans Wake* at the center and reading all other novels in its light, instead of the other way round? As I have already stressed, no reader is free in an absolute sense but is always subject to the historically specific constraints within which he or she is constituted as a reader. The answer, then, must depend on whether or not we still experience those needs which have marginalized this text since it first appeared, our ability to read in this or that manner being

[31] For an entertaining (and very serious) discussion of the serious/nonserious distinction, see Derrida, "Limited Inc."

determined to a large extent by the goals that we hope (consciously or unconsciously) to achieve, and the picture of the world we sustain or strengthen by doing so. Initially, we can be sure, such a reversal would have been impossible: Joyce's last book presented too great a challenge to the presuppositions of its early readers to register as anything but an anomaly, and the efforts of those who supported it and proselytized on its behalf (no doubt often more because of their faith in Joyce than in full recognition of what the new work had to offer) were largely directed toward minimizing its threat to the assumptions that upheld the existing canon. But do we still need to be protected from that challenge after the far-reaching shifts in our conception of literary texts in the last twenty years—shifts in which Joyce's writing, and *Finnegans Wake* in particular, have themselves played a significant part?[32] To many who have read Bakhtin, Barthes, Kristeva, Derrida, de Man, Heath, and Gasché (these names can stand for many more), *Finnegans Wake* may offer itself as the central text in the Western literary tradition. Thus David Lodge writes, apropos of Bakhtin's studies of the novel, "the later episodes of *Ulysses,* and the whole enterprise of *Finnegans Wake,* appear not as eccentric digressions from the great tradition of the novel, sidestrains of a maindrain, but the most complete fulfillment of the expressive potential of the novel that has yet been achieved."[33]

Let us imagine a reader who has succeeded, as Lodge believes Bakhtin did, in achieving a reversal of this kind. What are the predictable effects of this intellectual metathesis? To begin with, the face of the novel as a genre is radically altered, for those features we are accustomed to place at the heart of our dealings with the text become peripheral, as open to question as, say, the portmanteau words of *Finnegans Wake* have traditionally been felt to be. Plot, character, moral argument, teleological structure, chronological continuity, symbolism, emotional coherence, depiction of place, observance of lexical rules, authorial presence, linearity, identifiable voices, monolingualism, all these and more are rendered relative, seen as options with certain effects and certain drawbacks, available to be used, ignored, problematized, and joined with or played off others in innumerable combinations. In this light the tradition of the novel appears

[32]See Attridge and Ferrer, "Introduction."
[33]"Double Discourses," 1. The phrase "expressive potential" seems to point (dialogically, perhaps) in the opposite direction from the rest of the sentence.

an extraordinarily monochrome affair, so limited is the set of conventions within which writers have doggedly confined themselves. And no individual piece of fiction remains untouched: to take one's bearings from the experience of reading *Finnegans Wake* is to induce a close attention to the linguistic detail of the novel hardly encouraged by the search for psychological subtlety or moral significance or by the rush to a "represented" world of character and event. At the same time our hypothetical reader is freed from the remorseless demands of "organic form," with its injunction—formulated so well by Barthes—that nothing shall be counted as waste or noise (an injunction that not even *Finnegans Wake* has escaped, as witness Campbell and Robinson's *cri de coeur* in their *Skeleton Key: "There are no nonsense syllables in Joyce!"* [p. 360, their emphases]). All texts can be only sampled, all readings are partial, and every reading is different from every other one: a linear reading, for instance, is only one possibility among many. (Strictly speaking, it is not even that, because reading, we realize, always moves in several directions at once.)

To treat *Finnegans Wake* as paradigmatic, as the backbone of the literary corpus, is also to undo the opposition between narrative center and digressive periphery in every novel we read. One can, after all, keep reducing the most complex novel until one reaches a sentence at the level of "How Buckley Shot the Russian General" (and perhaps further), and at no particular stage is it possible to say that the "center," as an irreducible given, has been reached. Moreover, *all* novels are seen to be woven of narratives at every level—even in the most orthodox fictions, single phrases can encapsulate plots, whether culturally conventional or repeated from elsewhere in the text—and the absolute separation of "events" and "narration," "story" and "discourse," becomes impossible everywhere. The primacy and productivity of language are seen to operate as much in the telling of a convincing story as in the ruminations of a narrator or the interpolations of an arranger. The boundaries of the canon are breached, too. Texts that have been excluded because of their failure to conform to the norms of "unity," or "seriousness," or "realism," established for and by the main tradition, become readable—and, more important, enjoyable, because we are talking now not about a theoretical shift in modes of describing and categorizing literature but about a real shift in perception.

By the same token *Finnegans Wake* itself becomes readable in its own terms, not those of a naturalistic and humanistic tradition, as a text whose lack of center and equal lack of digression is as radical as it is productive. Every sentence in the *Wake* can be taken as the key to the entire work or can just as well be totally ignored. The pleasure that so many readers experience of tracing through the text a motif or an allusion—to find it coiling through a chapter, secreted within a word, scattered over a page, providing coherence in an otherwise chaotic passage, linking two sentences across a hundred pages, materializing when least expected, providing an absurd yet welcome note of familiarity in the midst of strangeness—need suffer no diminution from the awareness that a multitude of other motifs and allusions wait to provide similar pleasures in equal abundance. A sentence like the defense of Earwicker quoted earlier (pp. 215–16 above) can be savored for the local delights of its textual detail without being blunted by the overriding demands of a forward-moving narrative. It can be enjoyed as, among many other things, a game with misplaced literary or journalistic clichés on the model of the "Eumaeus" episode of *Ulysses* ("Slander, let it lie its flattest," "admittedly an incautious, but at its wildest, a partial exposure"): a dissolving of the boundaries between word and word and between language and language or, more accurately, a demonstration that such boundaries are always already dissolved ("ongentilmensky immodus," "silkinlaine testimonies"); an energizing of legal language by erotic displacements ("published combinations . . . visibly divergent"); an invocation of past codes and prohibitions—and the desires that break them—through the diachronic sedimentation of language itself (forest laws in "woodwards and regarders," "vert or venison"; the Old Testament in "garthen gaddeth green" ["gad" is "snake" in Pan-Slavonic] and "Jesses Rosasharon"[34]; medieval property and marriage agreements in "hwere sokeman brideth girling"); and a teasing out of interconnected references to clothing ("s*wool*th," "gown and pinners," "combinations," "silkinlaine," "wapt from wept"), writing ("pious author," "*shomer*" and "homogenius," "published . . . testimonies"), vegetation ("woodwards," "corn," "rushy," "nature," "vert," "garthen," "gaddeth" [to "gad" being to "straggle"], "green," "ripe"), and the childish sexual delights of urination/exhibitionism/voyeurism ("regarders,"

---

[34]This phrase also illustrates the internal diachronicity of the text, because it will trigger a memory for any reader who has encountered the passage already discussed in chapter 7 above, whether in the perusal of a critical work that quotes it or in a prior reading of the final pages of the text itself. Or, of course, it may remain in the memory to be re-evoked when the later passage is reached.

"shomers" [Hebrew for "watchmen"], "rushy hollow," "dubiously pure," "partial exposure"). Syntactically, the sentence can be relished as a token of the infinite productivity of grammatical rules empha- sized by Chomsky, here operating in the service of the interminable need to make excuses; and phonologically, as a rhythmic texture of sounds and stresses exploiting the patterns of nursery rhyme and popular idiom ("good and great," "chin Ted, chin Tam, chinchin Taffyd," "wapt from wept," "vert or venison," "garthen gaddeth green"). And what the project of centering *Finnegans Wake* would also show is that such enjoyment of writing's proliferating energies ex- tends to all texts; any work of literature can be seen to possess these qualities to some degree, to partake of the modes of textuality which have been variously described in terms of *écriture,* genotext, *signi- fiance,* heteroglossia, dissemination, rhetoricity, performativity, *scriptibilité.*

But would such a reversal of center and digression represent, at the level of the literary canon, the same operation that *Finnegans Wake* itself performs upon the distinction between progressive and di- gressive at the level of the text, the deconstructive operation I sketch- ed in part 2? Would it not be more like the inversion carried out by *A Tale of a Tub* or *Don Juan,* a reversal of priority that leaves intact the opposition itself, as well as the assumption that this opposition is a wholly given one?[35] We noted earlier that a crucial effect of the *Wake*'s dissolution of the distinction between center and periphery is to reveal the *constructedness,* and hence the radical instability, of any such distinction, and our thinking through of a hypothetical shift in the structure of the canon must take this effect into account. Such a shift needs to be understood as equally produced, not as the man- ifestation of inherent properties we have at last discovered after years of misapprehension. When I stated that the *Wake* would, after a re- versal of its existing relationship to the tradition of the novel, be readable "in its own terms," I meant—and could only have meant— "in the new terms made possible by the reversal." But that reversal is always itself reversible; as I suggested earlier, we would take little pleasure in Joyce's texts if we were to abandon entirely (supposing we could do so) the multitude of reading habits that enable us to trans-

---

[35]For all its radical import, Victor Shklovsky's notorious insistence that *"Tristram Shandy* is the most typical novel in world literature" remains a reversal of this limited kind ("Sterne's *Tristram Shandy,*" 57).

form writing, however provisionally and hypothetically, from a structure of differential signifiers to a field of signifieds (and perhaps even objects and events "in the real world"). *Finnegans Wake* can no more be *intrinsically* central to the body of texts constituting the English novel than it can be intrinsically at the edge—or *Middlemarch*, say, intrinsically at the center. The structure is more like that impossible figure of Derrida's "invagination" already referred to, where the inside is at the same time the outside. Which, after all, is the center of the fish on our plate, the backbone we fillet out or the flesh we eat?[36] As long as we need centers and digressions—and it is difficult to imagine not needing them—we will find them. The lesson of the *Wake* is that we do not stop finding them, and building on them, when we know that they are our own productions.

I am not suggesting that there is the remotest possibility of the anglophone cultural establishment's going back on its exclusion of *Finnegans Wake* from the central, defining core of the literary tradition, as enforced within the institutions of education and publishing. Indeed, the reasons I have given for the value of thinking through such a reversal are precisely the reasons why it will not happen within the context of current political and social systems. The canon is produced by and reinforces a set of values and assumptions upon which those systems depend for their degree of acceptance and their perpetuation; one has only to examine the governing political rhetoric of the major powers in the 1980s to find every notion that *Finnegans Wake* questions being given massive endorsement. The exercise of making the *Wake* a central and not a digressive text in our literary culture can be at present only a hypothetical one, but this is exactly its value, and the value of similar attempts to think against the grain of the instituted canon. Within the powerful processes of ideological inculcation such thinking can create a space where it might be possible to reassess the function and character of the literary and its potential importance for us as members of an always changing, always changeable society. Literature conceived on the basis of linguistic deviation has been a largely conservative force in the history of the West, naturalizing the potential disruptiveness of a language that exceeds or disappoints ideological models and placing the power to determine its

---

[36]Further speculation on this question would have to take into account Melville's disgression on the whale's skeleton in chaps. 102–4 of *Moby-Dick* and Rodolphe Gasché's brilliant discussion of that novel, "The Scene of Writing."

borders in the hands of those already dominant in the social and political system. It does not follow, however, that the adoption of a radical or progressive stance involves treating literature as an undifferentiated extension of the language currently classed as "ordinary" or "communicative" or "referential." On the contrary, the history of writing, in which I include the writing of poetry, fiction, and literary theory, shows that the question of difference—and the practice of making different—can become an instrument for the critical reconsideration of any such homogenizing characterization of language, a reconsideration whose implications go well beyond the problematic and pleasurable domain of the literary.

WORKS CITED

Aarsleff, Hans. *From Locke to Saussure: Essays on the Study of Language and Intellectual History.* Minneapolis: University of Minnesota Press, 1982.
———. *The Study of Language in England, 1780–1860.* Princeton: Princeton University Press, 1967.
Abrams, M. H. *The Mirror and the Lamp: Romantic Theory and the Critical Tradition.* New York: Oxford University Press, 1953.
———. *Natural Supernaturalism: Tradition and Revolution in Romantic Literature.* New York: Norton, 1971.
———, "Wordsworth and Coleridge on Diction and Figures." In *The Correspondent Breeze: Essays on English Romanticism,* 3–24. New York: Norton, 1984.
Aitchison, Jean. *Language Change: Progress or Decay?* London: Fontana, 1981.
Altieri, Charles. "Wordsworth's 'Preface' as Literary Theory." *Criticism* 18 (1976): 122–46.
Anttila, Raimo. *An Introduction to Historical and Comparative Linguistics.* New York: Macmillan, 1972.
Aristotle. *Aristotle's "Poetics": A Translation for Students of Literature.* Trans. Leon Golden. Commentary by O. B. Hardison, Jr. Tallahassee: University Presses of Florida, 1981.
Arnold, Matthew. "Preface." *Poems of Wordsworth.* London: Macmillan, 1879.
Atkins, J. W. H. *English Literary Criticism: The Renascence.* 2d ed. London: Methuen, 1951.
Attridge, Derek. "Closing Statement: Linguistics and Poetics in Retrospect." In *The Linguistics of Writing,* ed. Nigel Fabb et al., 15–32.
———. *The Rhythms of English Poetry.* London: Longman, 1982.
———. *Well-weighed Syllables: Elizabethan Verse in Classical Metres.* Cambridge: Cambridge University Press, 1974.
Attridge, Derek, and Daniel Ferrer, ed. *Post-structuralist Joyce: Essays from the French.* Cambridge: Cambridge University Press, 1984.

Works Cited

——. "Introduction: Highly Continental Evenements." In *Post-structuralist Joyce*, ed. Attridge and Ferrer, 1–13.

Attridge, Derek; Geoff Bennington; and Robert Young, eds. *Post-structuralism and the Question of History*. Cambridge: Cambridge University Press, 1987.

Barnet, Sylvan. "Coleridge on Puns: A Note to His Shakespeare Criticism." *Journal of English and Germanic Philology* 56 (1957): 602–9.

Barrell, John. *English Literature in History, 1730–80: An Equal, Wide Survey*. London: Hutchinson, 1983.

Barthes, Roland. *Elements of Semiology*. Trans. Annette Lavers and Colin Smith. London: Cape, 1967.

——. *Image-Music-Text*. Sel. and trans. Stephen Heath. London: Fontana, 1977.

——. *Mythologies*. Sel. and trans. Annette Lavers. London: Cape, 1972.

——. "Proust et les noms." In *To Honor Roman Jakobson*, 150–58. The Hague: Mouton, 1967.

——. *S/Z*. Trans. Richard Miller. New York: Hill & Wang, 1974.

——. "Theory of the Text" and "Textual Analysis of Poe's 'Valdemar.'" Both in *Untying the Text*, ed. Robert Young, 133–61.

Begnal, Michael H. "The Dreamers at the Wake." In *Narrator and Character in "Finnegans Wake,"* ed. M. H. Begnal and Grace Eckley. Lewisburg: Bucknell University Press, 1975.

Beja, Morris, et al., eds. *James Joyce: The Centennial Symposium*. Urbana: University of Illinois Press, 1986.

Bennett, Tony. *Formalism and Marxism*. London: Methuen, 1979.

Benveniste, Emile. *Problems in General Linguistics*. Trans. Mary E. Meek. Coral Gables: University of Miami Press, 1971.

Bialostosky, Don H. *Making Tales: The Poetics of Wordsworth's Narrative Experiments*. Chicago: University of Chicago Press, 1984.

Bishop, John. *Joyce's Book of the Dark: "Finnegans Wake."* Madison: University of Wisconsin Press, 1986.

Bloomfield, Leonard. *Language*. New York: Holt, 1933.

Bolinger, Dwight L. *Forms of English: Accent, Morpheme, Order*. Ed. Isamu Abe and Tetsuya Kanekiyo. Cambridge: Harvard University Press, 1965.

Booth, Wayne. "Did Sterne Complete *Tristram Shandy*?" *Modern Philology* 48 (1950): 172–83.

Bourdieu, Pierre. *Distinction: A Social Critique of the Judgement of Taste*. Trans. Richard Nice. London: Routledge, 1984.

Bowen, Zack. *Musical Allusions in the Works of James Joyce*. Albany: SUNY Press, 1974.

Brooks, Peter. *Reading for the Plot: Design and Intention in Narrative*. New York: Knopf, 1984.

Brown, James. "Eight Types of Puns." *PMLA* 71 (1956): 14–26.

Burgess, Anthony. *Here Comes Everybody: An Introduction to James Joyce for the Ordinary Reader*. London: Faber & Faber, 1965.

——. *This Man and Music*. London: Hutchinson, 1982.

Campbell, Joseph, and Henry Morton Robinson. *A Skeleton Key to "Finnegans Wake."* 1944. Rpt. Harmondsworth: Penguin, 1977.

Carroll, David. *The Subject in Question: The Languages of Theory and the Strategies of Fiction.* Chicago: University of Chicago Press, 1982.

Carter, Ronald, and Walter Nash. "Language and Literariness." *Prose Studies* 6 (1983): 123–41.

Cave, Terence. *The Cornucopian Text: Problems of Writing in the French Renaissance.* Oxford: Oxford University Press, 1979.

Chandler, James K. *Wordsworth's Second Nature: A Study of the Poetry and Politics.* Chicago: University of Chicago Press, 1984.

Chase, Cynthia. "The Accidents of Disfiguration: Limits to Literal and Rhetorical Reading in Book V of *The Prelude*." *Studies in Romanticism* 18 (1979): 547–65.

——. "The Decomposition of the Elephants: Double-Reading *Daniel Deronda*." *PMLA* 93 (1978): 215–27.

Chomsky, Noam. *Cartesian Linguistics.* New York: Harper & Row, 1966.

Christensen, Jerome. *Coleridge's Blessed Machine of Language.* Ithaca: Cornell University Press, 1981.

Christie, Will. "Wordsworth and the Language of Nature." *The Wordsworth Circle* 14 (1983): 40–47.

Cohen, Murray. *Sensible Words: Linguistic Practice in England, 1640–1785.* Baltimore: Johns Hopkins University Press, 1977.

Coleridge, Samuel Taylor. *Biographia Literaria.* Ed. James Engell and W. Jackson Bate. 2 vols. Vol. 7 of *The Collected Works of Samuel Taylor Coleridge*, gen. ed. Kathleen Coburn. Princeton: Princeton University Press, 1983.

——. *Poetical Works.* Ed. E. H. Coleridge. London: Oxford University Press, 1967.

Cook, Eleanor, et al., eds. *Centre and Labyrinth: Essays in Honour of Northrop Frye.* Toronto: University of Toronto Press, 1983.

Coward, Rosalind, and John Ellis. *Language and Materialism: Developments in Semiology and the Theory of the Subject.* London: Routledge, 1977.

Culler, Jonathan. "Jacques Derrida." In *Structuralism and Since*, ed. John Sturrock, 154–80. Oxford: Oxford University Press, 1979.

——. *On Deconstruction.* Ithaca: Cornell University Press, 1982.

Curtius, E. R. "Etymology as a Category of Thought." In *European Literature and the Latin Middle Ages.* Trans. Willard R. Trask. Princeton: Princeton University Press, 1967.

Danby, John F. *Shakespeare's Doctrine of Nature: A Study of "King Lear."* London: Faber & Faber, 1949.

De Man, Paul. *Allegories of Reading: Figural Language in Rousseau, Nietzsche, Rilke, and Proust.* New Haven: Yale University Press, 1979.

——. "Intentional Structure of the Romantic Image." In *The Rhetoric of Romanticism*, 1–17. New York: Columbia University Press, 1984.

——. "The Resistance to Theory." In *The Resistance to Theory.* Minneapolis: University of Minnesota Press, 1986.

Works Cited

Deming, Robert H. *James Joyce: The Critical Heritage.* 2 vols. London: Routledge, 1970.

Derrida, Jacques. *Dissemination.* Trans. Barbara Johnson. Chicago: University of Chicago Press, 1981.

——. "Economimesis." *Diacritics* 11.2 (1981): 3–25.

——. *Edmund Husserl's "Origin of Geometry": An Introduction.* Trans. John P. Leavey, Jr. Ed. David B. Allison. Stony Brook, N.Y.: Nicolas Hays, 1978.

——. *Glas.* Paris: Galilée, 1974.

——. *Of Grammatology.* Trans. Gayatri Chakravorty Spivak. Baltimore: Johns Hopkins University Press, 1976.

——. "The Law of Genre." *Glyph* 7 (1980): 202–32.

——. "Limited Inc."*Glyph* 2 (1977): 162–254.

——. "Living On." In *Deconstruction and Criticism,* ed. Harold Bloom et al., 75–175. London: Routledge, 1979.

——. *Margins of Philosophy.* Trans. Alan Bass. Chicago: University of Chicago Press, 1982.

——. *Positions.* Trans. Alan Bass. Chicago: University of Chicago Press, 1981.

——. *Signéponge/Signsponge.* Trans. Richard Rand. New York: Columbia University Press, 1984.

——. *Speech and Phenomena.* Trans. David B. Allison. Evanston: Northwestern University Press, 1973.

——. "Two Words for Joyce." In *Post-structuralist Joyce,* ed. Attridge and Ferrer, 145–59.

——. *La vérité en peinture.* Paris: Flammarion, 1978.

Devlin, D. D. *Wordsworth and the Poetry of Epitaphs.* London: Macmillan, 1980.

Doran, Madeleine. *Endeavors of Art: A Study of Form in Elizabethan Drama.* Madison: University of Wisconsin Press, 1954.

Dryden, John. Preface to *Fables.* In *Of Dramatic Poesy and Other Critical Essays,* 2:269–94. Ed. George Watson. London: Dent, 1962.

Duval, Edwin M. "Lessons of the New World: Design and Meaning in Montaigne's 'Des Cannibales' [I.31] and 'Des coches' [III.6]." *Yale French Studies* 64 (1983): 95–112.

Eagleton, Terry. *Literary Theory: An Introduction.* Oxford: Blackwell, 1983.

——. *Walter Benjamin; or, Towards a Revolutionary Criticism.* London: NLB/Verso, 1981.

Eco, Umberto. *L'oeuvre ouverte.* Paris: Seuil, 1965.

——. *The Role of the Reader: Explorations in the Semiotics of Texts.* London: Hutchinson, 1981.

——. *A Theory of Semiotics.* Bloomington: Indiana University Press, 1976.

Eliot, T. S. *The Use of Poetry and the Use of Criticism.* 2d ed. London: Faber & Faber, 1964.

Ellmann, Maud. "Disremembering Dedalus." In *Untying the Text,* ed. Robert Young, 189–206.

——. "Polytropic Man: Paternity, Identity and Naming in *The Odyssey* and *A*

Portrait of the Artist as Young Man." In *James Joyce: New Perspectives*, ed. Colin MacCabe, 73–104.

Empson, William. *Some Versions of Pastoral.* 1935. Rpt. Harmondsworth: Penguin, 1966.

Erlich, Victor. *Russian Formalism: History-Doctrine.* 1955. 3d edition. New Haven: Yale University Press, 1981.

Fabb, Nigel; Derek Attridge; Alan Durant; and Colin MacCabe, eds. *The Linguistics of Writing: Arguments between Language and Literature.* New York: Methuen, 1988.

Felman, Shoshana. "Rereading Femininity." *Yale French Studies* 62 (1981): 19–44.

Ferguson, Frances. *Wordsworth: Language as Counter-Spirit.* New Haven: Yale University Press, 1977.

Ferguson, Margaret W. *Trials of Desire: Renaissance Defenses of Poetry.* New Haven: Yale University Press, 1983.

Ferrer, Daniel. "Miroirs aux Sirènes." *Europe* 657/8 (1984): 99–106.

Fish, Stanley. *Is There a Text in This Class? The Authority of Interpretive Communities.* Cambridge: Harvard University Press, 1980.

Fónagy, Ivan. "Motivation et remotivation: comment se dépasser?" *Poétique* 11 (1972): 414–31.

———. *La vive voix: Essais de psycho-phonétique.* Paris: Payot, 1983.

Forrest-Thomson, Veronica. *Poetic Artifice: A Theory of Twentieth-Century Poetry.* Manchester: Manchester University Press, 1978.

Foucault, Michel. *The Archaeology of Knowledge.* Trans. A. M. Sheridan Smith. New York: Random House, 1972.

Fowler, Roger. *Literature as Social Discourse: The Practice of Linguistic Criticism.* London: Batsford, 1981.

Freud, Sigmund. *The Interpretation of Dreams.* Trans. James Strachey. Ed. Angela Richards. Harmondsworth: Penguin, 1976.

———. *Jokes and Their Relation to the Unconscious.* Trans. James Strachey. Ed. Angela Richards. Harmondsworth: Penguin, 1976.

———. *On Creativity and the Unconscious.* Sel. Benjamin Nelson. New York: Harper & Row, 1958.

———. "The Uncanny." 1919. In *Standard Edition*, trans. James Strachey, 17: 219–52. London: Hogarth, 1955.

Frow, John. "Annus Mirabilis: Synchrony and Diachrony." In *The Politics of Theory*, ed. Francis Barker et al., 220–33. Colchester: University of Essex, 1983.

Füger, Wilhelm. "Bloom's Other Eye." *James Joyce Quarterly* 23 (1986): 209–17.

Garvin, Paul L. *A Prague School Reader on Esthetics, Literary Structure, and Style.* Washington, D.C.: Georgetown University Press, 1964.

Gasché, Rodolphe. "The Scene of Writing: A Deferred Outset." *Glyph* 1 (1977): 150–71.

Works Cited

Genette, Gérard. *Figures of Literary Discourse.* Trans. Alan Sheridan. New York: Columbia University Press, 1982.

——. *Mimologiques: Voyage en Cratylie.* Paris: Seuil, 1976.

——. *Narrative Discourse.* Trans. Jane E. Lewin. Ithaca: Cornell University Press, 1980.

——. "Valéry and the Poetics of Language." In *Textual Strategies: Perspectives in Post-Structuralist Criticism,* ed. Josué V. Harari, 359–73. Ithaca: Cornell University Press, 1979.

Gifford, Don, and Robert J. Seidman. *Notes for Joyce: An Annotation of James Joyce's "Ulysses."* New York: Dutton, 1974.

Gilson, Etienne. *Les idées et les lettres.* Paris: Vrin, 1932.

Glen, Heather. *Vision and Disenchantment: Blake's "Songs" and Wordsworth's "Lyrical Ballads."* Cambridge: Cambridge University Press, 1983.

Godel, Robert. "F. de Saussure's Theory of Language." In *Theoretical Foundations,* 479–93. Vol. 3 of *Current Trends in Linguistics,* ed. Thomas A. Sebeok. The Hague: Mouton, 1966.

Goldberg, S. L. *Joyce.* Edinburgh: Oliver & Boyd, 1962.

Gombrich, E. H. *Art and Illusion: A Study in the Psychology of Pictorial Representation.* 2d ed. Princeton: Princeton University Press, 1961.

Gottfried, Roy K. *The Art of Joyce's Syntax in "Ulysses."* London: Macmillan, 1980.

Graham, Joseph. "Flip, Flap, Flop: Linguistics as Semiotics." *Diacritics* 11.1 (1981): 143–68.

Greene, Thomas M. "Anti-hermeneutics: The Case of Shakespeare's Sonnet 129." In *Poetic Traditions of the English Renaissance,* ed. Maynard Mack and George deForest Lord, 143–61. New Haven: Yale University Press, 1982.

——. *The Light in Troy: Imitation and Discovery in Renaissance Poetry.* New Haven: Yale University Press, 1982.

Gross, John. *Joyce.* New York: Viking, 1970.

Group μ. *A General Rhetoric.* Trans. Paul B. Burrell and Edgar M. Slotkin. Baltimore: Johns Hopkins University Press, 1981.

Hanley, Miles L. *Word Index to James Joyce's "Ulysses."* Madison: University of Wisconsin Press, 1937.

Harington, Sir John. "A Brief Apology for Poetry." 1591. In *Elizabethan Critical Essays,* ed. G. Gregory Smith, 2: 194–222.

Harris, Roy. *The Language Makers.* London: Duckworth, 1980.

——. *The Language Myth.* London: Duckworth, 1981.

Hart, Clive. *Structure and Motif in "Finnegans Wake."* London: Faber & Faber, 1962.

Hathaway, Baxter. Introduction. *The Arte of English Poesie,* by George Puttenham. Kent: Kent State University Press, 1970.

Hawkes, Terence. *Structuralism and Semiotics.* London: Methuen, 1977.

Hayman, David. *Ulysses: The Mechanics of Meaning.* 2d ed. Madison: University of Wisconsin Press, 1982.

Heath, Stephen. *The Sexual Fix.* London: Macmillan, 1982.

Heffernan, James A. W. *Wordsworth's Theory of Poetry: The Transforming Imagination.* Ithaca: Cornell University Press, 1969.

Heidegger, Martin. *Poetry, Language, Thought.* Trans. A. Hofstadter. New York: Harper & Row, 1975.

Heller, L. G. "Toward a General Typology of the Pun." In *Linguistic Perspectives on Literature,* ed. Marvin K. L. Ching et al., 305–18. London: Routledge, 1980.

Hindess, Barry, and Paul Q. Hirst. *Pre-capitalist Modes of Production.* London: Routledge, 1975.

Holenstein, Elmar. *Roman Jakobson's Approach to Language: Phenomenological Structuralism.* Trans. Catherine Schelbert and Tarcisius Schelbert. Bloomington: Indiana University Press, 1976.

Hollander, John. *The Figure of Echo: A Mode of Allusion in Milton and After.* Berkeley: University of California Press, 1981.

——. "Originality." *Raritan* 2.4 (1983): 24–44.

——. "The Poetry of Everyday Life." *Raritan* 1.2 (1981): 5–18.

——. *Vision and Resonance: Two Senses of Poetic Form.* 2d ed. New Haven: Yale University Press, 1985.

Homer. *Odyssey.* Trans. Richmond Lattimore. New York: Harper & Row, 1967.

Householder, Fred W. "On the Problem of Sound and Meaning: An English Phonestheme" (summary). *Word* 2 (1946): 83–84.

Hunter, G. K. "Humanism and Courtship." In *Elizabethan Poetry: Modern Essays in Criticism,* ed. Paul Alpers, 3–40. New York: Oxford University Press, 1967.

Huxley, Francis. *The Raven and the Writing Desk.* London: Thames & Hudson, 1976.

Jacobus, Mary. *Tradition and Experiment in Wordsworth's "Lyrical Ballads" (1798).* Oxford: Oxford University Press, 1976.

Jakobson, Roman. "Closing Statement: Linguistics and Poetics." In *Style in Language,* ed. T. A. Sebeok, 350–77. Cambridge: MIT Press, 1960.

——. "Fragments de 'La nouvelle poésie russe.'" In *Huit questions de poétique,* 11–29. Paris: Seuil, 1977.

——. "Metalanguage as a Linguistic Problem." In *The Framework of Language,* 81–92. Michigan Studies in the Humanities no. 1. Ann Arbor, Mich., 1980.

——. "A Postscript to the Discussion on Grammar of Poetry." *Diacritics* 10.1 (1980): 22–35.

——. "Quest for the Essence of Language." In *Word and Language,* 345–59. Vol. 2 of *Selected Writings.* The Hague: Mouton, 1971.

——. "What is Poetry?" 1933. In *Poetry of Grammar and Grammar of Poetry,* ed. Stephen Rudy, 740–50. Vol. 3 of *Selected Writings.* The Hague: Mouton, 1981.

Jakobson, Roman, and Linda R. Waugh. *The Sound Shape of Language.* Bloomington: Indiana University Press, 1979.

Works Cited

Jameson, Fredric. *The Political Unconscious: Narrative as a Socially Symbolic Act.* Ithaca: Cornell University Press, 1981.

——. *The Prison-House of Language: A Critical Account of Structuralism and Russian Formalism.* Princeton: Princeton University Press, 1972.

——. "Seriality in Modern Literature." *Bucknell Review* 18 (1970): 63–80.

Javitch, Daniel. "The Impure Motives of Elizabethan Poetry." *Genre* 15 (1982): 225–38.

——. *Poetry and Courtliness in Renaissance England.* Princeton: Princeton University Press, 1978.

Johnson, Barbara. *The Critical Difference: Essays in the Contemporary Rhetoric of Reading.* Baltimore: Johns Hopkins University Press, 1981.

——. *A World of Difference.* Baltimore: Johns Hopkins University Press, 1987.

Johnson, Samuel. *Johnson on Shakespeare.* Ed. Arthur Sherbo. Vol. 7 of *The Yale Edition of the Works of Samuel Johnson.* New Haven: Yale University Press, 1968.

——. *Lives of the English Poets.* 2 vols. London: Oxford University Press, 1952.

Jordan, John E. *Why the "Lyrical Ballads"? The Background, Writing, and Character of Wordsworth's 1798 "Lyrical Ballads."* Berkeley: University of California Press, 1976.

Joseph, Sister Miriam. *Shakespeare's Use of the Arts of Language.* New York: Columbia University Press, 1947.

Joyce, James. *Finnegans Wake.* 1939. 3d ed. London: Faber & Faber, 1964.

——. *Letters.* Ed. Stuart Gilbert and Richard Ellmann. 3 vols. New York: Viking, 1957–66.

——. *A Portrait of the Artist as a Young Man.* 1916. Ed. Chester G. Anderson. The Viking Critical Library. New York: Viking, 1968.

——. *A Shorter Finnegans Wake.* Ed. Anthony Burgess. London: Faber & Faber, 1966.

——. *Ulysses.* 1922. Corrected ed. Ed. Hans Walter Gabler et al. New York: Random House, 1986.

Kahn, Victoria. "Humanism and the Resistance to Theory." In *Literary Theory/Renaissance Texts*, ed. Patricia Parker and David Quint, 373–96. Baltimore: Johns Hopkins University Press, 1986.

——. *Rhetoric, Prudence, and Skepticism in the Renaissance.* Ithaca: Cornell University Press, 1985.

Keach, William. *Shelley's Style.* London: Methuen, 1984.

Kenner, Hugh. "Joyce and the 19th Century Linguistics Explosion." In *Atti del Third International James Joyce Symposium*, 45–52. Trieste, 1971.

——. *Joyce's Voices.* Berkeley: University of California Press, 1978.

——. *The Pound Era.* London: Faber & Faber, 1975.

——. "The Rhetoric of Silence." *James Joyce Quarterly* 14 (1977): 382–94.

——. *Ulysses.* Unwin Critical Library. London: Allen & Unwin, 1980.

Kermode, Frank. "The Final Plays." In *Renaissance Essays: Shakespeare, Spenser, Donne*, 219–59. London: Routledge, 1971.

————. Introduction. *The Tempest,* by William Shakespeare, xxxiv–lix. London: Metheun, 1954.

Keyser, Samuel Jay, and Alan Prince. "Folk Etymology in Sigmund Freud, Christian Morgenstern, and Wallace Stevens." *Critical Inquiry* 6 (1979): 65–78.

Klein, Ernest. *A Comprehensive Etymological Dictionary of the English Language.* 2 vols. Amsterdam: Elsevier, 1966–67.

Kranidas, Thomas. *The Fierce Equation: A Study of Milton's Decorum.* The Hague: Mouton, 1965.

Kristeva, Julia. *La révolution du langage poétique.* Paris: Seuil, 1974.

Lamb, Jonathan. "Hartley and Wordsworth: Philosophical Language and the Figures of the Sublime." *MLN* 97 (1982): 1064–85.

Land, Stephen K. "The Silent Poet: An Aspect of Wordsworth's Semantic Theory." *University of Toronto Quarterly* 42 (1973): 157–69.

Leavis, F. R. "Joyce and 'The Revolution of the Word.'" *Scrutiny* 2 (1933): 193–201.

————. *Revaluation: Tradition and Development in English Poetry.* London: Chatto & Windus, 1936.

Leech, Geoffrey N. *A Linguistic Guide to English Poetry.* London: Longman, 1969.

Leech, Geoffrey, and Michael Short. *Style in Fiction.* London: Longman, 1982.

Lemon, Lee T., and Marion J. Reis, ed. and trans. *Russian Formalist Criticism: Four Essays.* Lincoln: University of Nebraska Press, 1965.

Lentricchia, Frank. *After the New Criticism.* Chicago: University of Chicago Press, 1980.

Lerner, Laurence. "What Did Wordsworth Mean by 'Nature'?" *Critical Quarterly* 17 (1975): 291–308.

Levao, Ronald. *Renaissance Minds and Their Fictions: Cusanus, Sidney, Shakespeare.* Berkeley: University of California Press, 1985.

Levine, Jennifer. "Originality and Repetition in *Finnegans Wake* and *Ulysses.*" *PMLA* 94 (1979): 106–20.

————. "Reading *Ulysses.*" In *Centre and Labyrinth,* ed. Eleanor Cook et al., 264–83.

Lewis, C. S. *Studies in Words.* 2d ed. Cambridge: Cambridge University Press, 1967.

Lewis, Charlton T., and Charles Short. *A Latin Dictionary.* Oxford: Oxford University Press, 1879.

Litz, A. Walton. *The Art of James Joyce: Method and Design in "Ulysses" and "Finnegans Wake."* London: Oxford University Press, 1961.

————. *James Joyce.* New York: Twayne, 1966.

Lodge, David. "Double Discourses: Joyce and Bakhtin." *James Joyce Broadsheet* 11 (1983): 1.

————. *The Modes of Modern Writing: Metaphor, Metonymy, and the Typology of Modern Literature.* London: Arnold, 1977.

Works Cited

Longinus. *On Sublimity.* Trans. D. A. Russell. In *Ancient Literary Criticism,* ed. Russell and M. Winterbottom, 460–503. Oxford: Oxford University Press, 1972.

Lovejoy, Arthur O. *Essays in the History of Ideas.* Baltimore: Johns Hopkins Press, 1948.

Lovejoy, Arthur O., and George Boas. *Primitivism and Related Ideas in Antiquity.* Baltimore: Johns Hopkins Press, 1935.

Lyons, John. *Introduction to Theoretical Linguistics.* Cambridge: Cambridge University Press, 1968.

——. *Semantics.* 2 vols. Cambridge: Cambridge University Press, 1977.

Lyotard, Jean-François. "The Dream-Work Does Not Think." *Oxford Literary Review* 6.1 (1983): 3–34.

——. *The Postmodern Condition: A Report on Knowledge.* Trans. Geoff Bennington and Brian Massumi. Minneapolis: University of Minnesota Press, 1984.

MacCabe, Colin, ed. *James Joyce: New Perspectives.* Brighton: Harvester, 1982.

McCanles, Michael. "The Authentic Discourse of the Renaissance." *Diacritics* 10.1 (1980): 77–87.

McFarland, Thomas. *Romanticism and the Forms of Ruin: Wordsworth, Coleridge, and the Modalities of Fragmentation.* Princeton: Princeton University Press, 1981.

McHale, Brian. "Against Interpretation: Iconic Grammar, Anxiety of Influence, and *Poetic Artifice.*" *Poetics Today* 3.1 (1982): 142–58.

McHugh, Roland. *The Sigla of "Finnegans Wake."* London: Arnold, 1976.

McGann, Jerome J. *The Romantic Ideology: A Critical Investigation.* Chicago: University of Chicago Press, 1983.

McKnight, George H. *English Words and Their Background.* New York: Appleton, 1923.

Mahood, M. M. *Shakespeare's Wordplay.* London: Methuen, 1957.

Malkiel, Yakov. "Each Word Has a History of Its Own." *Glossa* 1 (1967): 137–49.

——. "Etymology and General Linguistics." *Word* 18 (1962): 198–219.

Marks, Emerson R. *Coleridge on the Language of Verse.* Princeton: Princeton University Press, 1981.

Martin, Jean-Paul. "La condensation." *Poétique* 26 (1976): 180–206.

Masson, David I. "Vowel and Consonant Patterns in Poetry." *JAAC* 12 (1953): 213–27.

Matejka, Ladislav, and Krystyna Pomorska. *Readings in Russian Poetics: Formalist and Structuralist Views.* Cambridge: MIT Press, 1971.

Merrim, Stephanie. "Cratylus' Kingdom." *Diacritics* 11.1 (1981): 44–55.

Miller, J. Hillis. "The Stone and the Shell: The Problem of Poetic Form in Wordsworth's Dream of the Arab." In *Untying the Text,* ed. Robert Young, 245–64.

Montrose, Louis Adrian. "Gentlemen and Shepherds: The Politics of Elizabethan Pastoral Form." *ELH* 50 (1983): 415–59.

Moss, Roger. "Difficult Language: The Justification of Joyce's Syntax in *Ulysses*." In *The Modern English Novel: The Reader, the Writer, and the Work*, ed. Gabriel Josipovici, 130–48. London: Open Books, 1976.

Müller, Max. *Lectures on the Science of Language*. 2d ser. London: Longman, 1864.

Nietzsche, Friedrich. *On the Genealogy of Morals*. Trans. Walter Kaufmann and R. J. Hollingdale. New York: Random House, 1967.

Noon, William T. *Joyce and Aquinas*. New Haven: Yale University Press, 1957.

Norris, Margot. *The Decentered Universe of "Finnegans Wake."* Baltimore: Johns Hopkins University Press, 1976.

Olshin, Toby A. "Genre and *Tristram Shandy:* The Novel of Quickness." *Genre* 4 (1971): 360–75.

Orr, John. "L'étymologie populaire." In *Essais d'étymologie et de philologie française*, 3–15. Paris: Klincksieck, 1963.

———. *Words and Sounds in English and French*. Oxford: Blackwell, 1953.

Ortner, Sherry B. "Is Female to Male as Nature Is to Culture?" In *Woman, Culture, and Society*, ed. Michelle Zimbalist Rosaldo and Louise Lamphere, 67–87. Stanford: Stanford University Press, 1974.

Owen, W. J. B. *Wordsworth as Critic*. Toronto: University of Toronto Press, 1969.

Palmer, Rev. A. Smythe. *The Folk and Their Word-Lore: An Essay on Popular Etymologies*. London: Routledge, 1904.

———. *Folk-Etymology: A Dictionary of Verbal Corruptions or Words Perverted in Form or Meaning, by False Derivation or Mistaken Analogy*. London: Bell, 1882.

Paris, Jean. "L'agonie du signe." *Change* 11 (1972): 133–72.

———. "Finnegans, Wake!" *Tel Quel* 30 (1967): 58–66.

Parker, Patricia A. *Inescapable Romance: Studies in the Poetics of a Mode*. Princeton: Princeton University Press, 1979.

Parrish, Stephen Maxfield. *The Art of the "Lyrical Ballads."* Cambridge: Harvard University Press, 1973.

Partridge, Eric. *Origins: A Short Etymological Dictionary of Modern English*. London: Routledge, 1958.

Patrick, Julian. "The Tempest as Supplement." In *Centre and Labyrinth*, ed. Eleanor Cook et al., 162–80.

Patterson, Annabel M. *Hermogenes and the Renaissance: Seven Ideas of Style*. Princeton: Princeton University Press, 1970.

Paulhan, Jean. *La preuve par l'étymologie*. Paris: Minuit, 1953.

Peirce, C. S. *Philosophical Writings of Peirce*. Ed. Justus Buchler. New York: Dover, 1955.

Pilkington, A. E. "'Nature' as Ethical Norm in the Enlightenment." In *Languages of Nature: Critical Essays on Science and Literature*, ed. Ludmilla Jordanova, 51–85. London: Free Association Books, 1986.

Piper, William Bowman. *Laurence Sterne*. New York: Twayne, 1965.

Plett, Heinrich. "Aesthetic Constituents in the Courtly Culture of Renaissance England." *New Literary History* 14 (1983): 597–621.

Works Cited

Pope, Alexander. *The Dunciad*. Ed. James Sutherland. Vol. 5 of *The Twickenham Edition of the Poems of Alexander Pope*, gen. ed. John Butt. London: Methuen, 1943.
——. *Pastoral Poetry and "An Essay on Criticism."* Ed. E. Audra and Aubrey Williams. Vol. 1 of *The Twickenham Edition of the Poems of Alexander Pope*, gen. ed. John Butt. London: Methuen, 1961.
Pratt, Mary Louise. "The Ideology of Speech-Act Theory." *Centrum* n.s. 1 (1981): 5–18.
——. "Linguistic Utopias." In *The Linguistics of Writing*, ed. Nigel Fabb et al., 48–66.
——. *Toward a Speech Act Theory of Literary Discourse*. Bloomington: Indiana University Press, 1977.
Puttenham, George. *The Arte of English Poesie*. Ed. Gladys Doidge Willcock and Alice Walker. Cambridge: Cambridge University Press, 1936.
Quint, David. *Origin and Originality in Renaissance Literature: Versions of the Source*. New Haven: Yale University Press, 1983.
Quintilian. *Institutionis Oratoriae*. Trans. H. E. Butler. Cambridge: Harvard University Press, 1920.
Rabaté, Jean-Michel. "Lapsus ex Machina." In *Post-structuralist Joyce*, ed. Derek Attridge and Daniel Ferrer, 79–101.
Ragussis, Michael. *The Subterfuge of Art: Language and the Romantic Tradition*. Baltimore: Johns Hopkins University Press, 1978.
Ramsey, Jonathan. "Wordsworth and the Childhood of Language." *Criticism* 18 (1976): 243–55.
Rand, Richard. "Geraldine." In *Untying the Text*, ed. Robert Young, 280–315.
Ricardou, Jean. "Time of the Narration, Time of the Fiction." *James Joyce Quarterly* 16 (1979): 7–15.
Richards, I. A. *Coleridge on Imagination*. London: Kegan Paul, 1934.
——. *The Philosophy of Rhetoric*. New York: Oxford University Press, 1936.
Ronat, Mitsou. "L'hypotexticale." *Change* 11 (1972): 26–33.
Said, Edward. "Abecedarium Culturae: Structuralism, Absence, Writing." In *Modern French Criticism: From Proust and Valéry to Structuralism*, ed. John K. Simon, 341–92. Chicago: University of Chicago Press, 1972.
Saussure, Ferdinand de. *Cours de linguistique générale*. Paris: Payot, 1960.
——. *Cours de linguistique générale*. Critical Edition. Ed. Rudolf Engler. Wiesbaden: Harrassowitz, 1967.
——. *Cours de linguistique générale*. Critical Edition. Ed. Tullio de Mauro. Paris: Payot, 1972.
——. *Course in General Linguistics*. Trans. Wade Baskin. New York: McGraw-Hill, 1966.
——. *Course in General Linguistics*. Trans. Roy Harris. London: Duckworth, 1983.
Schutte, William M. *Index of Recurrent Elements in James Joyce's "Ulysses"*. Carbondale: Southern Illinois University Press, 1982.

Senn, Fritz. *Joyce's Dislocutions: Essays on Reading as Translation.* Ed. John Paul Riquelme. Baltimore: Johns Hopkins University Press, 1984.

——. "Righting Ulysses." In *James Joyce: New Perspectives,* ed. Colin MacCabe, 3–28.

Shakespeare, William. *The Riverside Shakespeare.* Ed. G. Blakemore Evans. Boston: Houghton Mifflin, 1974.

Shipley, Joseph T. *Dictionary of Word Origins.* New York: Philosophical Library, 1945.

Shklovsky, Victor. "Sterne's *Tristram Shandy:* Stylistic Commentary." In *Russian Formalist Criticism,* ed. Lee T. Lemon and Marion J. Reis, 25–57.

Sidney, Sir Philip. *An Apologie for Poetrie.* In *Elizabethan Critical Essays,* ed. G. Gregory Smith, 1: 148–207.

Simpson, David. *Wordsworth and the Figurings of the Real.* London: Macmillan, 1982.

Skeat, W. W. *An Etymological Dictionary of the English Language.* 4th ed. Oxford: Oxford University Press, 1910.

Smith, G. Gregory, ed. *Elizabethan Critical Essays.* 2 vols. London: Oxford University Press, 1904.

Smith, Olivia. *The Politics of Language, 1791–1819.* Oxford: Oxford University Press, 1984.

Spark, Muriel. *The Prime of Miss Jean Brodie.* Harmondsworth: Penguin, 1969.

Spenser, Edmund. *The Faerie Queene.* Ed. J. Smith. Oxford: Oxford University Press, 1909.

Starobinski, Jean. *Words upon Words: The Anagrams of Ferdinand de Saussure.* Trans. Olivia Emmet. New Haven: Yale University Press, 1979.

Stead, Alistair. "Reflections on Eumaeus: Ways of Error and Glory in *Ulysses.*" In *James Joyce and Modern Literature,* ed. W. J. McCormack and Alistair Stead, 142–65. London: Routledge, 1982.

Steiner, Peter. "The Conceptual Basis of Prague Structuralism." In *Sound, Sign and Meaning: Quinquagenary of the Prague Linguistic Circle,* ed. Ladislav Matejka, 351–85. Michigan Slavic Contributions no. 6. Ann Arbor, Mich. 1976.

——. *Russian Formalism: A Metapoetics.* Ithaca: Cornell University Press, 1984.

Steppe, Wolfhard, with Hans Walter Gabler. *Handlist to James Joyce's "Ulysses."* New York: Garland, 1986.

Stetson, Erlene. "Literary Talk: Extended Allusions in *Ulysses.*" *James Joyce Quarterly* 19 (1982): 178–82.

Struever, Nancy. "Fables of Power." *Representations* 4 (1983): 108–27.

Tanner, Tony. *Adultery in the Novel.* Baltimore: Johns Hopkins University Press, 1979.

Tayler, Edward William. *Nature and Art in Renaissance Literature.* New York: Columbia University Press, 1964.

Thorne, J. P. "Generative Grammar and Stylistic Analysis." In *New Horizons in Linguistics,* ed. John Lyons, 185–97. Harmondsworth: Penguin, 1970.

Works Cited

Todorov, Tzvetan. *Symbolism and Interpretation*. Trans. Catherine Porter. Ithaca: Cornell University Press, 1983.
——. *Theories of the Symbol*. Trans. Catherine Porter. Ithaca: Cornell University Press, 1982.
——, ed. and trans. *Théorie de la littérature: Textes des Formalistes russes*. Paris: Seuil, 1966.
Tooke, John Horne. *Epea Pteroenta; or, The Diversions of Purley*. London, 1805.
Topia, André. "The Matrix and the Echo: Intertextuality in *Ulysses*." In *Post-structuralist Joyce*, ed. Derek Attridge and Daniel Ferrer, 103–25.
Trench, Richard Chevenix. *On the Study of Words*. New York: Widdleton, 1878.
Tuve, Rosemond. *Elizabethan and Metaphysical Imagery*. Chicago: University of Chicago Press, 1947.
Ullmann, Stephen. *Semantics: An Introduction to the Science of Meaning*. Oxford: Blackwell, 1962.
Valéry, Paul. *The Art of Poetry*. Trans. Denise Folliot. Vol. 7 of *The Collected Works of Paul Valéry*, ed. Jackson Mathews. Princeton: Princeton University Press, 1958.
——. *Oeuvres*. 2 vols. Ed. Jean Hytier. Paris: Gallimard-Pléiade, 1957–60.
Vico, Giambattista. *The New Science*. Trans. T. G. Bergin and M. H. Frisch. Ithaca: Cornell University Press, 1970.
Waugh, Linda R. "The Poetic Function and the Nature of Language." In Roman Jakobson, *Verbal Art, Verbal Sign, Verbal Time*, ed. Krystyna Pomorska and Stephen Rudy, 143–68. Minneapolis: University of Minnesota Press, 1985.
——. *Roman Jakobson's Science of Language*. Lisse: De Ridder, 1976.
Weber, Samuel. "The Critics' Choice." In *1789: Reading Writing Revolution*, ed. Francis Barker et al., 147–59. Proceedings of the Essex Conference on the Sociology of Literature, July 1981. Colchester: University of Essex, 1982.
——. *The Legend of Freud*. Minneapolis: University of Minnesota Press, 1982.
——. "Saussure and the Apparition of Language: The Critical Perspective." *MLN* 91 (1976): 913–38.
Weekley, Ernest. Preface. *More Words Ancient and Modern*. London: Murray, 1927.
——. Preface. *Words Ancient and Modern*. London: Murray, 1926.
——. *The Romance of Words*. 1912. 2d ed. London: Murray, 1913.
Wellek, René. *A History of Modern Criticism, 1750–1950*, vol. 2: *The Romantic Age*. New Haven: Yale University Press, 1955.
Whigham, Frank. "Interpretation at Court: Courtesy and the Performer-Audience Dialectic." *New Literary History* 14 (1983): 623–39.
White, Allon. "The Dismal Sacred Word." *Literature Teaching Politics* 2 (1983): 4–15.
White, Hayden. *Metahistory: The Historical Imagination in Nineteenth-Century Europe*. Baltimore: Johns Hopkins University Press, 1973.

——. "The Politics of Historical Interpretation: Discipline and De-Sublimation." *Critical Inquiry* 9 (1982): 113–38.

——. *Tropics of Discourse: Essays in Cultural Criticism*. Baltimore: Johns Hopkins University Press, 1978.

——. "The Value of Narrativity in the Representation of Reality" and "The Narrativization of Real Events." Both in *On Narrative*, ed. W. J. T. Mitchell, 1–24, 249–54. Chicago: University of Chicago Press, 1981.

Williams, Raymond. *Keywords*. London: Fontana, 1976.

Wilson, Edmund. "H. C. Earwicker and Family," and "The Dream of H. C. Earwicker." *New Republic* 99 (1939): 203–6, 270–74. Rpt. as "The Dream of H. C. Earwicker" in *The Wound and the Bow: Seven Studies in Literature*, 243–71. Boston: Houghton Mifflin, 1941.

——. "James Joyce." *New Republic* 61 (1929): 84–93. Rpt. in *Axel's Castle: A Study in the Imaginative Literature of 1870–1930*, 193–236. New York: Scribner's, 1931.

Wilson, Harold S. "Nature and Art." In *The Winter's Tale: A Casebook*, ed. Kenneth Muir, 151–58. London: Macmillan, 1968.

Wimsatt, William K. "In Search of Verbal Mimesis." *Day of the Leopards*, 57–73. New Haven: Yale University Press, 1976.

Wimsatt, William K., and Cleanth Brooks. *Literary Criticism: A Short History*. London: Routledge, 1957.

Wordsworth, William. *Lyrical Ballads*. Ed. R. L. Brett and A. R. Jones. London: Methuen, 1965.

——. *Poems*. Ed. John O. Hayden. 2 vols. Harmondsworth: Penguin, 1977.

——. *The Prelude: A Parallel Text*. Ed. J. C. Maxwell. Harmondsworth: Penguin, 1971.

——. *The Prose Works of William Wordsworth*. Ed. W. J. B. Owen and Jane Worthington Smyser. 3 vols. Oxford: Oxford University Press, 1974.

Wordsworth, William, and Dorothy Wordsworth. *Letters: The Early Years, 1787–1805*. 2d ed. Ed. Ernest de Selincourt, rev. Chester L. Shaver. Vol. 1 of *The Letters of William and Dorothy Wordsworth*. Oxford: Oxford University Press, 1967.

Yarborough, M. C. *John Horne Tooke*. New York: Columbia University Press, 1962.

Young, Robert. *Political Literary Theories*. London: Methuen, 1988.

——, ed. *Untying the Text: A Post-structuralist Reader*. London: Routledge, 1981.

INDEX

Index

Index

Index

Plato (*cont.*)
  Phaedrus, 23, 207
  See also Cratylism, Hermogenism
pleasure, 12, 14, 131–32, 151, 156, 216, 235
  Wordsworth's emphasis on, 12, 54, 67, 70, 78–79, 81
Plett, Heinrich, 35
Pliny, 228
poet, silent, 64–65, 71
poetic function, 128–30, 134–35
polysemy, 11, 167, 192–94, 226. *See also* ambiguity, pun
Pomorska, Krystyna, 127
Pope, Alexander, 60, 80, 85, 88
  Essay on Criticism, 47–49, 154
  use of pun, 190–92, 194, 202, 206, 208
portmanteau, 14, 172, 193–209, 217, 235–36
portmanteau-cliché, 178, 181
poststructuralism, 92, 97, 107, 126, 131
Prague Linguistic Circle. *See* Structuralism, Prague
Pratt, Mary Louise, 15, 128, 227
prescriptivism, 107, 114–18
Priestley, Joseph, 58
primitivism, 52, 55, 57, 61, 76
Prince, Alan, 113
Proust, Marcel, 221
pun, 108–9, 166–70, 172, 186, 188–94
  contrast with portmanteau, 14, 201–2, 206, 208
  and etymology, 108–9, 120, 123, 125–26
  See also ambiguity, polysemy
Puttenham, George, 128, 130
  Arte of English Poesie, 3, 8–9, 18–19, 24–45, 91, 219
  compared with Wordsworth, 54, 60, 67–68, 84
  De decoro, 36

Quint, David, 27
Quintilian, 21, 59, 68, 219

Rabaté, Jean-Michel, 170, 215
Rabelais, François, 10
Ragussis, Michael, 69
Ramsey, Jonathan, 87
Rand, Richard A., 100, 189
reading, as complex activity, 7, 11, 118–19, 141–42, 221, 227, 234, 236–37
realism, 161, 234

reason
  appeals to, 21, 24, 79
  insufficiency of, 3, 23, 36, 110, 123, 126, 189
récit. See story vs. discourse
referent, 44, 96, 129–35, 225–26, 232
register, 176, 204
Reis, Marion J., 127
religion, 38, 43–44
Reynolds, Sir Joshua, 83, 85
rhetoric, 19, 121, 140, 156, 160, 174
  classical, 64, 218
  vs. objectivity, 9, 16, 22–23, 91, 108, 110–11, 122
rhyme, 25, 120, 192, 194
rhythm, 132, 153, 172, 236. *See also* versification
Ricardou, Jean, 224
Richards, I. A., 75, 139
Robinson, Henry Morton, 211–12, 234
Romanticism, 7–8, 49–52, 57–58, 70, 73–76, 85, 130, 223
Ronat, Mitsou, 193
Rousseau, Jean-Jacques, 23, 57, 68, 157

Said, Edward, 92, 97
Sapir, Edward, 129, 135
Saussure, Ferdinand de, 6, 8–11, 15, 127, 133, 189, 208
  and difference, 141, 231
  and synchrony vs. diachrony, 9, 76, 90–126, 205
Schutte, William M., 180
Seidman, Robert J., 165
selection, theory of, 71–73, 76–82
Seneca, 20
Senn, Fritz, 126, 176, 183, 217
Shakespeare, William, 48, 86, 230
  King Lear, 39, 109
  Macbeth, 109, 189
  puns in, 188–89, 192, 194, 209
  Taming of the Shrew, The, 222–23
  Tempest, The, 39
  Winter's Tale, The, 32, 35, 38–39, 42, 44, 73
Shelley, Percy Bysshe, 51
Shipley, Joseph T., 122–23
Shklovsky, Victor, 236
Short, Michael, 106
Sidney, Sir Philip, 18–19, 25, 38, 40, 54, 107, 110
sigla, 199, 217
signifier vs. signified, 96, 104, 129–35, 186, 189, 193, 197
Simpson, David, 68

sjuzhet. *See* story vs. discourse
Skeat, W. W., 103, 110, 126
Smith, G. Gregory, 18, 29
Smith, Olivia, 57, 102
Smyser, Jane Worthington, 53
sociology, 5–7, 15
sound patterning. *See* patterning, sound
Spark, Muriel, 99
speech vs. writing, 57, 59, 92, 114, 116, 204, 226
spelling pronunciation, 113, 115–18
Spenser, Edmund, 38–39, 91
spontaneous, art as. *See* art, as spontaneous
sprezzatura, 19, 54
Starobinski, Jean, 208
Stead, Alistair, 174–75
Steiner, Peter, 127–28
Steppe, Wolfhard, 163
Sterne, Laurence, 10, 218, 228–30, 236
Stetson, Erlene, 171
story vs. discourse, 207, 224, 234
structuralism, 95, 111, 230
    literary, 3, 13, 29, 75, 92, 97, 118–19, 219–20
    and scientific model, 5–6, 29, 90, 97
Structuralism, Prague, 3, 127–28
Struever, Nancy, 125
stylistics, 3, 108, 128, 184
supplement, 23, 35, 43–44, 50, 76, 81, 100, 157
    added text as, 26, 40–41, 62
    art as, 20, 28, 36–43, 46–49, 72
    art as avoidance of, 49–52, 63, 69–70
    digression as, 224, 226
    Finnegans Wake as, 198, 209
    literary language as, 26–28, 40, 42–43, 68, 88, 130
    as surrogate nature, 31–33, 75
    and theory of selection, 69–82
Swift, Jonathan, 186, 228–29, 236
synchrony. *See* diachrony vs. synchrony
synecdoche, 166, 168, 170
syntactic deviation. *See* deviation, syntactic
syntagmatic relations, 94–96

Tanner, Tony, 197
taste, 5–6, 15, 34, 36
    in neoclassicism, 47–48, 85
    in Romantic period, 54, 72, 74–75, 78–85
    See also decorum, judgment
tautology, 161, 175, 180

Tayler, Edward W., 19–21, 24, 32, 41, 43
Tennyson, Alfred, Lord, 152
Thorne, J. P., 184
Todorov, Tzvetan, 108, 127, 132–34, 136, 157
Tooke, John Horne, 102, 125, 204
Topia, André, 91, 170
Trench, Richard Chevenix, 99, 110
Tuve, Rosemond, 29
Twain, Mark, 102

Ullmann, Stephen, 134, 156
Ulysses, 10, 126, 200, 214, 218, 233
    "Aeolus," 144–45, 162, 174, 179–80
    "Calypso," 138, 161, 165, 182
    "Circe," 38, 143–45, 147, 163–64, 166, 169–71, 174, 180, 187
    "Cyclops," 159, 174
    "Eumaeus," 13, 160, 172–84, 186–87, 200
    "Ithaca," 162, 183, 187
    "Lestrygonians," 147
    "Lotus-Eaters," 145, 182
    "Nausicaa," 160, 165
    "Oxen of the Sun," 160, 180, 203, 224
    "Penelope," 50, 144, 159–60, 165, 171, 187
    "Sirens," 12, 136–57, 162–74, 180, 183–84, 186–87
    "Telemachus," 144, 164–65, 183
    "Wandering Rocks," 162
    See also Finnegans Wake, and *Ulysses*
Uncle Charles principle, 173
universalism, 34, 63, 67–68, 72, 74–75, 77, 92, 178

Valéry, Paul, 29, 132–33, 154–55
versification, 25–28, 65–67, 73, 78, 130. *See also* rhythm
Vico, Giambattista, 68, 107, 110, 123, 125, 210
Virgil, 47
visual patterning. *See* patterning, visual
Voltaire, 102

Walker, Alice, 18, 26
Waugh, Linda R., 128–29, 132, 134–35, 150
Weber, Samuel, 124, 213, 230
Weekley, Ernest, 103–4, 109–10, 112, 119, 125
Wellek, René, 74, 85
West, Rebecca, 159
Whigham, Frank, 40

Index